WOMAN
IN THE
WILDERNESS

Miriam Lancewood

WOMAN
IN THE
WILDERNESS

My Story of Love, Survival
and Self-discovery

piatkus

PIATKUS

First published in Australia and New Zealand in 2017 by Allen & Unwin
First published in Great Britain in 2017 by Piatkus

13 5 7 9 10 8 6 4 2

Copyright © 2017 Miriam Lancewood
Maps by Jo Pearson
Internal design by Anna Egan-Reid

The moral right of the author has been asserted.

Most names have been changed to protect places and people's privacy.

The author has made every effort to ensure the accuracy of the information within this book was correct at time of publication. The author does not assume and hereby disclaim any liability to any party for any loss, damage, or disruption caused by errors or omissions, whether such errors or omissions result from accident, negligence, or any other cause.

A CIP catalogue record for this book
is available from the British Library.

Trade Paperback ISBN: 978-0-349-41824-7

Printed and bound in Great Britain by
Clays Ltd, St Ives plc

Papers used by Piatkus are from well-managed forests
and other responsible sources.

This book is dedicated to my loving adventurer, Peter.
He showed me the way of freedom and randomness.

Oh, mothers
Kiss your children every night
Let the truth be their light
Make them go and let them be
Like my mother did with me.

Oh, fathers
Sing your children a tender song
About the earth where they belong
Sing your love and set them free
Like my father sang to me.

—Miriam Lancewood

—— CONTENTS ——

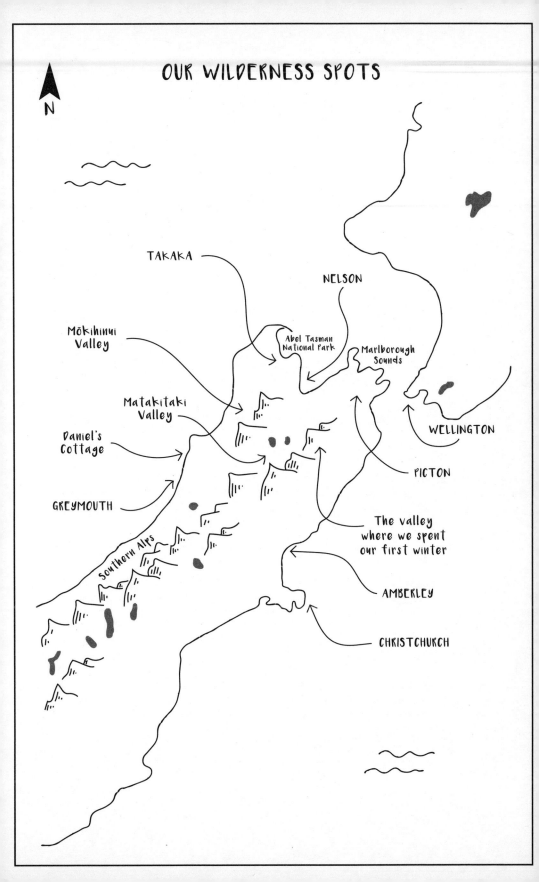

TE ARAROA TRAIL, AOTEAROA NEW ZEALAND

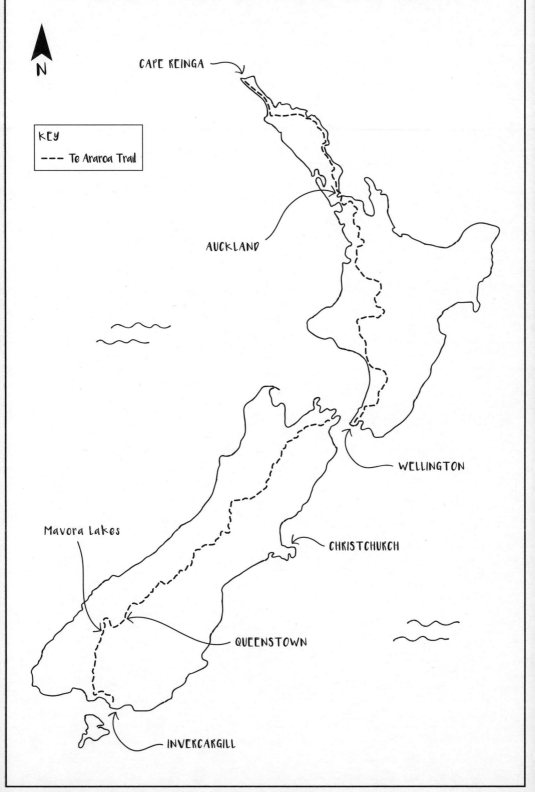

N

KEY
- - - Te Araroa Trail

CAPE REINGA

AUCKLAND

WELLINGTON

CHRISTCHURCH

Mavora Lakes

QUEENSTOWN

INVERCARGILL

THE WILDERNESS

It is a beautiful winter's day and I am walking with my bow and arrows on the side of a mountain, in search of a wild goat. I clamber into dense forest, and make my way up through vines and fallen logs. Gradually, the trees become smaller, and the moist, leafy soil gives way to rocky patches. The sun has warmed the dark rock face, and I sit down to admire the world around me. This beautiful valley is our home for the long winter. There is no wind and everything is utterly still. I marvel at the silent grandeur of the majestic peaks covered with untouched white snow. Below me, the river has shaped the landscape according to its own random way. The swift river and the slow forest are growing together in harmony.

Directly above me, I notice more flat rocks to climb on to. Maybe there are goats living underneath that little overhang? They like warm, dry places with good views, and might come back in the late afternoon. I quietly climb a little higher to take a closer look.

Eventually, I arrive at an open spot between some small trees. I don't see any goats, but I realise that I am now so high up that I can see our little camp down in the narrow valley below. I can even see Peter! He is a tiny figure with a red jumper, almost swallowed up by the great landscape. It was only this morning that I kissed him goodbye, but it feels as though I haven't seen another human being for ten years.

Peter, look this way! I think excitedly.

As I watch, I see him stand up. Maybe he is looking up at the mountain? I can't tell for certain, but I jump up and take my jacket off, waving it from left to right to try to get his attention. After a few seconds I see Peter pick up his little mat and wave it slowly in the air in response.

I feel tears well up in my eyes. We are waving at each other, touching each other over a great distance. I am looking at the wilderness and at Peter: the two dearest beings in my heart.

CHAPTER 1

FREEDOM IS FOR FREE

I was nervous. I could feel my cheeks glowing and I tried to cool them down with the backs of my hands, but to little effect. As I walked slowly towards the door, I rehearsed what I was going to say. My manager, Virginia, had also become my friend over the last year and I didn't want to disappoint her. I knocked on the door.

'Come in.'

Virginia was sitting at her desk, busy with papers, computer, schedules and timetables. Her beautiful dark hair fell smoothly behind her shoulders. She was a little plump, and that strengthened her position and softened her character.

'Take a seat, Miriam. How are you?' she asked cheerfully, shifting her purple shawl behind her shoulders. 'What can I do for you?'

I lifted a folder off the chair on the other side of her desk in order to sit down. 'Good, thank you.' I took a deep breath. 'I'm sorry, Gin,' I began, 'but I'd like to resign.' I waited a second before I continued. 'I like the school and all, but I am ready for something else.' Then I smiled, because I had reached the end of the lines I'd practised in my head.

At first Virginia looked slightly amused, then I saw a little surprise in her eyes. 'Why?' she asked. 'Have you got another job?' She placed her hand kindly on mine for a moment. Her shawl fell back to the front again.

'Oh, no,' I replied. 'I'd like to live in the wilderness.'

Virginia raised her eyebrows.

'The bush, nature, way up in the mountains,' I added.

Her mouth fell open. 'Really? But . . . why?' she asked.

'Well, it's just that the wilderness makes me feel alive,' I offered. Virginia still looked a little perplexed. 'I would like to try it, to see if I can survive, to see if it transforms my mind and my body,' I said.

'I see . . . but, will you still come out to town sometimes, do you think?' I could see Virginia trying to make sense of what I was telling her.

'Well, our plan is to go into the mountains for three months at a time, then we will come out to restock our supplies before returning to find another place in the wilderness,' I explained. 'We are going to do this for four seasons—one year.'

'But how will you shower?' she asked suddenly.

Shower? I thought. It took me a split-second to digest this unexpected question. 'Well, I'll just wash in the river!' I blurted out.

'Even in the middle of winter?' A flash of disbelief crossed Virginia's face. 'Oh no, you have to come out once a month! At least when you have your period, surely!'

I couldn't help myself: I laughed, and shortly afterwards Virginia laughed too. A rush of excitement filled me: this was really happening. I was about to embark on a great adventure.

On a beautiful autumn day in April, the teachers and the students at the school I worked at held a farewell party for me. They had organised a buffet, and afterwards I sang a song for everybody, outside in the courtyard. I was nervous about performing in front of a big group, because my voice had failed me on past occasions, but I was determined to say goodbye properly and with style. I sang a song that I had written myself: 'Get out for freedom, 'cause there is no key . . . Remember, freedom is for free.'

Later, when we were inside, I was trying to break up a piece of chocolate cake with a plastic fork totally unsuited to the task when Virginia came over to me.

'We'll certainly miss you, Miriam,' she said.

'That's very nice of you to say, Gin.' I smiled at her.

'I mean it. But I have to admit living in the wilderness still seems a strange choice to make,' she said honestly. 'I mean, you've had offers to work as a teacher, become an athlete or even a musician. How come a pretty young woman like you would choose to live in poverty and isolation in the mountains?' Her big brown eyes looked puzzled.

'Well—' I started, glancing down at my cake.

'I've seen those movies about young men who rebel against their parents,' Virginia went on. 'Guys who come out of difficult upbringings and escape into the wild. But you have a very good relationship with your family, don't you?'

I nodded. 'Oh, very much so! I really couldn't wish for better parents. I don't see them often, of course, but we are very close.'

'And they are OK with the fact that you'll be running around in the mountains?' Virginia chuckled.

'Oh, yes.' I beamed at her. 'They're very encouraging.'

'Well, that's why you have so much confidence, then!' she exclaimed. 'Your parents obviously gave you the courage to set out on your own.'

I had never thought about it that way, but perhaps Virginia was right.

'So . . . you're not rejected by society,' she continued, 'but you still choose to walk away from it. Even though, so to speak, you have a beautiful table laid out for you with an abundance of food, you're leaving the house—quite literally.'

'I guess some part of me finds it all meaningless.' I looked at her apologetically.

Virginia took a thoughtful sip of her soft drink. 'What do you mean by that?'

'Working your life away for money or status, fighting your way up the social ladder, buying more things that you don't really need . . . All of that.'

'And freezing in the mountains is a better option?' Virginia's eyes sparkled.

'Maybe not,' I replied, laughing. 'But I'll give it a try!'

After a brief pause, I added, 'I remember one particular night when I was about sixteen, I looked out of my window into the dark forest. As I did, I thought about how, once upon a time, our ancestors lived in those great forests, slept on the ground next to their animals. Now we are so reliant on living in houses, surrounded by comforts. What an enormous change.'

'Mmm, yes.' Virginia took another sip. 'So, do you feel humans have lost touch with the earth, then?'

'Well, don't you? Reconnecting with Mother Earth sounds a bit new-agey—' I pointed at the mountains through the window— 'but out there is a different world, Gin.'

She turned round to look at the faint shapes in the distance.

'The timeless beauty is just astonishing,' I said shyly. 'I want to try living without any barrier between the naked earth and myself. Cooking on fires, drinking pure water, sleeping on the ground . . . The wilderness might be able to teach us something, if we have time to listen.' I waited for Virginia's response to this outlandish statement.

She simply raised her eyebrows and nodded. Then her face lit up. 'Hey, you'll also learn all the survival skills for when the pandemic comes and everybody heads for the hills. I'll come running to you guys, then!'

I laughed, relieved by the change of topic.

Virginia put down her cup, then mimed drawing a bow to shoot an animal. 'Can you imagine me shooting a goat?' she cried.

'Wait until you're hungry enough!' I replied, then I heard my colleague Rose calling to me from outside the classroom. I put my plate with the untouched cake down next to Virginia's cup. As we walked together out to the courtyard, she grabbed my hand. 'Good luck, darling, I admire your courage. Please look after yourself, won't you?'

'Thank you, Gin. I will.'

The school gave me a most practical gift: a merino shirt, top and hat. I said a small speech to thank everybody, then I tried to hug my ten students. Most of them were secondary-school dropouts with behavioural issues, and every one had a problematic background and struggled to be part of society. I had helped them with finding jobs, writing reference letters and attending court cases. These youngsters were growing up in a world that I myself had never known. I had not always found it easy to work with them, especially not the gang-affiliated kids. Some of them didn't want to hug me, because they were glad to see me go—or perhaps because hugging was not part of gang 'protocol'.

One of my students was Sam. He was very tall and fat, and liked to get drunk most evenings, but he was a gentle giant. Big Sam did give me a hearty hug; he actually lifted me off the ground, and swirled me round so that my legs flew out behind me. It was such a funny sensation that it gave me the giggles, and even made my gang puppies smile (or snigger—I could never quite tell).

Fifteen-year-old Jimmy from Samoa was one of my favourite students. I remember when I first read his file. He had lived in the United States and had participated in big gang fights, then back in New Zealand he had been in a juvenile prison for theft and violent assaults. Other students had recognised his infamous name and warned me about him, so that I almost trembled when he first knocked on my door. But, by the end of his first day, I couldn't help but like the small and shy Jimmy. Later that year, I had organised a camping trip for the students and had learned that tough Jimmy was actually terrified of the darkness and ghosts. So, when I left the school, I gave him a little malachite gemstone that my mother had given to me when I was ten years old and was also afraid of ghosts. Jimmy seemed genuinely pleased to have it.

So Jimmy was happy, Virginia was happy, and I was happy. I considered it a good closure. This was the day I had looked forward to all year: the exhilarating moment when I would turn the page over into a new life. As I drove home, I felt euphoric. My heart was bursting with energy, and I smiled all the way. School was out. I had plenty of savings in the bank, I had New Zealand residency, and I had the freedom to live wherever I wanted.

A strong wind gust wobbled my car a little. How I loved that invisible force! As it slid down the mountaintops and into the valley, the wind threw the long blond tussocks into the air and tickled under the outstretched boughs of old trees. It carried seeds and bent the yellow flowers to kiss the ground. It gained strength on its way across the treeless plains, and now it was trying to blow my car off the road.

Our little home, a white wooden cottage surrounded by an ancient stand of native kahikatea trees, was half an hour's drive from the school. As I neared the house, I saw Peter out harvesting the pumpkins in the big vegetable garden. I waved to him, hooting jubilantly. It seemed fitting to make a lot of noise to celebrate my resignation.

I jumped out of the car and hugged Peter enthusiastically. I looked into his shining blue eyes, and in my best Ed Hillary voice announced, 'I knocked the bastard off!'

'Well, aren't you a good Kiwi now?' Peter chuckled.

I had met Peter in a restaurant in South India four years earlier. With his eyes full of enthusiasm, he had told me how he had walked on foot across South India in 45-degree-Celsius heat, climbed Himalayan ranges without maps or guides, and caught waves in the ocean at night during a lightning storm . . .

I had listened open-mouthed. In my years of travel, I had never met such a bright-eyed, intelligent man who had so boldly traded his house and job for a life of adventure. The attraction I felt to him was not only because of his knowledge and wisdom, his zest for an adventurous life, his ability to live simply, or even his strong body; there was an undeniable spark of love between us present right from the beginning. It is a spark that has never gone away. I knew then that I had found a truly remarkable man.

Two years after I met Peter, I had come with him to his home country, New Zealand. Peter and I yearned for natural places; we were always longing for peace, beauty and space. In my eyes, there was no greater beauty than the uninhabited, rough wilderness of New Zealand's steep and unforgiving mountains, extended forests, great rivers, lakes and wild animals. The mere sight of the mountains always made me feel very happy. The rural areas of the Netherlands that I had grown up in had some space, but no great wilderness. Once upon a time there would have been big forests, swamps and marshes, but now most people lived in cities that had grown together. Between the towns were fertile, green agricultural fields, divided by man-made canals. I had left a very orderly world behind, and I was now longing for something wild.

Peter had told me stories of his time in India during the seventies, when he had walked with sadhus in the Himalayas. I wanted to wander in the mountains and find peace, just like these spiritual holy men. But India has countless villages for food and other necessities, and quite predictable weather patterns; the high mountains here in New Zealand are uninhabited, and, apart from the occasional speargrass root and snowberries, there is very little to eat—besides wild animals. In order to make our move into the wilderness, we were forced to organise our life very carefully.

'How many cups of tea do you drink a day, sweetie?' I was sitting at the table with pen, paper and a calculator, working out the details of the supplies we would need to take with us.

Peter furrowed his brow. 'I don't know. Maybe six or so?'

'OK. That makes twelve a day, a hundred and twenty for ten days, two hundred and forty for twenty days . . . So that's about three hundred and sixty a month, or a thousand and eighty for three months.'

Since we planned to take a minimum of food with us, we had to calculate every teabag, spoonful of honey, gram of milk powder, flour, yeast, rice and beans to last us the winter. Peter had dried vegetables from our garden in the warm autumn sun. We had buckets in which we would store our food safely in the ground, and I had made a list of the contents of each one. Everything was meticulously organised, just like in the stories I had read about Arctic expeditions.

We also studied books about edible plants and mushrooms to prepare ourselves for gathering wild food. We counted on finding edible plants, berries and mushrooms, and I planned to learn to hunt wild animals like rabbits and goats, but if I failed to get anything, we wouldn't starve. I had grown up in a household of anthroposophy—a system established by Rudolf Steiner that uses mainly natural means to optimise physical and mental health—and I had been a vegetarian from birth. It was only when I arrived in New Zealand and learned about the ecological problems with introduced mammals that I saw it was ethically justifiable to shoot wild animals for food. Over the years, Peter and I had met several hunters, and one of them had a bow and arrows. The moment I saw that young man, I had known that I also wanted to learn how to hunt wild animals in the traditional way. So, I had bought a beautiful bow and many expensive arrows, and I had practised diligently every day for an hour in the garden on a fixed target.

We had decided to spend our first season in south Marlborough. We would set up a tent near an old hut called Base Hut that was not visited much during winter, but had four-wheel-drive access. It was Peter's idea to ask our good friend and neighbour Ricky to give us— along with all of our supplies—a lift to Base Hut in his four-wheel-drive truck. We didn't plan to live in the hut, but it had a firebox inside that would allow us to cook food on rainy days. This, we felt, was a very good place to start our life in the mountains.

We had bought an annual hut pass, which allowed us to stay in any hut that was maintained by the Department of Conservation (DOC), and we set out on lengthy walking sessions in preparation for our new life, carrying heavy backpacks on ten-day hikes. We walked off track with our bulky burdens, pushing through dense vegetation on rough ridges and impenetrable gullies. We waded through freezing rivers in sandals to train ourselves to endure numb feet. We tried lighting fires in the rain, and we discovered that wool was warmer than synthetic garments. I bought blankets in second-hand shops, and I hand-sewed jackets and trousers to keep us warm in the freezing weather.

Before we could leave, we also had to get rid of all our excess belongings. We had rented a furnished cottage so we had relatively few possessions. Except for one box of books, which we stored with Ricky, we gave everything away—laptops, mobile phones, clothes, shoes, wall hangings, alarm clocks and so on. I discovered it was much easier to accumulate things than to discard all the goods I had grown attached to, but when I looked at our two packs and our twelve buckets of food, I smiled. It was exhilarating to be so free of possessions.

After many weekends of training and reading a wide range of expedition books, I felt absolutely confident that we could survive in our tent near that hut in the wilderness. I couldn't wait to test my abilities.

On the morning of our departure, a beautiful autumn day in early May, I called my parents.

'How will we know that you're still alive?' my mother asked anxiously.

'You have to trust it, Mama,' I replied. 'We will be so careful, and I will write you long letters. We'll meet hunters who will post them for me.'

'Will they do that?' my mother asked, surprised.

'Yes. Hunters are very reliable people, and I'll put stamps on the envelopes so they'll only need to drop the letters in a postbox.'

My dad offered me a last piece of advice. 'Good luck with your bow hunting. Don't get lost!'

Mum sent kisses through the phone. *'Dag liefke!'*

I was suddenly aware that these were the last Dutch words I would hear for a long time. My dear, sweet parents. I felt a lump in my throat. *Will everything be all right?* I wondered.

'Mouse is here!' I heard Peter shout.

I swallowed my tears and ran outside to help lift the heavy buckets and boxes into the back of Ricky's truck, while Peter fixed all our gear firmly in place with ropes.

Ricky, our neighbour, was an energetic 37-year-old, with the bounce and verve of a teenager. Somehow, he had escaped the seriousness that often seems to come with having to support children who live with an ex-partner. He resembled a young dog, always looking for someone to play with. We had nicknamed him Mouse because he was quick, fast and tireless. He was a very good pig hunter, and to him no obstacle was ever too big. He did everything with great enjoyment.

When he had heard about our plan, he had been as excited as we were. His green eyes twinkled at the prospect of being part of our adventure. As well as taking us into the mountains with his truck, he told us he would also chainsaw a stack of firewood for us. Then we would spend one night together at the Base Hut campsite, as a kind of farewell party, while eating a meal of some of his wild pork.

Peter and I had a very good friendship with Mouse. The only friction was caused when his wife, Debbie, was around. She was a small but tough lady who was also an excellent pig hunter; she always caught the biggest boars. In their garage, one could admire her trophies: a long row of big pig tusks. Her appearance could be described as both beautiful and ugly—it depended on her mood. She was sometimes friendly, but sometimes prickly, tired and grumpy.

When Debbie had said that she wanted to come with Mouse to drop us off into the mountains, I'd had trouble concealing my feeling of disappointment. I had envisioned an evening of laughter and story-telling, but now I worried that if there was a bad atmosphere it might smother our enjoyment.

Mouse was in the driver's seat and Debbie sat next to him. Peter and I sat in the back with a box full of feijoas between us.

'You got everything?' asked Mouse.

Peter looked at me.

'I think so,' I said.

'Well, you'd better be sure, because it's too late now,' said Peter nervously.

I glanced over my shoulder at the buckets on the back of the truck. '*Ja*, we've got everything.'

'*Ja!*' Mouse laughed as he started up the truck. 'You got your German organising your expedition, Pete?'

'I ain't no German, Mouse!' I said, also laughing.

'You sure sound like one!' Mouse teased.

'The Dutch are actually just swamp Germans.' Peter winked at me. 'They can organise everything—every inch of your life, if you don't watch it.'

As we drove out of our valley for the last time, I looked out at the willow trees with yellow and red leaves that hugged the stream which ran through the paddocks.

'Who knows when we will be back here,' said Peter.

'Never!' I whispered, and laughed. I felt so excited.

'Never' wasn't true, of course; in the springtime, we would be on this road again, though not to our old cottage but to Mouse's house.

Peter's arm was leaning on the box of feijoas, his hand near my knee. I slotted my left hand into his.

'Thanks for doing all the packing.' He smiled at me.

'My pleasure.' I squeezed his hand a little.

We drove quietly along the road towards the foothills of the Southern Alps. Out of the window I saw endless rows of grapevines. The fruit had recently been harvested and the stalks looked deserted. The vineyards slowly gave way to paddocks full of sheep. Peter selected two small feijoas, wound down the window and threw them into the grass on the side of the road.

'One day, we might come back here and find a feijoa tree,' he said.

After about an hour, we turned off on to a quiet, corrugated gravel road, which we continued along until we saw a sign: FOUR-WHEEL-DRIVE ONLY—PROCEED AT YOUR OWN RISK.

'Can you stop here for a sec, babe?' said Debbie. She was holding a pair of binoculars and leaning out of the window to look at the valleys and ridges on her side.

'Any sign of pig rooting?' asked Mouse, as he brought the truck to a halt.

'Maybe. There's a gully over there with a bit of pigfern, some bare patches, bit of fresh rooting going on, I'd say.'

I was sitting behind her and quickly wound down my window to show my shared interest in hunting, even though I really had no clue what to look for. I wondered whether I should ask for the binoculars, or if that would be the wrong move. 'Do wild pigs live at such high elevation?' I asked.

'Oh, yeah. They live wherever they get left alone,' she answered.

'I've seen big boars living by themselves on the mountaintops. Very tough fucking beasts, I tell ya,' said Mouse, pulling a blue woollen jumper over his shirt.

'Where do the pigs run when you chase them from the tops?' I looked at him in the rear-view mirror.

He smiled at me. 'Nowhere. They're buggered, 'cause my dogs will get them in no time.'

'Poor pigs.' Peter sighed. 'You ought to leave them alone.'

'Poor Pete, you're too soft!' Mouse laughed. 'Pete couldn't hurt a fly,' he said to Debbie, putting his foot down to get the truck moving again.

Mouse forded the river many times. At one point, we drove through a deep stretch and water nearly came over the bonnet. I had visions of the truck breaking down in the middle of the river, water flowing through the doors and our precious buckets floating away downstream. The more I thought about it the more it seemed a real probability.

'Don't look so nervous, Miriam!' Mouse had seen my face in the rear-view mirror. 'I've got a snorkel on my truck. The water can come up to here.' He indicated with his hand on his chest.

'Have you ever actually been that deep under the water?' I asked disbelievingly.

'Yeah, that's when he bloody drowned his truck!' Debbie laughed.

'What do you do when that happens?' I was preparing myself for the worst-case scenario.

'That's when you get out and start walking,' answered Mouse.

We crept past a big slip that had wiped out half of the road, and Mouse was forced to drive over the small bushes on the other side. We looked down at the river below.

'Reminds me of the Himalayas,' said Peter. 'It looks like this, except everything there is on a bigger scale.'

'One bus goes over the edge there every week,' I added.

'A bus every week?' Mouse yelled over the engine noise. 'Where do they get all their buses from? They must waste a lot!'

'India big country, no worries!' Peter yelled back.

The truck climbed over a big rock with one wheel in the air, and the whole vehicle tilted on a dangerous angle. I looked at the ropes over our buckets and was glad that Peter had tied them securely.

Then we came to a 40-metre-long mud pool. On the right side was a vague track into the bushes that other people had taken to avoid the mud. Debbie tried to point out where to go, but Mouse was too hasty; he drove straight into the mud.

I held my breath when I felt the truck beginning to sink and I stared blankly at the windscreen, listening for a change in the engine sound. The wheels seemed to be losing grip and the back tyres were slipping in the ooze. We were moving precariously slowly, but thankfully we never came to a complete halt and we finally made it to the other side. Debbie spent the next five minutes telling Mouse that she had seen the escape route, but he—as usual—didn't listen. I was wondering whether to support Debbie or Mouse; in the end I said nothing.

Everybody was relieved when at last we saw Base Hut. It had been built at the foot of a steep, forested hill. There was a grass clearing on one side, and the river on the other. The hut, which was clad with iron sheets and had a corrugated-iron roof, looked a little forlorn and dilapidated. It appeared to have been standing there for a long time by itself.

Mouse was the first to jump out of the truck. 'We made it!' he exclaimed. 'So you might be huddling in this grotty little shack for the next three months while the rain thunders on the roof.'

'Or maybe you will get snowed in and you won't be able to open the door,' added Debbie.

'Holy fuck! Where will you go for a shit?' Mouse laughed.

I walked into the hut, my eyes resting on an empty woodshed on my way. When I stood in the doorway, it took a while for my eyes to adjust to the dim interior; there were only two small windows, and they hadn't been cleaned for a very long time. It was cold and it stank of mice. The walls, which had once been white, had turned brown over the years. On my left were four iron bunks with plastic-coated mattresses. In the middle was a table with three chairs, one of which was broken. On the right was the little firebox, with a few pinecones and newspapers on the floor. There was a small kitchen bench, but no sink or tap. A metal bucket stood next to the sink for collecting water from the river. On the lower bench was a stack of plates. When I lifted the top plate, black mouse droppings scattered on to the ground. Somebody had left an old billy and frying pan, but forgotten to clean them.

'Jeez, do we have to stay here for the night?' Debbie gasped, stepping inside behind me.

'I guess so.' I felt as uncomfortable as she did. I opened one of the windows to let some fresh air in. 'Once we get the fire going it will be all right.' I sounded more optimistic than I felt.

Mouse cut more firewood with his chainsaw in one hour than we could have cut with an axe in a week. He worked as an arborist, and I had seen him hanging from trees, with his knee hooked in a branch, chainsawing with one hand while keeping his balance with the other.

While Peter and Debbie stacked the firewood, I suggested burying the food buckets. Mouse offered to give me a hand. We took our time deciding where the best place would be, but when we finally started digging we discovered that the soil was only five centimetres deep. It was nothing but river stones. Even in the forest, the tree roots made it impossible to dig a hole.

Mouse sat down in the grass and laughed cheerily at our naivety.

'We'll just have to hide them,' I said, sitting down next to him. 'And cover them with moss and branches.'

I was nervous. If anything happened to our food it could be disastrous. I envisioned all kinds of scenarios. Hunters might see a little bit of white bucket and steal the food. Or their dogs would sniff out the flour. And what about rats? They could chew through the lids in a heartbeat.

'So, how do you like your new house?' Mouse asked, as he dragged two of the heavy buckets towards a natural hollow.

'I think I'd rather sleep in the tent outside than in that dirty hut,' I said mournfully. 'Tomorrow we will pitch our tent.'

'Not many women would choose to live in a tent in the winter.'

'Not many men would either!' I laughed and cocked my head in his direction.

'True,' he admitted. 'You are quite unusual, not needing the luxury of a clean, dry house though,' he said, picking up his buckets.

'I enjoy a simple life, walking in beauty, cooking on a fire, washing in the river. It makes me feel so alive.' I opened the palms of my hands. 'The best things in life are free!'

'Freedom is for free!' He smiled at me.

'Wouldn't you like to live in the wilderness for some time?' I asked.

'Yeah, I like the bush, but I'm more of a people person, really,' Mouse said. 'I'd feel too isolated up here in the mountains.'

I looked at his shining eyes and his mouth that looked like a dolphin's. The world was always a happy and carefree place with Mouse around.

While Peter cooked a tasty curry with Mouse's wild pork, the hut slowly warmed up with a crackling fire. Two candles on the table lit up our dinner. We ate with the occasional comment or joke, but I felt a little tense and slightly on my guard with Debbie around. Soon after we had done the dishes, we decided to get into our sleeping bags to keep warm. I quickly selected the least dirty mattress, checking first to see whether the black stains would rub off the plastic coating. Then I crawled into my sleeping bag, and made a pillow out of my jumper. *This is the last night my sleeping bag will be clean*, I thought.

'Is everybody warm?' Peter asked.

'I'm cooking,' said Mouse. He always took every sentiment to the extreme.

'When the fire dies down it will be cold,' said Debbie.

Nobody knew what to say any more. When it was silent for a while, Debbie said, 'Goodnight, everybody.'

'Goodnight,' I replied.

Every ten minutes, Mouse turned over and his bed squeaked.

'Stop turning round so often, Ricky,' Debbie snapped.

Then, to my horror, I heard mice running around. They made a lot of noise with a plastic bag, and Peter got up and put the bag away.

When it was quiet again, I lay there wondering whether the mice would investigate my sleeping bag next. They might run over my face by accident. I felt very uncomfortable and suddenly very hot. I wished I had pitched the tent; I would have felt much more at ease in my own enclosed space.

After some hours of half sleep, I woke up again.

This time there were rats in the ceiling. They couldn't come inside, but they were running up and down in the otherwise silent night. Mouse switched his headlight on, walked with his clean socks over the dirty wooden floor and grabbed the broom.

'You're going to sweep the rats out, are you?' Peter's voice piped up.

'Watch this,' Mouse whispered. He zigzagged through the room, with his eyes on the ceiling to detect the rats' positions, then he bashed the head of the broom with deafening force against the ceiling. The result was absolute silence. Mouse bashed the broom another few times for good measure. It was only a thin ceiling and the rats must have been shell-shocked by the sudden noise.

'See,' said Mouse triumphantly. 'It worked.'

The next morning Debbie was packing the truck before we had even finished breakfast.

'We have to head out quickly in case it starts raining and the river comes up,' Mouse reasoned, stroking his wife's back. Maybe it was because of the sleepless night, but Debbie looked rather pale and fragile. When it at last came time to say goodbye, she was already waiting in the truck.

I hugged Mouse's wiry body. I didn't want to let him go. I suddenly realised that he might be the last person we would see for a long time.

'We will miss you,' I said.

Smiling cheerfully, he told us he was happy for us and promised to pay a visit if the river allowed it. 'Good luck with the hunting,' he said to me. 'Remember: sun on the back, wind in your face!'

I nodded and tried to return his smile.

Then they drove away. Mouse forded the river with much bravado, water splashing up over the bonnet. Just before the corner, he tooted, and we could hear the drone of the engine for another minute or so.

Then the silence arrived.

CHAPTER 2

WINTER

Peter turned round and put my arms over his shoulders. 'Now it's just us!' he said, embracing me. I kissed him softly on the forehead.

In the sky above us, a big hawk appeared, gracefully following the path of the river below. When it saw us, it flapped its brown wings wildly to change course, then disappeared over the other side of the mountains—which, to us, was the other side of the world.

I took a deep breath. 'I feel like we have finally come home.'

Peter nodded. 'This is the world we were all born into.'

I took his hand and looked out at the valley and forest all around us. 'Amazing feeling, to be so alone in such an isolated place, isn't it?' I said.

'It is. The nearest house is a good three days' walk from here. This time of year, most people leave the mountains alone and stay inside until the spring.'

I looked up and saw some clouds drifting over the ranges. They were moving fast; there must have been a lot of wind on the tops.

'What do you think will happen to us?' Peter wondered.

I thought for a while before responding. 'I don't know. I really can't picture the future.'

'Because it's totally unknowable.'

'Yes, it's actually as though we have no future. Just the great timeless void, an infinite mist.'

Back at the hut, I rekindled the fire and made two cups of tea, which I carried over to Peter, who was sitting on a rock near the river.

'This is absolutely, amazingly beautiful, isn't it?' I looked at the crystal clear water, which cascaded down from the mountains. The big round rocks, worn smooth by the current, shimmered in the sun.

'Yes, and vast parts of this island are like this, too.' Peter leaned back on to the rock.

'I just feel so lucky to be here, to actually live in this beauty.' I looked at the rocky outcrops on the other side of the river, the dense forest in the distance, and the old trees nearby. When my tea was finished, I made another cup. We had no clock, but I guessed it was probably ten in the morning. I thought of Virginia and Rose, who would be sipping their coffees at the table by the window in the staff room. We were now in such different worlds.

After my initial elation, an uncomfortable feeling was creeping to the surface, a kind of realisation that sent a flash of panic through my body. It was the one thought that clashed with all my fantasies of living peacefully in the wilderness: the *What now?* thought. What was I going to do next?

I thought of things to do and remembered I hadn't seen the toilet facilities. The long-drop was built 70 metres from the hut. It was a deep hole with a wooden structure on top; the only thing about it that resembled a modern toilet was the white seat. A soggy roll of paper sat in the corner. I lifted the lid and looked into the hole. The smell was so horrible that I quickly closed the lid.

If I sit on that toilet with the door closed, I'll be suffocated, I thought.

I felt a little apprehensive. The hut and toilet were worse than I expected, and I forced myself not to think of the months ahead. I jumped into action instead.

The hut desperately needed cleaning, so I collected a bucket of water from the river, found an old towel and started washing the grimy walls, dirty windows and even the stains on the mattresses. We would definitely sleep in the tent, as the hut obviously belonged to the rats and mice, but in bad weather we could at least shelter in a clean hut.

Peter saw me running back and forth with buckets. 'Why don't you sit down for a minute?' he asked. But I had been running around for years and I found it difficult to sit still. I took the dirty frying pan from the shelf and scrubbed it clean with sand from the river, then I did the same with the cutlery and the billy. Next, I searched around for the best place to camp, eventually pitching the tent underneath some trees with a flysheet strung over the top as an extra roof. The tent would be our bedroom, the hut our living room during bad weather; the river was our tap, fridge, shower, dishwasher and washing machine, and the whole valley was our garden. Our home in the wilderness. I started to feel better about the place.

Several times Peter offered to help me but, dreading the moment when all the chores were done, I preferred to do everything on my own. I needed to fill up the empty day. Finally, after I had tied a rope between the trees for a washing line, I sat down. I couldn't think of anything else to do.

What time could it be? I wondered.

The sun was just touching the top of the mountains. It felt as if it was four o'clock, but it could also be three o'clock. The day seemed endless.

This was the one thing all our hiking trips and training had not prepared me for: boredom. Being occupied with walking every day was relatively easy when compared to just . . . living. If I had been a hiker, I would have shouldered my pack and begun to walk to the next hut. If I had been a hunter or a fisher, I would have declared it a day and walked back to the car. But I could go nowhere.

I joined Peter, who was calmly reading an old newspaper in the sun.

'I think it'll be a bit of an adjustment in the beginning, don't you?' I sounded far more coherent than I felt.

'Oh, yes, a major adjustment.' Peter nodded. 'The mind needs to calm down. It could take days to ease into the rhythm of this place. Maybe weeks.'

Those first days were indeed a major adjustment, on many levels. Sometimes I felt comfortable and at home; other times I felt insecure about the future. But mostly I felt bored and restless. I no longer had a job, a project or stimulation like social contacts, email, music and all the rest. It felt as though I was going through withdrawal symptoms. My mind was running too fast, my thoughts were all over the place and endless memories flashed by. My head felt chaotic compared to the silence of nature, whose gentle rhythm was much slower than my busy self.

I was glad to be able to talk with Peter about the difficult process of slowing down. He hadn't ever lived in the wilderness before either, but he did seem to understand the nature of the mind a little better than I did. Even though he appeared tranquil compared to me, he said he knew exactly how I felt; he had not found a million chores to do, but he had read all of the old newspapers and magazines in the hut from cover to cover. His suggestion was that we just go through the boredom and restlessness, and do nothing for a while.

Nothing.

That was the last thing I wanted to do. Nothing meant boredom, the dreaded void, horrible emptiness. Nothing was the unknown.

I had discovered I was afraid of nothing. I would be forced to face this fear in the weeks to come.

On the first morning that we awoke to sunshine, we built a big fire outside the hut. I like fires. Since the age of five, I have been fascinated by two things, both taught to me by my very patient father: building tree huts and lighting fires.

We had brought with us flour, yeast and an old-fashioned camp oven, which is basically a big iron pot with a flat lid. Peter had learned to use camp ovens when, as a 20-year-old, he worked as a cook on cattle stations in the Gulf of Carpentaria in Northern Australia. In order to bake bread in our camp oven, we would need dense wood for our fire; Peter explained to me that if we used soft wood like pine we would end up with ashes and no embers, which would leave our bread uncooked in the middle. It took about two hours for the dense wood we gathered to become red-hot embers.

Peter then kneaded the bread dough, and placed it in the camp oven. When the dough had risen to the lid, he moved the burning logs aside and created a hollow in the heart of the glowing embers. He placed the camp oven in the hollow, then moved coals on top of the flat lid with a little shovel.

After an hour, I anxiously lifted the lid, and together we gazed upon a beautiful golden-brown loaf of bread. We smiled from ear to ear as we ate our first hot slices. It was delicious. It tasted of independence.

A colourful little bellbird with a shiny green back and yellow tummy was singing in a tree nearby. Its ruby-red eyes studied us from different angles.

'Watch its beak carefully,' said Peter quietly.

The bird sang with much enthusiasm, but sometimes its beak opened without making any noise.

'Some of the sounds we can't hear!' I whispered.

'Some of the high notes, yes.'

'What else in this world are we missing without knowing it?' I wondered.

'That's for us to find out, Miriam,' Peter said, and the bellbird flew away.

In our first week, a black-and-white billy goat had walked past our camp. I ran after him and bleated 'meeeh, meeeh, meeeh' to see if he would call back, but the goat just wandered casually off into the forest. I hadn't made any attempt to shoot it, because we were still eating Mouse's pork.

A week later, though, it was time for me to go in search of more meat. While I had practised shooting at a target, I didn't have much experience with actual hunting. However, I was eager to learn a new skill.

When I thought of the word 'skill' it brought back memories of Peter's brother, Mark, who owned a large sheep station. We had visited him three years earlier, during my first month in New Zealand.

During that visit, Peter, Mark and I had been standing around the kitchen bench, drinking cups of tea and chatting while, with a big hunter's knife, Mark cut slices of some pork-and-venison salami made from animals he had hunted himself. The two brothers couldn't have appeared more different. Mark, with his super-short hair, talked, acted and looked like a typical farmer: practical, no nonsense, straight to the point. A bit blunt at times. The way he was standing showed he was as strong as an ox—a force to be reckoned with. With a serious face and laconic tone, he was busy summarising the political state of the world.

'With over-population and natural resources being increasingly stripped, the pressure will intensify and it's only a matter of time before some sort of disaster strikes.' He looked us briefly in the eyes, and nodded. 'Yes, the entire shaky system will fall down like a bloody house of cards.' With the tip of his knife he picked up a piece of salami and put it in his mouth.

'But how?' I asked.

Both brothers were now looking at me with bemused expressions, as though I was the only one who had never contemplated an apocalypse before.

'Genetic-engineering disaster,' said Peter. 'Or a Third World War.'

'Climate war. Pandemic,' Mark added.

'Stock-market collapse like in 1929.' Peter shook his head slowly. 'There could be any number of causes.'

'Yep,' said Mark. 'When the shit hits the fan, money will be worth nothing and everybody will have to fend for themselves.' He moved the sliced salami across to us.

I was somewhat surprised by Mark's words. Peter and I had just spent many years travelling in Asia, where the problems of over-population and resource shortages of all kinds are very apparent—but these things were not at all obvious to me here in New Zealand.

'If law and order break down,' Mark continued, 'I know what I'll do.' He leaned forward conspiratorially. 'I'll blow up the bloody bridges so that no one can get to my property.' He pointed out of the window, and I looked at the endless green hills and patches of forest that belonged to Mark and his family. 'With the bridges gone, only people with skills will be allowed on my land.'

Skills, I thought. *Skills*.

'I've got plenty of guns to defend my family with. Above the door is my three-o-eight, just in case I need it quickly, and I've got other guns in my safe.'

'Enough for a small army!' Peter laughed.

I envisioned myself, in this imaginary post-apocalyptic future, standing on the edge of the bridgeless river.

'What skills do you have?' Mark and his mates would shout from the other side.

'Physical education teacher,' I would call back.

'What?' the survivalists would cry out at such a useless answer. What survival value would *that* offer to the community?

'Physical edu—'

BOOM!

Miriam's dead.

My imagination then went straight to a great cannibal feast—since nothing would be allowed to go to waste in those future days, of course.

If an apocalypse ever comes my way, I had reasoned then and there, *I should probably make sure I have some survival skills . . . just in case. And anyway, even if nothing happens at all, at least I will have enjoyed the process.*

I had therefore decided I wanted to learn how to hunt like our ancient ancestors did. As a child, I had made bows and arrows with my father, out of the bamboo in the garden, and Robin Hood had been my hero. Hunting seemed to suit me nicely, I thought, so about a year before our move into the wild I had bought a traditional recurve bow. My beautiful bow has no sights, and the aiming has to be done intuitively—'intuitive shooting', they call it, which sounded just right.

So, when we had finished all of Mouse's pork and it came time for me to set out in search of more meat, I took my bow, put my knife in its sheath and headed confidently off along a path into the forest. I imagined this must have been what it was like for early Native American hunters, striding through the wild landscape, bow and arrows slung over their shoulders. Here I was, hunting in the wilderness of New Zealand. What a fantastic, epic adventure!

I followed the track up the mountain, listening out for any sound and careful to be silent. I thought I heard goats bleating in the distance, but when I got closer discovered it was only the voice of the river. I hid behind trees, sat still, sniffed everywhere and looked for any goat droppings or tracks in the dirt. But the whole world was motionless—even the birds were silent. I stared at the forest on my left but I didn't dare venture too far off the path for fear of getting lost. I suddenly felt uneasy in this impressive expanse of forest, where nothing was quite familiar.

I spotted a big boulder in a grassy clearing. Mouse had told me that goats liked open clearings, so I crept over and hid behind the rock. I put an arrow in my bow, in preparation for a fine shot. I slowly lifted my head, half expecting to see a goat standing there, waiting for me, at my desired 20-metre distance. But no. Nothing. Not even a complacent rabbit or a lost hare.

I bleated in a last, desperate attempt to trick a goat into the clearing. 'Meeeh! Meeeh!'

The only answer was silence and a fading sun.

Disappointed, I turned and walked quickly back to our camp. I was suddenly fearful of the encroaching darkness.

'How far did you go?' Peter asked when I returned. 'What did you see?' He was excited to hear about my first hunting attempt.

'Um, not so far actually.' I felt a little ashamed. 'I didn't see anything,' I mumbled.

'Oh, well, you can only try,' Peter said encouragingly. 'There is plenty more time to learn to hunt.'

The clear days were so warm that we were able to sit out in the sun wearing only a T-shirt, but as soon as the sun disappeared behind the mountains the cold air descended upon us. Our tent was beneath evergreen trees, and their branches kept us warm during the long nights, when the valley was invaded by frost and the first morning light revealed white crystals in the grass.

We went for many beautiful walks on those clear days. Peter often led the way, walking a little distance ahead of me. I felt very safe in the wild with Peter. On my own I would have been afraid of losing the way, but with him around I had no such fear. He had a good sense of direction, and even if we did get lost he would know what to do. He walked elegantly; I never saw him placing his feet casually or roughly. He disliked following a trail, and would instead walk right through the forest to rocky creeks and canyons, leading us to lofty viewpoints, enchanting green meadows and secret little caves. One time, he spotted a big old pine and we climbed into its branches and sat four metres above the ground, at the same level as the birds, and looked out over the entire valley.

'This looks a bit like Scandinavia,' I said, pointing to the pines in the valley.

'Or perhaps Canada,' he said, finding a comfortable place to sit. 'Those trees are firs, pines and macrocarpas. From the 1850s, they tried to farm this area, burning all the dry ridges with fire, but they couldn't burn the moist gullies.' He pointed to a stand of beautiful old native beech trees that had survived. 'Because of all the burning, the valley eroded so much that they decided to sow pine seeds out of a fixed-wing plane.'

'How do you know that?' I asked, scratching some nice-smelling gum off the tree.

'I met an old guy last year who selected the seeds for the operation when he was young.'

'But why were they concerned about whether this was eroding or not?'

'Because without vegetation the area was prone to flash-flooding. The whole lower river valley filled up with rocks from these mountains here and all the farmland flooded regularly.'

I looked at the beautiful contours of the big pines. Some of them were as slim as a pencil; others had long side branches or were the shape of a cone.

'It's good for us—we won't get overrun with trampers. New Zealanders these days don't really like to see introduced trees.' Peter laughed.

'Even though their forefathers planted these trees themselves?'

'Yeah, the ideology has changed. People would rather go to pristine native forest.' He smiled. 'There is only one rule with ideologies and that is the fact that they change all the time.'

Peter was leaning back against the trunk of the tree, his legs folded and curled round the branch. His long, wavy hair fell behind his shoulders; in the sun it looked golden, and in the shadow silver. He always has an aura of stillness when he is in nature. He dislikes haste and hurry, and tries to enjoy every moment of the day. Now, his blue eyes gazed over the landscape, taking in the detailed beauty. His big ears were sticking out through his hair; he tries to hide them, but I like his elf ears. He can hear so many things, often over great distances— sometimes he can even hear my thoughts.

After some weeks of exploration, we decided to move deeper into the mountains to South Hut, which we had never been to and were curious to see. We set out on a sunny day, with all our belongings and two weeks' worth of food. I always hiked in sandals. In the past I had worn boots, but my wide feet always suffered from painful blisters. My light sandals prevented this, and also had the advantage of drying out quickly after the numerous river crossings—which was useful now, as our route took us along a broad riverbed and over big boulders.

I looked at the rushing river for a moment, dreading taking the first step into the ice-cold water. The water was bone-achingly cold and made me shiver instantly, and the torrent pulled at my legs. I started to feel very nervous about my clothes, which were wrapped in only a few plastic bags that would not remain watertight if I was swept away by the river. What's more, if I fell in, we didn't have a car to go back to—Peter would have to pitch the tent and put me in my sleeping bag to prevent hypothermia.

'Use your walking stick as a pivot!' yelled Peter over the noise of the river.

The rushing water was confusing—I couldn't see the bottom properly—and the current was throwing me off balance.

'This way!' Just as I was about to plunge into a deep channel, Peter pointed with his stick to a shallower point. I slowly waded out of the river, my sandals filled with small gravel.

'Aren't you cold?' I shouted.

'Freezing!' Peter called back. 'Keep on walking!'

But I had to stop and empty the pebbles out of my sandals first. I wobbled dangerously on one leg underneath my heavy backpack, while Peter slowly walked into the forest.

The path left the valley floor behind and climbed steeply into the mountains. Permanent frost was already visible in the shadowy parts of the valley abandoned by the sun, but the climb was so strenuous that I quickly warmed up again. Eventually, the trees opened out to a view over the valley. On the other side of the gorge was a vertical rock face. Wind funnelled in between the crevices, making the trees above the river sway softly.

It was a beautiful, gentle sight. The dance of the treetops.

'This beauty and purity will transform the mind, don't you think?' said Peter. His eyes were full of wonder. 'All the great religions have one basic message. Christ, Buddha, Muhammad, Lao-tzu—they all speak about the transformation of the mind.'

I nodded, looking out at the powerful river, which had cut so effortlessly through the hard rocks. 'Whatever it might mean, this pure and wild place should change our consciousness.'

The last half an hour of the climb was exhaustingly steep. It was amazing to finally see the small white hut sitting in the colossal landscape. Before we could reach the hut, however, we had to cross a wet, slippery swamp. I sank up to my knees in the black mud.

'Why did they build the hut here?' I sighed in frustration, sloshing through the freezing bog.

Inside, the hut was damp. Sunlight had not reached it for weeks. But there was an open fire and firewood in the shed. The interior looked light and clean, thanks to three windows.

'Hey, no sign of mice! And what a nice hut, with all this light,' I exclaimed merrily as I started to unpack our bags.

'Should we sleep in the hut, rather than the tent?' I asked. 'How many visitors will come in the next month, do you think?'

'Well, last year four people came in June, and six in July.' Peter was flicking through the hut book. 'Listen to this entry from a hunter who came last winter: *I found two ruptured tins of peas in this hut. They froze solid overnight!*'

We exchanged an astonished look.

'Here's another from July last year,' Peter continued. '*This is the coldest hut I've ever stayed in—measured minus seven inside the hut. Welcome to Siberia!*'

I looked out of the window at the pines scattered among the alpine beech forest.

'Oh god, here's another bit of news.' Peter kept reading the entries. 'This is written by a possum trapper who spent a few days here in June last year. *The fucking fireplace ain't working—DOC concreted the fire bed. Without a draw to keep the fire going, it smokes like a bastard!*'

'What does that mean?' I stared at the open hearth.

'In the old days there would have been boulders on the floor of the fireplace to allow the fire to suck the air from the outside. But, with the concrete plugging the gaps between the boulders, there's no air for the fire to burn properly. We'll try it out, but we might have to open the window to get a draught.'

When Peter lit the fire we discovered that the angry possum trapper had been right: the hut filled up with vast quantities of smoke. We sat in our smoke-hole until our eyes were stinging and watering and Peter was forced to open the window. The freezing draught rekindled the fire, and the air in the hut cleared up within seconds.

'How are we going to keep warm?' I worried that maybe we weren't equipped for the icy temperatures that might hit us in the coming months—this was only the beginning of winter, after all.

'We'll just have to build bigger fires,' said Peter. 'The good thing with an open fire is that you can put big logs on it. But the winter rain will come soon, so we'd better get the woodshed filled right up.'

———

Urged on by the imminent wet weather, we anxiously set out on firewood missions. Once the wood was saturated, it wouldn't dry out again until spring. I decided to collect the washed-up logs on the riverbed that had been dried out by the wind. To get to the river, I had to go down a slippery slope covered with clumps of speargrass. This severe, spiky grass is common in the New Zealand high country, and we'd had enough experience with it to know that it can inflict serious injury if you aren't careful. The root of the speargrass is edible, but we had never dared go near enough to any plant to try it.

When I found a suitable log on the riverbed, I lifted it on to my shoulder. On my way back to the hut, I spotted another log. Recalling the weight-training sessions I'd done as a teenager when I was a competitive pole-vaulter, I judged that I would be able to carry a second log and, after a few attempts, I managed to position one log on each shoulder. This might have been bordering on extremism, but I started to feel a great excitement in my heart. Our life had become a proper expedition! I slowly shuffled back up the hill between the speargrass clumps, through the forest, across the creek and at last back to the hut, where I dropped the logs on the ground and collapsed theatrically.

Peter stood in the door of the hut with his mouth hanging open. 'One log is heavy enough, but two logs is insane,' he exclaimed. 'Soon you'll be cutting off one breast to shoot your bow better!'

I laughed, then jumped back to my feet and lifted Peter 20 centimetres up in the air, in order to further demonstrate my strength.

Peter grinned. 'OK then, watch this, Miss Amazon,' he said as I returned him to the ground.

Taking the axe in both hands, he positioned himself in front of one of the logs. With his feet set apart, he lifted the axe behind his head. His knees came forward, his hips followed, his chest was round like a drawn bow and, with a brilliant whip-like movement, he swung the axe right into the heart of the log.

'I can do that.' I reached impatiently for the axe's handle.

'No, no, you've only seen half the act.'

Peter reset his position. He looked at the log, took a deep breath and once again made his whole body move like a whip. Transferring all his strength to the axe head, he hit the log in exactly the same place so that a crack appeared.

'Wow, that is incredible! Let me try,' I said, and Peter handed the heavy axe to me.

Imitating Peter's serious expression, I positioned myself in front of the log. I moved my body like a whip and hit the log. The axe landed five centimetres from Peter's split, and it just bounced off the log.

'You see,' Peter said, when I had hit the log in 10 different places. 'It's not as easy as it looks.'

Carrying the logs had left streaks of mud on my neck and I felt warm enough to have a wash in the cold river. I carried my blue enamel cup, yellow Sunlight soap and a little red towel to the riverbed. The bright colours looked nice among the grey stones.

I undressed and stood naked at the edge of the roaring river, the cold breeze caressing my skin. I splashed water over my body then washed myself with the soap as quickly as possible. I towelled off and immediately put my clothes back on. Once I was warm again, I wet my hair with cups of water and soaped my head.

I bent forward, looking at the forest upside down, and put my head into the fast-flowing river. The freezing-cold water gave me an immediate headache. The earth disappeared, my long hair flowed downstream, and for five seconds I directly experienced the heart of the river. It was exhilarating. It made me feel cleaner than all of the hot showers of my life put together.

Our days in South Hut were very cold, and the nights were freezing. The fire made a small difference, but we didn't have enough wood to keep it going all night. Peter always likes to have a cup of water next to his bed at night, but this was pointless because it turned to ice during the frosty nights. It was so bitterly cold that we could see big plumes of our breath inside the hut at all times.

One late afternoon we were waiting for the rice and beans to cook, while the rain drummed on the corrugated-iron roof. The freezing draught from the open window chased what little heat there was out of the room. I had put on all of my jumpers and jackets and wrapped my woollen blanket round me. Peter sat in front of the fire.

He slowly lifted the lid of the billy to taste a bean and check if it was ready.

'I don't like it any more, Miriam.' His face was gloomy and his voice cheerless.

'The beans?' I asked hopefully.

'No. I don't like this hut in this swamp, the smoking fire, the freezing temperatures—all *this*.'

He looked at me. 'This is nonsensical! I am sitting in front of a fire and ice is forming on my back! What are we doing here?'

I didn't know what to say. He indeed looked cold with his blue nose and white cheeks, but I felt somewhat disappointed. We had barely been in the mountains for a month. This was only the beginning of our expedition life, and I expected much more severity, yet Peter sounded as though he wanted to bail out.

It was silent for a little while. I looked at my finger with a black dash on it; I had touched the hot handle of the billy when it came out of the fire, and it had left a slight scar.

'Well, why don't you eat more? You've been eating so little lately.' I made an effort to sound cheerful and supportive.

'I'm so cold that I'm not hungry during the day,' he answered dolefully.

That didn't make sense to me: if I felt cold, I would eat more, not less.

I looked at all the food in the corner of the hut. Three days ago, we had walked back to Base Hut to get more flour, rice and beans.

'We still have another two weeks' worth of rations,' I said hesitantly. 'I don't feel like walking them back down again.'

'No, me neither.' He gazed at the wooden floorboards. 'This is only the *beginning* of the winter. Can we even endure these conditions?' His blue eyes were filled with concern. 'In the summer this hut is no doubt fantastic, but it is horrible in winter.'

'East Hut is better.' Luckily we knew this, as we had explored East Hut the previous year. 'As soon as our food is finished, we'll move back to Base Hut and then we will go to East Hut.'

I also felt cold and miserable at times, but I never considered going back to where we had come from. The lure of adventure was too attractive—I felt like an explorer from the old days. Yes, our voyage was accompanied by physical hardship, freezing temperatures, monotonous food, endless rain, cabin fever and other miseries, but I also felt so alive. We were touching the real world, with its extreme elements of rawness and wildness. When I dragged wood from the riverbed, washed in the cold rivers or lit a fire at night, my heart and soul felt full of energy.

For me, there was also an element of curiosity. What would happen if Mark's words were true and our world's systems did collapse for whatever reason? Would Peter and I be able to survive? We had brought most of our food with us so we were not starving, but what would it be like if the day came when we had to rely on our hunting and gathering alone? Could we even survive if we had no extra rations? This was a good experiment, I thought. I was beginning to see that a life of survival would actually be dauntingly arduous.

Since my first hunting excursion, I had set out with my bow many more times, but apart from one hare—which immediately ran away—I had not seen anything. After Peter's gloomy fireside confession I resolved to try setting a trap for a possum. Meat might give us the warmth and energy we so sorely needed.

Brushtail possums were first introduced to New Zealand from Australia by early European settlers in the 1850s, and are today designated a major conservation pest. In New Zealand, most people would never think of eating a possum, but Peter and I needed meat. I had no experience with trapping and killing possums, but Mouse and Peter had once showed me how and it had seemed simple enough. The only thing I was afraid of was catching a finger when setting the trap, but everything went well—everything, that is, except for the fact that no animal stood in my trap. I had sprinkled flour and curry spices around the trap, but the possum was not fooled.

The next morning, we both woke up with hunger pains. Our big meals of rice and beans filled us up, but the nights were so long and cold that we burned up all our food by the time the sun came up again. We were losing weight just by enduring the freezing conditions.

On the third morning, Peter went out to check the trap.

'We have a possum!' I heard him call.

A brown possum about the size of a cat was sitting in the trap. It had soft dark-brown fur, a fluffy tail and a small head with black eyes and pink ears. It had little claws and rat-like teeth.

'You kill it,' I said quickly. Peter had a lot of experience with possums, I knew.

'You're the one who wants to be a hunter. You should have a go,' Peter replied.

We both dreaded killing the possum.

Hesitantly, I grabbed its tail with my left hand then hit the possum on the head with the back of our axe—but, to my horror, I didn't hit it properly and it didn't die. It looked up at me with terrified big brown eyes. With shaking hands, I hit the possum several times more.

'Between the eyes!' Peter yelled.

I had envisioned that killing a possum would be straightforward, but the reality for an ignorant beginner was sickening. I lost my grip on the tail, and the battered possum dragged its trap a metre away from us.

Peter stepped in and took hold of its tail, and, with one accurate hit, the possum went down at last.

It was only when the possum was lying lifeless in the grass that I felt I could breathe again. My heart was beating wildly and I felt like crying.

'Do you want me to skin it?' Peter asked, pulling the possum from the trap.

'No, no, I'll do it,' I answered. I was trying desperately to overcome my shock and be practical, but my voice sounded broken. My hands still shaking, I picked up the possum and laid it out in front of me. I looked at its still body. Just moments ago it had been living; now it was dead. Where had the life gone?

I tried to recall Mouse's instructions on how to skin an animal, but all of a sudden I couldn't remember anything. I didn't want to look like a wuss, though, so I pretended I knew what I was doing. I tentatively cut the skin round the paws, but I pulled it too roughly and it ripped. A lot of fur came out and it stuck to the meat. I tore pieces of skin off the animal, and even more grass and sand got stuck to the meat.

Peter came back and looked at my mess. 'Can't you remember how Mouse and I did it?'

'Yes, I do remember!' I lied. 'This is the right way!' I sounded angrier than I meant to be.

'Why don't you let me show you?' Peter was starting to get annoyed. 'Look at all the dirt on the meat.'

'I'll do it. Just leave me to it!' I had tears in my eyes.

I finally managed to pull most of the skin off, then I cut the stomach open and hesitantly moved my hands into the possum's still-warm body to pull out its intestines. All the blood and intestines fell on to the ground. It stank and it was revolting.

I felt horrible.

I slowly washed the possum in the river in a feeble attempt to get the dirt off the meat. It was more difficult than I thought, and the meat still looked dirty. When I finally came into the hut with the dripping possum, Peter looked at it with disgust.

I placed the meat on the cutting board and walked quickly out of the hut and into the forest. The tears pricked my eyes. One big tree had created some space around itself, its big branches reaching out like arms. I was able to step easily up on to the first branch. I sat there and cried about my messed-up possum, Peter's irritated words and, most of all, for taking the life of this beautiful creature that had done nothing wrong. What a misery I had caused. What a gruesome horror all this had turned out to be. Why should we kill these innocent animals?

Eventually I walked back to the hut. Peter saw my red eyes and hugged me. 'Taking a life is not easy, is it?' he said kindly. He found it just as horrible as I did.

'I don't want to be a hunter or trapper.' The tears had come back into my eyes.

'You don't have to be if you don't want to,' he said, kissing my eyes. 'Here, you can have the first taste.' He shyly handed me a plate—his token of friendship.

Peter had prepared the meal, as I had no idea how to cook meat. Since I used to be a vegetarian, not only killing an animal but also cooking and eating the meat was totally new to me. I wasn't sure whether I'd like it. Peter had boiled the fat possum in the billy until the meat fell off the bones. He set the meat apart, then he fried one precious carrot and onion with Indian spices and added the possum meat. We ate it with fried rice. It was absolutely delicious, and we especially enjoyed the much-needed fat.

'So what do you think—will you trap or hunt again?' Peter asked later on.

'Well . . . I'll give it another try.'

We slept well that night. We felt warm during the night and we didn't wake up with hunger pains the next morning.

The possum gave us three meals.

We were rolled up in our sleeping bags. Wearing gloves, I held my book up in the cold air. We had brought books with us that we would be able to study a hundred times over and still learn something new. I was trying to focus on the texts of the ancient Chinese philosopher Lao-tzu. Half of the time, my thoughts wandered off into unimportant memories, until I read: *If I really know what it means to live in the great Dao, then it is above all busy-ness that I fear.*

'What do you think that means?' I asked Peter, after reading it out loud.

'Well, if you're busy, you're occupied. Then it's very easy to lose awareness. Without busy-ness there is time and space to look at yourself, to find a way out of your mental prison.'

I wormed myself out of my sleeping bag and put some more wood on the fire to heat up the possum stew that was in the billy.

'And what is the great Dao?' I asked.

'That's a question we might find an answer for together.' Peter smiled at me.

I looked out of the window. It was drizzling outside, and a thick layer of mist obscured the forest beyond the swamp. Just when I started to wonder what my mental prison might be, I saw two figures sloshing through the swamp. My eyes lit up.

'People!' I exclaimed. 'What an unlikely day to have visitors.'

Excitement had come to our doorstep!

Peter leaped out of his sleeping bag and we hastily made space in the small, cluttered hut.

I opened the door and shouted, 'Good afternoon!'

The two hikers seemed surprised to see me.

I was extraordinarily happy—meeting people in this wet, miserable place felt like winning the lottery. When they reached the hut, I sat them down inside, gave them a hot cup of tea, and enjoyed looking at their faces, bodies, posture, clothes and equipment. I absorbed everything with a passion.

They told us that they were farmers from the west coast of the North Island. The rain didn't bother them. 'If you don't work in the rain, you don't work' was their refreshing motto. They were both in their forties. Matt was quite handsome, tall, broad-shouldered and strong. He sat down with his back to the wall and his cup of tea in his hand. He looked relaxed, and I realised how unusual it is to see somebody completely—both physically and mentally—relaxed.

His friend Jack was a little smaller with short dark hair and brown eyes. He first spent 10 minutes trying to find the muesli bars in his pack then, once he found them, decided to unpack the rest. Everything was neatly piled on his bunk. I could see that he was thinking ahead, organising his gear in an attempt to create order—a little safe space with his few belongings in the midst of the infinite wilderness. I observed him carefully, because he reminded me so much of myself.

'What's that you've got on the fire, mate?' Matt asked with a smile.

'This is possum stew,' Peter answered solemnly.

'You're eating a possum?' Jack looked surprised.

Peter laughed, and offered them a spoon. They each tried it and had to admit that it did taste good.

We sat together in that tiny hut while the darkness fell. They had brought four candles and we relished the cosy luxury of having light at night. We talked about hunting, farming, family and world politics. The topic of conversation was secondary to Peter and me; the fact that we had visitors was much more important.

'Are you saying that you have no clock here?' Jack said. 'You don't know what time it is?'

'No.' Peter chuckled. 'There's no need for a watch here, is there? What does it matter whether it is ten o'clock or eleven o'clock?'

'We eat when we are hungry and sleep when it is dark,' I added merrily.

Jack looked at his watch. 'So would you be asleep now if we hadn't turned up?'

'For sure,' I replied. 'Probably an hour ago!'

'But it's barely eight o'clock! You must sleep more than the average toddler.' Jack was laughing.

'Well, yes,' Peter said. 'It's amazing that the body can sleep that much, but apparently it's possible.'

Matt and Jack found this astonishing. We explained to them that we like to live spontaneously, leaving our fate in the hands of chance and randomness, making space for the unexpected. Peter asked whether they knew of any remote valleys we might spend the next season in, and Jack answered that he would recommend the Matakitaki Valley, Bob's Hut perhaps. He showed us on the map where it was hidden.

All four of us slept in the hut that night. I worried about waking up the others, so I lay very still in my sleeping bag. I slept so little that, the next morning, I resolved to pitch the tent for the second night.

In the morning, they donned their wet raincoats and set off into the swamp with their rifles. I admired their stamina. Later in the day they returned with the head of a beautiful chamois.

'Where is the rest of the animal?' I asked.

'We shot it a long way away and we could only bring the head and back steaks with us.'

Peter and I fell silent. I was quite shocked; I thought sadly of the animal that had died for nothing and the good meat that was rotting away needlessly.

We had another good evening together, with shared food and stories. Peter and I slept in our tent, which we had pitched underneath the trees. We had collected some ferns to make our thin yoga mats a little more comfortable, and I was curious to see how we would survive the cold winter night. We were dressed in all of our clothes, including hats. I pulled the sleeping bag right over my head and made an air-hole to breathe through. My nose felt half frozen, but slowly the temperature in the tent began to rise. Our bodies were warming it up and, to our great surprise, our small tent proved warmer than the hut, especially during the cold early-morning hours. We decided that, from now on, we would sleep in our tent and use the hut only for rainy days.

The next morning Matt and Jack went out hunting very early. When they returned, Matt smiled happily at us.

'Show me your map of the area.' His voice sounded buoyant, as he described to us in great detail a long, complicated route. 'And here,' he said, pointing with a blade of grass at a spot on the map, 'you will find a young deer hanging in a tree. It will give you enough meat for the next few weeks.'

'Why don't you want it?' I asked, amazed.

'Oh, it's way too much meat to carry all the way out,' Matt said. 'Plus my wife doesn't like the taste of wild venison.' He shrugged.

Peter looked at me in disbelief, his eyes shining. We were delighted.

We hugged Matt and Jack goodbye, promising to stay in touch. They disappeared off across the swamp, the chamois head sticking out of Matt's pack.

'Have a good journey,' I said softly as I watched them go. In Matt's pack was a 10-page letter I had written to my parents. When my mother and father opened the envelope, in their summery garden on the other side of the world, they would smell the smoky paper and know that I was alive and well.

The moment the hunters were gone we set off with our empty packs to the tree that Matt had directed us to. It took us several hours, and I will never forget the moment we came round the corner to see this enormous beast hanging in a tree. I had grown accustomed to possum-sized animals and discovering the skinned deer felt like meeting a moose in Alaska. Peter cut as much meat off the bones as possible, and we returned to South Hut with about forty kilos of meat, which we hung outside in the trees. The cold temperatures kept away any flies, and we ate the venison for four weeks.

After what felt like weeks of rain and showers, I woke up one morning to the sound of intense silence. I zipped open the tent to find little snowflakes drifting slowly down to earth like tiny butterflies. A soft white blanket concealed the secrets of the land. It was magical.

That afternoon the wind changed and the weather cleared up. To see the blue sky after days of cold rain and snow was an absolute delight. Peter ran immediately to the first little spot in the sun. When I brought him a cup of tea, he was beaming with happiness: my sweet sun-worshipper in his shorts and T-shirt in the snow.

I walked into the white forest. The beech trees with their evergreen leaves were bending under the heavy snow. I saw little paw prints in the white carpet: possums had been running around in the night. The snow absorbed all sounds and everything was soft, silent and new.

When we finished our basic provisions, we decided to return to our supply buckets at Base Hut. We refilled the woodshed, then walked back down into the valley with what was left of the venison. When we arrived at the riverbed, we found a flock of Canada geese resting there. The first goose signalled to its friends, and soon they were all honking. Their calls sounded beautiful, but so melancholic; it was almost as though they were begging to be left alone. It is legal to shoot Canada geese in New Zealand, in order to control their numbers, and due to the damage they cause to pastures and crops. Most hunters don't eat them, and it is sad to see them wasted. Possums and goats are problematic in terms of conservation too, of course, but I have a particular fondness for geese since they remind me of the last free animals in the Netherlands: the migrating geese that fly in a V-shape through Europe. Eventually the Canada geese flew away, one by one, embracing the wind.

As we descended into the lower valley, we felt the temperature rising, and we were glad to see Base Hut. It suddenly seemed bigger than we remembered. With the sun on the hut and the brilliant little firebox we were going to be toasty warm.

'We won't call this Base Hut any more.' Peter grinned. 'We'll call it The Hotel. It's so comfortable! Feel how warm it is.'

I sat down in the dry grass with my face in the sun and soaked up the warmth. We had been living in the mountains for nearly two months now, but it felt like an eternity. During those first two weeks I had been so bored, but the wilderness had forced me to yield and gradually, day by day and week by week, time had slowed down.

If I live the rest of my life in the wilderness, I thought, *I will have a very long life.*

I didn't miss anything from the world I had left behind.

I realised that my experience of nature had begun to change. I was tuned in to the rhythm of the forest, river and mountains. Beauty had become more apparent and intense. When I looked at the mountains, I saw not only their outward shapes, but also colours and moods. And slowly, over the weeks and months, I smelled the subtle breeze, the perfume of the forest and the approaching rain. I noticed changing clouds and delicate colours in the sky.

After a week in the warm Hotel, we were ready to move to East Hut. The sky was blue and the land was white with frost when we set out with our heavy packs. As we walked through the frozen grass, ice gathered on top of my toes and my feet became so cold that it was actually a relief to step into a river that was just above freezing point; the water gave a sudden boost to my circulation and my feet felt warm afterwards. The crisp air was invigorating and the valley looked pristine and miraculous.

After about an hour, we entered an old mānuka forest with big round boulders scattered between the trees. Beams of sunshine filtered between the trees with their tiny green leaves. Everything was covered in a thick carpet of soft green moss.

'This, my sweetie, is the real Lothlórien,' said Peter.

We sat on a boulder to eat some bread and looked into the magical forest. A little grey bird with long skinny legs and a white belly dropped out of the sky in front of our feet: a native robin. It investigated us with much curiosity, examining the breadcrumbs with its shiny black eyes, then flew on to a branch to sing with a surprisingly loud voice. The bird seemed to have no fear of us.

East Hut was high in the mountains and built in a fantastic spot, with a brilliant view into the valley below as well as a beautiful panorama of the mountaintops. Just outside the hut was a little grass clearing, which ended abruptly above a river gorge. I carefully approached the edge, and looked down into a deep ravine with a wild river at the bottom.

The interior of the hut was simple, clean and light. There was ample firewood and a big firebox. I had never felt happier. We built our camp on a dry spot under the trees near the hut.

It was now midwinter and we had many severely frosty nights and clear, sun-filled days, during which we went out on walks. After all the rainy days at South Hut, it felt like the best weather in the world. During the cold nights, icicles formed on the corrugated-iron roof and, melting in the morning sun, they would crash one by one to the ground. One day I went to collect a bucket of water out of the stream near the tent and by the time I got back the surface was already frozen over.

During these long winter months, we ate many possums and were not hungry. I felt happy and privileged to live in such natural beauty, but there was one thing nagging at me: I was very disappointed with my efforts as a bow hunter. I had expected myself to have a little bit more enthusiasm for hunting; I had hoped I would confidently roam the wilderness, and that, even after failure, I would still show stamina and endurance. Instead, I had gone out just once or twice and, after coming back empty-handed, I had all but given up on hunting.

'You know what your problem is?' Peter said when I expressed this to him. 'Your Robin Hood image.'

I looked at him blankly.

'You think you'll be able to hunt animals straight away. Maybe you should start at the beginning,' he said kindly. 'Be by yourself in the forest for a few hours. Go for a walk and sit somewhere quietly. See what you see.'

So I followed his advice. First I walked up and down the path. Then I hiked along the riverbed. At last, I felt confident enough to wander into the forest by myself without getting lost. I sat down on logs and began to notice signs: hoof prints in the mud, old droppings, damaged bark on trees and many other subtle indicators of the presence of animals.

Before I could learn to hunt for animals, I had to learn to watch for them. I resolved to give hunting another go, and to learn to be more patient.

'What do I look like?' I brought my face close to Peter's, pretending to look in a mirror. We were standing beside the fire.

'Good.' Peter laughed.

'Well, without a mirror, I have to trust your judgement!' I kissed him.

'What about me?' Our noses touched. 'Doesn't it bother you that I look so old?' asked Peter.

'Doesn't it bother you that I look so young?' I replied, putting the billy on the hook above the fire. 'You're old, and I'm young. Why should young be better than old?'

'True.' Peter nodded. 'But there aren't that many young women who'd like to live with a man thirty years older than them.'

'But I don't want to live with any older man—only with you!' I hugged Peter in his three woollen jumpers.

'Lucky me!' He laughed.

'You are fit and healthy and very wise. Lucky me!' I kissed him again.

'Well, yeah, your advantage is that you can avoid some of the mistakes that I made in my life.' He picked up our cups.

'Yes indeed. More people could learn from intergenerational dialogue,' I said. 'Older people can learn from younger, and vice versa.' I added tea leaves to the water in the billy. 'Do you learn much from me?' I looked at him with a grin.

'From you I have learned that two people can live in harmony with each other.'

Once, when Peter and I had first met in India, we were talking with another traveller when she had asked quite bluntly whether Peter was my father; I had felt so embarrassed at the time. Some friends back in Holland imagined their fathers when I mentioned Peter's age to them—they thought he must be old, slow or decrepit, and that I had lost my mind. Others supposed that my relationship with my own father must have been so bad that Peter was his replacement. 'Let them think,' my mother had always said when I was a child and worried about what other people might think. As it turned out, it proved to be a helpful piece of advice for me later in life, too.

During that whole winter, neither of us ever had an accident or fell ill. My only problem was dandruff. In the past I had cured it with special shampoo, but this time it came back so badly that I often scratched my hair in my sleep.

'Do you know that you're waking me up because of your scratching?' Peter said one morning.

'It's dandruff,' I replied quickly.

'Let me have a look,' he said. 'I've heard that some ancient cultures used to wash their hair with urine.'

'What?' I turned round and frowned. 'Piss?'

'Yes! It must be an awfully strong product. Apparently they only used women's urine . . .' He laughed.

And so the idea was born to wash my hair with urine. On the appointed morning, I peed into a tin. It was dark yellow and had a good strong smell. I carried the tin down to the river, wet my hair then slowly poured the urine over it. I sat in the sun for a horrible, stinky half-hour to let it soak in. Peter had the giggles and pinched his nose at me. Then I went back to the river, and found a deep pool between the rocks to rinse and wash my hair with soap to alleviate the stink. And, thanks to what turned out to be the most affordable and best product in the world, my dandruff was cured—and it has never come back.

The midwinter days were short and the nights long. We cooked our food before dark, then sat round the firebox for 'a quarter candle' so that we only used one candle every four days. During our precious time with light, Peter would read to me from *The Lord of the Rings*. In the beginning I noticed that my thoughts wandered off and I missed big parts of the story; it was only after several weeks that I was able to listen effortlessly. After reading, we would move to our tent, where we would lie quietly in our sleeping bags and listen to the peculiarly clear sounds of the forest at night. Owls called to one another through the trees, possums laughed and screamed, and many other nocturnal animals came out of their shelters to wander their own pathways. Below us, the water rushed endlessly in the gorge.

The nights were neither completely quiet nor totally dark: the moon lit up the mountains and forests. We often gazed at the stars in the crystal-clear sky, and wondered why there was something rather than nothing in the great universe.

It was an amazing feeling to sleep under the stars. In the first weeks, I had been afraid to go outside at night, as I didn't know what the wild animals would do. But I no longer had any fear because our valley felt like my home. We often slept deeply for 12 hours, and the effect of so much good rest was an increased energy. After three months, I felt more energetic than ever before in my life, and this energy brought with it the delightful feeling of living in a very healthy body.

Half of our life was spent collecting wood and cooking over fires. I would usually light a fire in the early morning to make tea and toast our bread. During the cold winter months, I mastered the art of lighting a fire, and I had come to love our joyous companion; the fire was a kind of living being that always rekindled my spirits. Just watching it calmed my mind. It had taught me its main principles: it always needs space and air. And, once a fire is burning well, it detests being disturbed in its heart. Fire and human beings have a lot in common that way.

Fire-lighting, though, also had its costs. My hands were stained with soot from feeding half-burned logs into the fire, and smoke had crawled into every particle of my body. It was impossible to wash the smell out of my hair or clothes. I washed my T-shirts and trousers often in the river, but within hours they would return to their smoky state. The smoke was part of me, like perfume was part of a rose.

After many weeks I volunteered to go back to The Hotel for a resupply and set off with an empty pack, focused on getting there quickly. I walked briskly down the path into the valley, waded through the river many times, brushed through overgrown pathways, and ran when the terrain was flat. When I entered Lothlórien, it suddenly seemed ludicrous to hurry. There was absolutely no logical reason to be so hasty; in fact, it was safer to go slowly. I stopped, looked at the beauty around me and realised that I did everything at great speed. It was an automatic response to my life in school and the workplace. Nature, however, had plenty of time. I discarded the invisible whip.

'Hey, Miriam!' Peter's smiling face appeared in front of the tent entrance.

'What?' I whispered. I was just putting the sleeping bags back in the tent, after airing them out for a few hours.

'Harry is here!' Peter was barely moving his lips and pointing at the hut.

'Harry?' My mouth fell open and a little smile appeared on my face too.

I crawled silently round the tent after Peter to spy on the area in front of the hut . . . and there was Harry, our good neighbour, sunbathing on the grass: a proud and beautiful hare. Of course I was not going to shoot our visitor.

Our need for food meant that we trapped many possums in our area, except for one. We had named him Percy and we often saw him around the camp. He didn't need to be afraid of us, as the traps were far away from the tent, and it was nice to make friends with some of the animals around us. We nearly always had a camp animal or bird that we did not disturb. It was heartening to see wild creatures in their natural environment. They reminded us of how few free creatures one saw in human-dominated places.

One morning I woke early, when it was still dark. I poked my head out of the tent, trying to discern whether dawn was breaking yet. When I heard the first birds singing I grabbed my clothes and crawled outside. The sky was grey, but I knew it would be blue by the time the sun revisited this part of the world. I collected a few dry branches and lit the fire to boil some water for tea. When Peter came out, he too admired the glorious day. We ate our toast while sitting round the fire.

'Look at this brilliant day!' I said. 'We should go for a long walk.' I was already putting the billy, tea and milk powder into a little backpack.

In the forest we saw signs of severe frost. The creek was still running, but a shield of ice had grown over a waterfall, clinging to vegetation and rocks. On the side were thin icicles, growing longer with every icy drop. The shady walls were completely covered in ice sculptures.

We ascended into the alpine vegetation and eventually stepped into snow. We came to a little stream with ice crystals clinging to the bank. I was hot and sweaty from the climb, so I quickly undressed and washed myself. The water and the cool breeze were so refreshing, and soon my skin was tingling and radiating warmth from within.

Peter was studying the mountaintops. 'This is the best day for a climb to the top,' he said. 'Do you want to have a go?'

The glimmering white snow reflected the bright sunlight, and the sky above was such a deep blue that it was almost purple. The snow was so hard that in most places we could walk on top of it. My wooden walking stick sank into the ice, and with every thrust a magical blue colour appeared in the deep holes. Only the sound of our footsteps and sticks disturbed the silence that lay so firmly on the land.

The view from the top was absolutely stunning. There was no wind and everything was silent. We saw ranges upon ranges of mountains covered in snow. There was no sign of any human mark: the whole world was white and empty. The sun was so strong that we felt warm in shorts and a woollen jumper. We stood looking at a silent, enchanted world.

On our way down we noticed a steep slope on the side of the mountain; it was a soft and snowy shingle slide. We only had to lift our knees and we slid and jumped down the mountain. The climb to the top had taken us many hours, but it only took us twenty minutes to come down. The sensation was amazing, like effortlessly skiing down a silky white sheet.

We stopped for a rest, and Peter reached into his pocket, revealing a piece of newspaper.

'A cup of tea!' I hugged him. What a brilliant idea to bring some paper to light the fire.

He broke some dead branches from a bush and made a little fire on top of the stones. I scooped some snow into the billy and brought the water to the boil.

'Ice tea!' Peter laughed. 'We always drink our tea in beautiful spots, eh?'

I couldn't think of anything in the world that would be more enjoyable than walking up a mountain, lighting a little fire and drinking a cup of hot, milky tea.

By mid-August, we were coming to the last of our flour, rice, beans and dhal. After many months round the campfire and countless walks in the snow-capped mountains, it was time to walk out again. We were reluctant to leave our beautiful spot behind. The eastern valley had become our home, and we were dreading the reunion with civilisation. We feared that a culture shock was awaiting us in the world of speed and noise, but without our rations we had little choice.

It took four days to walk out of the mountains to the sealed road where we would be able to hitchhike. During the walk, we reflected upon our time in the wilderness.

'Remember how we thought that the purity of nature would transform our minds?' Peter stopped and stood still at one point, resting his chin on his walking stick.

'Do you feel transformed?' I asked.

'Yes and no,' he said. 'The reality is always different from what you think, isn't it?' He tapped the bottom of his stick against mine. 'I realise now how small our minds are and how utterly limited our thinking is, relative to the vastness of all existence.'

'Well, I feel transformed,' I said. 'I feel super energetic! Because of the long sleeps, or maybe the power of the mountains—who knows? Perhaps all nature can do is give energy, so that the mind can find a way to transform itself.'

'Oh yes, I feel very energetic too,' Peter agreed. 'Mental and physical rest is so important at all ages. The art of doing nothing is undervalued, I reckon.'

'Well, that's what I found the most difficult: doing nothing.' I smiled at him, then we continued on our way.

Eventually we left the mountains for the plains; the air grew soft and the temperature was noticeably rising. Everywhere around us we saw signs of spring. The lush grass was covered with little purple flowers, and noisy bees were busy collecting the pollen. Some trees were covered in yellow blossoms. There were so many magnificent colours.

We slowly walked down the long valley, until we came to farmland. Every paddock was fenced off and secured with electric wire.

'Everything is so straight and square!' I exclaimed.

'It's to control the uncontrollable.' Peter looked at me with a smile. 'But, of course, nature only needs time. One day it will all revert to its natural order.'

I looked around. I saw the farmland with different eyes. Life had been put in a prison here; it was only allowed to grow a certain way. Human order meant control. The wilderness was the opposite: it looked chaotic, but had its own, everlasting order.

Finally, we arrived at the sealed road. After 10 minutes, a big red BMW approached us and came smoothly to a halt. The driver's window rolled down and a handsome man in a suit put his right arm on the ledge. I caught a whiff of sweet aftershave. A little smile was playing around his thin lips. He looked puzzled at our clothes and walking sticks. Eventually his blue eyes met mine. I started to smile.

With a twinkle in his eyes, he leaned forward and asked, 'Where have you guys come from?'

CHAPTER 3

SPRING

It was late afternoon. The air was moist and lush, full of spring. An unhurried bumblebee led the way down our old road. Every hill, pothole, tree and bush was so familiar to me, yet it felt as though we had been away for a lifetime. We walked past our former cottage, and soon arrived at Mouse's place—a modest wooden house on a lifestyle block with a few sheep, flowering fruit trees and a backdrop of pines.

'What?' Mouse yelled from the kitchen window as soon as he spotted us. 'How did you get here?'

A moment later he appeared in the doorway with an astonished look on his face.

'Walked, hitchhiked and walked,' Peter replied, as we hugged Mouse tightly.

'Hey, fucking hell, it's amazing that you guys survived up there!'

As I looked at Peter's beaming face, I was overcome with a sense of accomplishment: we had endured the long winter months in the mountains.

'How was the weather?' Mouse asked. 'We had nothing but rain! I tried to come and visit you guys twice, but I couldn't cross the rivers. *Twice!*'

'Most of the time we had very clear skies and heavy frosts at night,' said Peter. 'Lots of snow too.'

'I want to hear all your stories,' Mouse said. 'But come in first. I'll make us a brew.'

We took off our sandals and I hesitantly stepped on to the clean blue carpet. Two boars' heads stared at us from where they hung silently on the wall, their final astonished expressions frozen for eternity.

Mouse switched on the electric jug, which instantly made a surprisingly loud noise. 'What would you like to eat?' he asked. 'What have you missed most?'

'Fruit,' we both chirped.

He put a big bowl of mandarins and apples on the table, then poured the hot water into the cups.

'So quick.' I pointed at the jug. 'Compared to gathering wood and lighting a fire to boil water.' I looked at Peter. The way he returned my smile made me feel as though we shared a secret about a world nobody else understood.

Mouse opened the fridge to get milk and my eyes rested on all the food inside. For a moment I felt like a bushman in New York, looking at the abundance of food that threatened to tumble out, but of course I had grown up with fridges like these. When I was a child, we used to have four kinds of cheese and three types of yoghurt—both products I now saw as luxuries.

'Hey, did you shoot anything with your bow?' Mouse looked expectantly in my direction, placing the cups on the table.

'Um, well . . . no, not really,' I replied. Mouse had taught me so much about the theory of hunting that I now felt like a failed pupil.

Peter came to my rescue. 'We had plenty of meat, though. Possums and lots of venison.'

'Huh, how did you get the deer?' Mouse tilted his head to indicate he was ready for a good story.

One tale after another rolled out. I started, Peter finished, and vice versa. One of us cheerfully acted out a scene, while the other did the voice-over.

'You should have seen the guy's face when Peter said we were eating possum!' I shrieked.

'Priceless!' Mouse laughed. He then added in a more serious tone,

'Sometimes it must have been bloody tough though, eh?'

'Sometimes it was freezing cold.' Peter shook his head. 'Boy oh boy, you wouldn't believe it. Frozen tent, frozen waterfalls, everything frozen solid! But, you know—' Peter put down his cup of tea— 'when you wake up at three o'clock in the morning because you've already been asleep for eight hours, all those stupid old memories come up and plague you, over and over again.'

'Really?' Mouse's face showed some concern.

'Yes, all that unresolved conflict is patiently waiting to come out.' Peter slowly stroked his beard with two fingers. 'Like spiders in the basement.'

'Yeah,' Mouse said. 'I guess we keep ourselves busy all the time to avoid thinking about that crap.'

'There's very little to do out there after dark, so you have no option but to let it come up.' Peter took a sip from his tea.

'Then what?' Mouse asked.

'After some months, it disappears. To sit through a very quiet winter, even just once in your life, is very purifying—mentally, I mean.'

'Physically too,' I added. 'Because we had so much sleep, we are completely recharged.'

'Interesting shit, eh?' Mouse lifted his eyebrows.

We drank our tea in silence for a moment.

'So, what's been happening here?' Peter asked.

Mouse's eyes searched for a moment. 'Well, jeez, not much really. Same old, same old, I guess.'

The phone rang, which caused an automatic rush of adrenaline to course through my body.

Mouse jumped up. 'Help yourself to anything. I might be on the phone for a while. Business call.'

Peter switched on the television and loud voices suddenly filled the house. He zapped between CNN, BBC, Al Jazeera, Russian TV and CCTV from Beijing to learn as much as possible about the current world situation. I ran to the computer in another room. When I typed in my password, I was surprised to feel a nervous anticipation and urge to get to my email quicker. I felt like an addict finally getting a hit of my drug of choice. The hour I spent reading emails felt like five minutes and I was jerked back to reality by the sound of Debbie's voice.

I tried to smile heartily, and so did she. I gave her small body a hug. Then she laughed and said, 'I can smell wood smoke on you!'

While Peter helped in the kitchen, I escaped to the clean white bathroom to wash off the smoke smell. While my nose lingered on a fresh-scented towel, I saw myself in the mirror. I was surprised at my reflection. *Is that me?* For the first time in months, I saw my own face. Somehow I had forgotten what I looked like, because Peter's face had become more familiar to me than my own.

Over the following days, we had more showers, washed our clothes and drove to the supermarket for new supplies. The evening before we were to leave again, we sat around the table.

'Now, do you guys actually know where you are going next?' Mouse asked.

'Well, three people we met in the last four months told us about Bob's Hut,' said Peter. 'That's in the Matakitaki Valley. They all said it is beautiful primeval forest, remote and not often visited.'

Mouse frowned. 'Have you seen the hut? Have you actually been there yourselves?'

'No, we haven't, but we're sort of relying on random advice.' Peter met Mouse's eyes.

'How come you don't have a plan? Like, go there in spring, here in summer, over there in autumn—that kind of thing?'

'If you plan everything, you don't allow much space for the unexpected.' I shrugged. 'The unexpected is often the most interesting!'

'Marvellous things that might change our entire life could happen to us, but you can't plan for those things,' Peter added.

'Horrible things could happen to you, too, which might end your life!' Mouse bent over the map. 'OK. So it's the Matakitaki. Where's that then?' he asked, his green eyes sparkling beneath long eyelashes.

Peter pointed to a region of a national park where the natural forest had never experienced human interference. There we would find truly pristine wilderness.

Next morning, with Mouse's truck loaded up with his four-wheel bike and our restocked supply buckets, we headed out over some mountains and then cruised down a large river valley, eventually turning off on to a deserted dirt road. At the end, we transferred to the four-wheel bike with a trailer and drove past the farmland and into the trees. The forest felt like another world—green, lush and full of life—and the sun lit up the path.

'Hold on tight,' Mouse instructed before he took off at a stupendous speed through creeks and hollows full of mud and over large rocks. Peter was forced to wrap himself round me, and I held Mouse's body tightly to prevent being flung off on the sharp corners. We were driving at such an absurd speed, and it was also wonderful to be so close to Mouse, that I laughed the entire trip. When we could drive no further, I rolled off the bike, still crying with laughter.

'What's so funny?' asked Mouse with genuine surprise in his voice.

We hid our food buckets in the forest, covering them with moss and stones, then hiked with our heavy packs over a forested hill and into a wide river valley where tough and wiry matagouri bushes grew abundantly. Their impressive thick spikes kept grazing animals at bay while providing convenient housing for many birds and rabbits.

We were extremely glad to finally find the small wooden hut on the edge of a clearing. It was right at the edge of a gigantic red beech forest. About a hundred years ago, a farmer—Mr Downie, we presumed—had cleared the land for his sheep and built Downie's Hut from the trees he had cut down. In recent years, the old shingle roof had been hastily covered with corrugated iron to stop leaks. The hut was about four by four metres, and it was so dark inside that it took a while before I could see the open fireplace, four bunks with mattresses and the wooden bench beneath a small window.

I examined the hut with interest. It was like moving into a museum, with those dark, rough-cut planks as walls, original slats in the ceiling and ancient names and dates carved into the wood.

'Hey, did you see that stoat?' Peter exclaimed while I was furiously sweeping the floor. I looked up, but I was too late.

'That's lucky. He'll hunt all the mice and rats for you!' said Mouse. 'How long will you guys stay here, do you reckon?' He was breaking up some old firewood to light a fire to make tea.

'Once we've shifted all the buckets, we'll make a camp near Bob's Hut. So fairly soon, I imagine,' Peter said.

After dinner we crawled into our sleeping bags to keep warm.

'It's nice to look at a fire, eh?' Mouse was lying comfortably in his bed, with his arms under his head. 'My old man only let us have a fire when he was home. He guarded his big pile of firewood like a fucking maniac. He'd give us a real bad-ass beating if he discovered we'd lit the fire while he was out.'

'Really?' I gasped. I could not imagine a childhood with such violence.

'Oh, yeah,' said Peter from his dark corner of the hut. 'In those days you got beaten at home *and* beaten at school! Corporal punishment was completely normal back then.'

'Yeah, at school I had the choice of doing homework or receiving the cane.' Mouse grinned. 'The beating that the teachers gave me was nowhere near as bad as what my father would have given me, so I always chose the cane!'

'What, every day?' I imagined a thin little boy volunteering for a beating.

'Well, in the end they couldn't see the point of it. So the headmaster took me under his wing. He gave me a uniform and helped me with homework.' He chuckled at his own ingenuity.

I thought of my own upbringing, during which I never received a beating for anything. It sounded as though Mouse had grown up 30 years before I did, but he was only a dozen years older than me. Times had changed a lot.

The next morning, Mouse got up at first light. 'Well, good luck, guys,' he said. His face looked slightly concerned. 'I'm not sure if I'll be able to come and visit you here. It's kind of far away,' he said apologetically while we wormed ourselves out of our sleeping bags.

'Oh, don't worry, we'll be fine.' I smiled confidently and hugged him. 'I'll send a letter via the first hunter we meet.'

We waved goodbye and watched through the tiny window of the hut as he loped off through the wet grass. After about 50 metres, he started to run.

Later that morning the sun disappeared behind dark clouds and it started to drizzle. Then it rained steadily, and then it bucketed down.

Peter looked somewhat forlorn standing in the dark hut in his big black Swanndri jacket and shorts.

'Your hair is all curly with the humidity.' I hugged him.

'We need wood.' He gave me a kiss. 'Wood, Miriam,' he repeated with some urgency in his voice. 'So we can bake our bread.' I looked at his serious face. 'After the winter, all the wood here is soaking wet.'

'Tomorrow it will clear up, things will dry out, and we'll fill that shed right up!' I said optimistically.

But it didn't clear up. The next day it rained more, and the day after that even more. In fact, the rain never seemed to stop. In between showers, I ran to the riverbed for wind-dried logs, while Peter set about splitting a waist-high red beech log. We burned the driest pieces and set all the wet split wood against the walls so that the flames would dry it out. We burned wood in order to dry wood, which, in turn, we then burned to dry new logs. On and on it went. Day in, day out.

We waited for weeks inside that old hut, which stood gloomily in the cold, slanting, merciless rain or wet snow. The river rose to monstrous proportions. Flooded side creeks blocked the way up the valley and to the road out. The light in the hut was so dim that reading a book was impossible unless you stood right by the window. We played chess, read books by the window, cooked beans, cut wood, kept the fire going and drank endless cups of tea. Meanwhile, the birds went about their spring business and the hares ran about oblivious. Of all the creatures in this valley, we seemed the least suited to life in this place.

I sat in front of the one window for days, searching for figures in the swirling mist.

If only someone would come, I thought. *A hunter, hiker, fisher . . . Anybody would be fantastic.*

I imagined two men leaning over the kitchen table, discussing their hunting destination with a cup of steaming-hot coffee in their hands.

'Matakitaki!' I whispered in their imaginary ears. But my telepathy never worked, because nobody ever came.

'You know people say they would head for the hills when the system collapses, right?' I said while cleaning out the billy one day.

'Yeah.' Peter was busy blowing into the fire, turning smoke into flames.

'Imagine they came out here. I don't think many would handle it—psychologically, I mean. After the first week, they would get restless and suffer from cabin fever. They would want to know what had happened to their family. They'd feel agitated just with the separation from the rest of humanity, don't you think? Mouse, for example—he could barely stand one night. He couldn't wait to run back home.'

I paused. The rain was drumming on the roof.

'If we had a choice, I'd go out now to find another place where it isn't raining.' I sighed. 'It's been raining non-stop for weeks now!'

'Yes, I agree. The reality, however, is that, even if we could cross the rivers, we have nowhere to go. The wilderness is our only home at the moment. So this is it. Right?'

I looked out of the window at the patterns of fog gathering between the trees.

'Yeah, we're totally subject to the weather.' I smiled wryly.

'This is not a rainy holiday after which we can return to our normal life with a normal house,' Peter said. 'This is our life, so we have to adapt.'

A couple of times, when the rain turned to drizzle, I went out hunting. In shorts and sandals, I walked through the long grass. The waterlogged green stems felt very soft on the skin of my calves. Parts of the clearing had become swamp, and my feet disappeared up to my ankles. When I saw a hare sitting on the stones in the distance, I fired an arrow. Bright sparks flew up when the arrow hit the stones. The hare was long gone, and my arrow was bent. It would never shoot straight again.

I set out a possum trap several times, but didn't catch any possums. They, too, were hiding from the rain. So we ate beans for dinner, and lentils. Every day. Beans. Dahl. And rice. For weeks.

We had a lot of time in that gloomy old hut. Since we couldn't really read books, I had come up with an interesting form of entertainment: I would name a country, and Peter would describe some of the landscape from pictures he had seen. He knew the general climates and vegetation from his studies. He had read many books about historical and political events, and he now told me these stories. That's how I learned a bit more about the wider world.

One night we discussed Iraq with its ancient culture, and Peter veered off on to 'The Epic of Gilgamesh', which I found particularly interesting.

'Gilgamesh was a legendary, but real, king from around 2700 BC who wanted to overcome mortality,' Peter began. 'So he decided to build the first city. He asked permission from the goddess Ishtar. She answered, "This gift of civilisation I will give to you, but remember: you cannot give it back." So Gilgamesh built Uruk. Its city walls were the symbol of separation from the wilderness, but without a direct relationship with nature; people soon felt lonely and isolated and their achievements seemed irrelevant in the face of death.'

'Wow! You cannot give civilisation back,' I said. 'We haven't learned much in five thousand years. Now we have bigger cities and feel even lonelier and more isolated.'

We lay silent for a while.

'The walls might come down one day,' I said.

'Might take a while though,' Peter said.

There was a long-drop toilet near the hut. The hole had been dug a long time ago, and over the years it had slowly filled up with human waste, soil and rainwater. One morning I sat down on the wooden toilet and looked at the wet snowflakes drifting on to the soft moss. I heard my poo falling down . . . and then, to my utter horror, I felt a backsplash. A mixture of rainwater and shit had just hit my bum! Other people's shit! I sat completely paralysed for a few seconds, digesting this nightmarish event. Then I jumped into action and ran whimpering through the driving rain with my trousers still round my ankles to wash my buttocks roughly in the creek.

I detected a little twinkle in Peter's eyes when I entered the hut. 'What happened?' he asked innocently.

'Backsplash,' I said gravely, reaching for the soap—I planned to head straight back outside for another cleaning session.

He pointed to a box in the corner of the hut. 'I always put newspaper down first for that very reason,' he said with a grin on his face.

After three weeks of rain, we became irritated with each other over the smallest things.

'Where are the rolled oats?' Peter asked impatiently one morning.

'I put them in the bag in the corner, or maybe back in the bucket. Oh no, maybe on that hook over there? For god's sake, just look! They can't be far away!' I snapped.

'You are getting so angry with me these days. I really get the feeling you don't like living with me any more,' Peter said to me one afternoon. The tone of his voice made my tears well up. I apologised for my grumpiness and hugged him. I was overcome with just how dependent we were on each other in this lonely hut in the inhospitable mountains. It felt like walking through a desert with one bottle of water, only to discover that the bottle was lost. Peter was my most precious person. I had to treat him carefully, because he was my partner, my best friend and my sole companion in the wilderness.

One night when we went to bed, the rain drumming on the roof, we heard the sound of thunder in the distance. A lightning strike illuminated the hut, followed by an ear-splitting thunderclap that shook the bunks and brought with it a waterfall of rain outside. Talking was impossible because of the frighteningly loud noise. It did occur to me to worm myself into Peter's bunk, but that seemed very childish and quite pointless.

Then the rain eased and the gales started. Wind came right through the tiniest gaps, and we could hear branches in the forest outside crashing violently against each other. There was a dead tree looming over the hut, and I was afraid that it would come down in these strong gusts and flatten the hut. I grew more anxious by the minute, wondering whether we would survive the night. *Will we make it to the morning?* I fretted. My mind filled with images of our crushed bodies, devoured by stoats and wild pigs. Suddenly an enormous crash made me screech. A terrific bang shook the ground and my heart leaped into my throat.

To my amazement, we both survived the night and the roof remained intact. In the morning, I opened the door and smelled the crisp, invigorating southerly air that always brought good weather. A glorious blue sky! The end of the monsoon! I opened my arms to the heavens. I felt like Noah after the great flood, ready to send my dove out to look for land.

'Blue sky!' I yelled out to Peter.

We walked to the river, where we were welcomed by a stunning view over the high, snow-covered mountains. We had never seen these peaks; they had been hidden for almost a month by the endless cloud. Just 20 metres from the hut, we discovered that a huge living tree had fallen over—the source of the enormous crash I had heard during the night. And as for the dead tree I had been so worried about during the night? It remained where it had been before the storm: leaning over the hut.

We embraced and congratulated each other. We had survived the rain! To experience a clear sky after 25 days of rain felt like the greatest joy ever—almost worth sitting through all that rain for. Almost.

I had a burning desire to leave immediately for Bob's Hut. 'I'm going to the next hut to bring supplies, and I'm going to come back with news that the upper valley is wonderful!' I said.

I immediately started packing the big bags of rice and flour. I couldn't stand to spend even one more day in the stinky, dark dungeon of the hut. I was itching for an exciting solo expedition.

'Should you be in such a hurry?' Peter looked slightly concerned. 'The river might still be high.'

'Oh no, I'm sure the rivers will have gone down.' I continued packing. 'I'm going to make the most of every good day. Hey, the sign says four hours to Bob's Hut. That's not far!' I kissed Peter goodbye with great optimism. 'See you tomorrow!'

It felt extraordinary to walk off into the Great Unknown, alone, on such a splendid day. I navigated the mud, climbed over steep banks, round fallen trees and across creeks. The track was quite clear and easy, and I felt content. But after an hour the path entered a different kind of forest where it was deadly quiet. No little breeze, no singing birds, no babbling streams. The sun vanished behind the clouds and it felt as though it was suddenly twilight. Between the still, silent trees, I felt very uncomfortable and out of place. The trees on this eerie mountain were telling me to turn round. 'Turn round . . . Turn round . . .'

Swirling mist rolled into the trees when the path ascended, and every hundred metres the air became colder. I went over a small pass where there was still some snow. When I looked back, I saw my own footprints. *If I never return*, I thought nervously, *at least they'll be able to follow my footsteps and find my body.*

I grew more anxious by the minute.

I crossed a side river with little trouble and later came to a bridge that I had seen on the map. I'd never seen a structure like this before: one wire for my feet, two for my hands. If I slipped off the bottom wire, I would fall in the grey river or crash on to the black rocks far below. I laid my walking stick horizontally across the two top wires and hesitantly stepped on to the single bottom one. The ice-cold river rushed beneath me at tremendous speed.

Don't fall in, echoed the voice in my head, while my knuckles turned white from holding on tightly. Towards the end, the wires were so high that I could hardly reach them and I almost lost my footing. With immense relief, I finally made it to the other side.

The path continued up the cold mountain, through the dark, wet, slippery forest. My progress was alarmingly slow and I was totally out of energy. I felt like Little Red Riding Hood waiting for the wolf to come. Instead of a wolf, though, I spooked a big stag. He was drinking from a stream and ran away, crashing loudly off through the otherwise silent forest.

Then all of a sudden my trail disappeared.

I stood still and stared at the sinister forest all around me. The decaying black beech leaves covered any trace of a path. Fearfully imagining myself vanishing into the darkness, I turned round and round on the spot, frantically searching for the orange triangle of a trail marker, but all I saw was a thicket of weirdly entwined trees. I peered at the patch of light above that penetrated the thick, dusky forest. The day seemed to be waning fast. I walked a little further on into the distance where I could see an opening between the trees that could be a path. But, when I got there and found nothing, I hurriedly retraced my steps. Everything seemed suddenly strange, but somehow I discovered my missed turn.

The track climbed again, and eventually I saw the bright light at the edge of the forest. I followed the orange markers on iron poles into a big swamp, which was completely covered in a thick layer of snow. A narrow creek flowed through the thick tussock. Plants had covered the surface and I thought it was quite shallow until I stepped right into the freezing water and it reached my thighs. My woollen jumper, which was tied round my waist, was instantly soaked. I gasped for air and, in panic, I started to cry. I thought about dying of hypothermia, and all sorts of other frightful situations flashed through my mind. I was at the end of my tether.

I tried to run, but instead of going faster I stumbled over the snow-covered boulders that were now in front of me. I told myself to calm down. I'd heard stories of people who lost their minds in the woods. The palpable menace stole their rationality, turning them hysterical; I felt I was fast going down that same road.

Then I saw a tiny white hut in the distance. When I reached the door, my eye fell on a grave in the snow right underneath the window. To arrive at a one-man cemetery after such a spooky trip was the last thing I needed. The grave was marked with a big wooden cross engraved with the words REST IN PEACE, BOB. It appeared that Bob had been an old gold miner, and his shovel now hung on the hut's wall as a memorial to his life here. *He must have died in or near this hut*, I thought. *Of a disease? From an accident?* I shivered.

When I opened the door, I saw that the clean, light-filled interior was a great deal better than Downie's Hut. This hut was perhaps three by five metres. I looked in the hut book and realised that nobody had been here all winter. Outside, the last light revealed an enormous rocky mountain standing aloof and silent over the hut. I had found myself in a very, very isolated and uninhabited place. This was the rugged wilderness I had been looking for, but now that I had found it I wasn't quite sure what to think. I felt as if I was all alone in the world.

I changed into my spare woollen leggings and shirt, and lit the fire. I hung my wet shorts and woollen jumper on a line above the fireplace, and soon started to feel warm again. When I went to bed I closed my eyes and thought of Bob—or rather his spirit, which might still be wandering around.

'Hello, Bob,' I whispered.

No reply.

As I lay there in the silent night, I found that my normal chatter-thoughts vanished and I was left with nothing but fear—the fear of seeing a ghost. I felt as though I was 12 years old again. I hid my head in my sleeping bag for a long time until I couldn't breathe. I thought of the gemstone I had given to Jimmy to protect him from his fear of ghosts.

Then I remembered something I had read in Lao-tzu: *What you want to destroy, you must first allow truly to flourish.* So I took a deep breath, and let the fear come. I was inviting the very ghost I was afraid of. I waited and stared into the darkness. No ghost voices spoke. Nothing happened at all. I lay there in the silence and saw that it was, in fact, the unknown I was afraid of.

Somehow, this simple discovery made me feel immeasurably better, and I started to breathe again, and eventually drifted off to sleep.

In the middle of the night I woke up sweating in my sleeping bag, and I knew that warm northerly weather probably meant more rain. And, indeed, in the early morning it bucketed down. Fearing that the rivers would rise, I frantically packed my bag—I didn't fancy spending three weeks alone in this hut with Bob's ghost!

I raced down the mountain, shuffling without even thinking about it over the wire bridge that had been so problematic the day before. I was forced to come to a halt 20 minutes later by a raging side river that had been so easy to cross on my way up. I looked at the murky brown water rushing past. The river wasn't wide, but the current looked furious.

I inspected the wash-out route. Where would the river take me and spit me out if the current pulled me off my feet? Eventually deciding to risk it, I entered the river. I placed my long walking stick between the rocks and leaned into it. Several times the current pushed my pole away. The flow was strong—very strong. The river pulled at my legs, as big boulders rolled past on their way down the riverbed.

Then I remembered my mother's well-tested drama exercise: *If you envision yourself as a tree, nobody can possibly lift you.* I could hear her voice as though she was standing right next to me. Imagining my roots going far into the earth, I stood like a solid tree in the middle of the roaring river. The water came up to my waist and the level was still rising, but the river could not move me. Adrenaline made all of my senses acute. I was conscious of every breath. Step by step, I moved myself slowly forward, all the way to the other side.

With my light pack, I walked quickly the rest of the way back to Downie's Hut; I didn't even notice anything ominous about the forest and arrived quite cheerfully around mid-afternoon. The weather had completely cleared, and I felt a little silly for racing down through the rain.

Peter was surprised to see me and hugged me tightly. 'You should have waited, sweetie. Don't risk crossing swollen rivers. In nineteenth-century parlance, they called drowning "the New Zealand Death" because so many people died crossing rivers here.'

That night in bed, I thought of what could have happened in that river. For the first time that day, I was truly afraid that I might have drowned, and I could feel my heart beating in my throat. It was such a strange sensation, because I had not felt any fear when I crossed the river eight hours earlier. My fear was caused by my thoughts. *Is that always the case?* I wondered.

We woke the next morning to a clear sky. My fears of rivers and ghosts forgotten, I convinced Peter to take our gear and walk up to beautiful Bob's Hut. We didn't set off until late morning, because the packing had taken us some time. That didn't matter, I assured Peter, because it wasn't far anyway.

When I tried shouldering my pack, though, I discovered that it was so heavy I couldn't lift it. I was forced to sit down on the ground, put the straps over my shoulders, roll sideways in order to lift a knee then, with help of my walking stick, eventually stumble up and on to my feet.

With our heavy packs, our progress over the muddy tracks was very slow.

'This is not going to take four hours. We'll be lucky to get there before nightfall!' Peter turned and waited for me while I closed the 15-metre gap between us. 'You're always in a hurry because you're so goddamn restless,' he said.

I staggered past him without saying a word.

'We could have packed everything today and left early tomorrow morning, but because you are so impatient now we're both in danger!' Peter yelled after me.

He was quite right. I couldn't argue with the truth, but I wouldn't admit it either, and that just made Peter even more furious.

'And what is so heavy in these packs anyway?' he carried on. 'We really should chuck some stuff out. This is ridiculous. All that toilet stuff for starters—your face cream in that glass container!'

I lifted my head to attempt to defend myself, the drizzle slowly soaking my clothes, but I found no excuse.

'Surely you don't need that in the wilderness,' Peter continued. 'If you're worried about getting a wrinkle on your face, you should run back to town.'

OK, enough. I thought. I never said it aloud, but I vowed then and there never to go on a long hike with Peter ever again. Any resupply missions, I decided, I would do on my own from now on. Our life was perfect—as long as we didn't walk long distances together with heavy backpacks. We had clearly reached our limit. Little did I know that one day I would break that vow.

We finally reached the hut in the last light of the day. I silently lit the fire and Peter cooked dinner without saying much.

'Well, it's good to be here,' he eventually said, nonchalantly flicking through the magazines left by other hikers.

I looked up in surprise, then laughed.

'Why are you laughing?' he asked genuinely, then he saw my face and smiled.

'Oh, nothing, sweetie,' I replied.

Slowly the weather cleared up and the forest dried out. We were surrounded by beautiful rocky outcrops and were living in the shadow of many stunning snow-capped mountaintops. On warm afternoons we heard avalanches bringing thousands of tonnes of snow and ice down from the tops of the near-vertical faces.

Bob's Hut looked out over a huge boulder field where two rivers met. Everywhere around us were little streams and creeks cascading down vertical cliffs. We often looked through a notch in the mountains at one particularly majestic pyramid: its tops were covered in pure snow, but the vertical cracks and chasms were bare, for no vegetation or snow could hold on to anything. The exposed rock face reflected the colours of the sky: some evenings it almost looked reddish; during the day it was black in the shadow; when the sun shone straight on it, it appeared light brown.

When the soil started to dry up underneath the trees, we made a comfortable tent camp near the hut and, except for rainy days, we spent most of our time outside.

One day when we came back from a long walk Peter spied a Canada goose sitting on her eggs in the high grass next to the river. He walked closer to see if she would fly away, but the brave mother did not move an inch. From that day, we began to try to find eggs left without mothers to guard them. I forgot my bow for the time being, and focused on egg-hunting. The idea of eating eggs was very appealing.

After a few afternoons of walking over the stones, I finally found a beautiful ring of feathers so delicately woven together that it withstood the gale-force wind that often swept the valley. I could hardly force myself to take the eggs. I could hear the mother's wild honking in the distance, and I took only two eggs, careful not to touch the other three.

Tears came to my eyes. I felt so heartless and so sorry for the mother. *I'm stealing her children* went through my head—something I had never thought when buying eggs in the supermarket. Now here I was, crying over taking two goose eggs.

When I returned to the hut, Peter looked at the eggs, and not at my red eyes.

'Now, we don't know what stage the embryo is at, right?' Peter held the two precious, warm eggs in his hands. 'In Vietnam, they want the embryos. They actually eat them—sometimes raw! So there's no problem either way, OK?'

He broke the eggs carefully into a cup. The yolk was not like that of a hen's egg from a supermarket; this yolk had some kind of blood-thing in it.

'You want to eat this?' Peter looked at me.

'Um . . .' I didn't want to eat it, but I didn't want to sound pathetic either.

He grinned, fished the embryo out of the cup, and threw the egg in the frying pan. We had an omelette with fresh bread and we felt like the kings of our wild castle.

One day while I was toasting bread over the fire, I heard a sound we hadn't heard for almost two months: an engine. *Wop-wop-wop-wop.* A small blue helicopter appeared from behind the mountaintops. It was an astonishing sight, like seeing aliens dropping from the sky. I waved cheerfully to the pilot, hoping to make him land and talk to us.

He hovered noisily above the ground, turning the whole place into an unbelievable whirlwind. When the chopper blades finally slowed down and the flurry of leaves and branches floated back to earth, a man climbed out with a small dog in each hand.

Paul was living on the West Coast. The helicopter was his own and he flew it to remote areas to spend nights trapping possums. He tried to make a living selling the much sought-after possum fur. He was friendly, in his mid-forties, with a little belly. He was shy, yet sometimes had bold moments of directness.

'You're a bow hunter?' He looked at me disbelievingly, taking a seat on a log beside the fire.

'Yes. No. Well, I have a bow.' I looked at my bare feet and dirty toenails. 'And arrows,' I added. That was the truth of the matter. 'Deer are too big for me to shoot, and I haven't seen any sign of goats,' I said apologetically.

'No, there aren't any goats around here. Maybe chamois on the tops, but mostly deer and possums. Every area has its own animals,' he explained. He took off his hat for a second to scratch his short blond hair.

'That East Matakitaki Hut is real nice too,' he said, gratefully accepting tea and a slice of camp-oven bread. 'Next week I'm going to trap possums up there. I can fly your food there too, if you want.'

Peter's eyes lit up.

'It's only ten minutes with my helicopter.'

This was lucky for us, especially after the difficulty we'd had carrying our supplies up here to Bob's Hut.

We drank our tea and I gazed up at the early stars in a very cheerful mood now that our future—free of arguments over carrying heavy packs—was secured.

We talked all evening, and in the morning we sat round the fire again with a cup of tea.

Paul patted the little dogs next to him. 'You were talking about goat-hunting, right?' he said to me. 'Well, I know the most beautiful valley in the world and nobody goes there. It's full of goats, deer and chamois. No huts or tracks, and it will take three or four days to walk in there.'

We both jolted to a new state of alertness.

'What's it called?' Peter moved closer to Paul to avoid mishearing this crucial information.

'Paul's Paradise.' Paul grinned. 'Top-secret location, very high in the mountains. It's pretty cold in winter and spring, but if you want to go there this summer I can fly your supplies in there for you.'

'Do we have to walk blindfolded?' I joked.

'No huts, you were saying?' Peter said.

'I'd like to build a hut, so that I can stay somewhere when I'm hunting.' Paul smiled when he saw my starry eyes. 'I'm a builder by trade and can fly in material like corrugated iron for the roof, firebox, walls, piles, the lot. I'll teach you how to build.'

I had to refrain from jumping into his arms and bear-hugging his stocky body out of sheer gratitude and delight. I couldn't believe our incredible luck. We had just met the best man in the country.

We spent the rest of the day fantasising about our little hut in the wilderness. I thought of Mark with his skills requirement, and already felt the pride of being able to shout back: 'I build huts!'

Before Paul flew away again, I gave him some mail to post to my parents. There was a letter for them to forward on to my older sister, Hanna, and eventually it would reach my younger sister, Sofie. I knew that all of them were looking forward to receiving a message from me in the wilderness. I had written all about the weather that ruled our daily life, and described the full moon coming up over the mountains and how it lit up the snow on the tops so extraordinarily. I knew my portrayals were a big contrast to their world of schedules, social meetings, bills, mortgages, work and stress—with a holiday at the end of it all.

Without all the busy-ness and distractions, I wrote, *I'm confronted with my own fears and limitations, which are not always easy to face. I've discovered I am afraid of being alone, for instance. So I've started to practise, and every time it becomes a little easier. I sit by myself in the forest for an afternoon, feeling restless and uncomfortable. I have to resist running back to*

Peter. Then I focus on the beautiful trees and ferns, and slowly I start to feel more at ease. Hopefully the fear will disappear altogether one day.

When I closed the bulging envelopes, I wondered if my family could even imagine the place I was living in: a timeless land protected by ancient rhythms, where humanity is obsolete and control pointless. A land in which the forest is a guardian and fire our closest friend, the wind a bringer of change and the sun our salvation.

A week later Paul returned. I went with him in his helicopter to collect a month's supply of food from Downie's Hut to stash at East Matakitaki Hut. The chopper left the earth slowly at first, then we whooshed into the air. The flight was breathtaking. I smiled continuously as I gazed out over the tops of the trees that we had walked beneath so slowly. The river looked so different from above. The mountains were remarkably untouched and wild, without any sign of a human imprint.

'Great feeling of freedom, isn't it?' I looked at Paul's face for a second.

'This—' he cocked his head towards the nose of his helicopter—'is my freedom in my life!'

We both laughed joyfully.

Paul flew me back to Bob's Hut, and a few days later Peter and I walked to East Matakitaki Hut together. The hut was built in a beautiful grass clearing. On one side was a fast-flowing crystal-clear river; on the other, old beech trees hugged a steep mountain. When we looked up the valley, we saw stunning snow-capped mountains. The government had built this hut 60 years ago for professional deer cullers, and the original construction had since been improved by the Department of Conservation.

Mice had found their way into the hut via the chimney, so I insisted on sleeping in the tent. Not far from the hut, beneath the beech trees, was a conveniently flat spot to set up our tent. Apart from the occasional rainy day, we mostly lived outside round our fire.

When the brilliant weather arrived, we started to explore our surroundings. All around us were many mountain passes, but no marked trails. The sky was blue, the air was fresh and clear, and a little breeze brought the scent of yellow flowers in the grass. One day we followed the river that meandered through the dense beech forest. The only time the evergreen forest showed any change in colour was when new leaves budded in the springtime. A beautiful red tint emerged from the trees. We climbed up the valley until we came out in a lovely meadow, where Peter sat down in the sun and took his shirt off.

'Heliopathy!' He smiled. 'Get some sun on your white skin.'

I took off my shirt too. 'Ta-da!'

I danced to make Peter laugh, then I curled in next to his body, put my ear on his heart, caressed the blond hair on his chest and kissed his flat stomach, which was still tanned from the winter sun. I closed my eyes and smiled. How I loved the natural perfume of his body.

'Such soft skin you have,' he said, stroking my back.

We made love in the soft grass and imagined that we were Adam and Eve. It was so strikingly beautiful and serene. We had not a worry in the world. Crickets were chirping, robins were singing and fantails came around. Some geese were resting just 50 metres away. We were no threat to any of them. The whole valley seemed enchanted. We were simply part of the exquisite beauty of the world.

'Miriam, come, have a look!' Peter called out to me. We were out collecting firewood, and Peter took me down to the river.

'Blue ducks,' he whispered excitedly, while we crawled through the grass. 'Hear the whistle they make?'

Peter's bright eyes met mine. It was wonderful to see such rare birds. Their unique sound was quite extraordinary: a whistle, a ffffio—from which it gets the name whio in te reo Māori—louder than the rushing water, and therefore more effective than the usual quacking. Oblivious to their audience, the little blue-grey ducks were floating and diving into the fast-flowing river as if it were a pond.

'Do you see the flap of skin at the tip of the beak?' whispered Peter. 'It helps with sifting invertebrates from debris by touch in the turbulent water. They're diving for insects on rocks at the bottom. Many bird lovers would give an arm and a leg to see this.'

Over the months, Peter taught me the names of all the living things we saw around us. He viewed the natural world as a miraculous wonder, and slowly his curiosity and knowledge became mine too.

On the map Peter had seen a lake that lay at the foot of one of the great towering peaks around us. So, one clear morning, we set out for the lake, and climbed the mountain behind our camp. We reached the last of the trees and in front of us lay a huge boulder field. While I gazed at the endless, moon-like landscape ahead, Peter jumped to the first stone like a mountain goat, his hair dancing in the wind.

'You have to keep the momentum going!' he called over his shoulder, hopping to the next stone.

When I leaped after him, he yelled, 'Watch out for the tippers!'

'What are they?'

'Big stones that look solid, but suddenly tip you over if you step on the wrong side.'

Trailing behind Peter, I soon jumped on to a tipper and was mercilessly thrown on to the unforgiving surrounding rocks. It didn't cause much more damage than a small bruise, but I felt dazed and quite upset.

'What happened?' Peter had come back for me, and stretched out his hand to lift me back to my feet.

'A tipper.' Tears were almost in my eyes. The fall had given me a fright. I hugged Peter's strong body until I felt less shaky.

Together we climbed into the alpine vegetation. We looked at the beautiful, delicate flowers in between the patches of snow. They looked so fragile, yet grew in one of the most hostile places on earth. I had felt so vulnerable after falling on to the rocks, but these plants had to tolerate exceptionally harsh conditions on the wind-blasted scree fields. They would see metres of snow, torrential rain and intense heat. Every plant and animal that lived here knew how to endure: a trait that I, too, would acquire over the years.

When we finally came to the lake, which lay buried underneath the snow, it felt as though we had reached the top of the world. Everything around us was pure, pristine and such a bright white that I could barely open my eyes. While we stood taking in the astonishing view, we heard a strange snigger coming from the sky. Looking up, I spotted a beautiful big black-backed gull with a white belly: the king of the mountains. He floated gracefully across the deep blue sky. Soon, others joined him, all sniggering as they circled above us. We looked up at them; they looked down at us. After a while, they had had enough and soared off to another mountain in the distance.

'Don't you wish you could fly?' Peter was gazing at the small dots above the mountain.

I wriggled myself underneath his arm. 'Yes,' I said, and we laughed.

I had all but given up on bow-hunting, but I did hope to see a deer. One quiet afternoon, I walked away from the path on to a carpet of moss between the gnarly old trees. The moss looked lovely but I couldn't feel it, so I took off my sandals to fully experience its softness. The sunshine looked pleasant but never reached my skin, so I took off my clothes to feel its warmth.

If a deer saw me now, I thought, *it would just see a naked ape—just another animal in the forest.*

I walked slowly over fallen tree trunks, and found by chance a little pond. I drank the clear water. A hind had been there too, and not long ago; her hoof prints were still visible in the mud. I stood perfectly still for a long time, hoping to see her. Then I curled up next to the pond and watched the changing patterns the sun made on the moss. It was so very peaceful to lie there alone and with nothing on. With my shorts, T-shirt and sandals, it can be easy to forget that I am really just another kind of animal.

When all our food was finished, we walked out of our valley and into the other world. After three days' hiking through the forest, we reached the dirt road and farmland.

After some time, a car came by and stopped. The driver was dressed in black with dark sunglasses concealing his eyes. His passenger was a Buddhist monk: an American in bright orange robes who had just come out of a seven-day retreat in a cottage nearby.

'How wonderful! We've also just come out of the mountains,' I exclaimed. 'We lived over there for three months.' I pointed at the big forested valley on our left. I wanted to talk to him about 'the art of doing nothing' (which he would probably call meditation) but the orange-clad man declined to be heartened by my smile and appeared particularly uninterested. As we drove along, he complained wearily about the obligatory politics within his Buddhist Sangha back in California.

'He didn't seem very Zen!' I said to Peter after they had dropped us off.

'No, rather stressed-out actually. That's a pity. It's such a stunning place here.'

We turned and gazed back at the familiar snow-capped mountains. Little dots appeared in the clear blue sky and we heard the beautiful, melancholic honking of a flock of geese. Twenty or more were flying our way in a brilliant V-formation. They were moving slowly and rhythmically and gradually passed us, on their way to the grassy plains. We watched them until they disappeared out of sight. We could hear their honking for a long time, before it too faded away.

CHAPTER 4

SUMMER

'I bet you never thought you'd end up here when you were walking out of the mountains!'

Mouse grinned at me.

The boat, with its humming engine, skimmed over the small waves. The sky was blue, with small puffs of white clouds hovering on the horizon. We had left the harbour in Picton more than an hour ago, and now we were sailing between the quiet islands in the Marlborough Sounds. Mouse was steering his boat with one hand and pointing with the other at the seals that were lazing around on the blackened rocks in the summer sun.

He slowed the boat down, then opened one of the dog boxes. A slim black dog jumped out on to the deck.

'See how Bella's sniffing?' Mouse said. 'She can smell a pig in the scrub, if the wind is right.'

The dog pointed towards Arapaoa Island. Mouse opened another dog box and three more impatient dogs leaped out, bumping into my legs. They jumped into the sea and swam the short distance to shore. While I watched them disappear into the prickly gorse, Mouse studied his GPS tracking device to follow his 'girls', as he called them.

We floated there peacefully. The sun was high up in the sky and now that we had stopped moving, it was getting hot. Since it could take some time for the dogs to find a pig, I rested on top of the dog boxes and watched Peter, who was admiring the scenery. He held the boat's railing with one hand, while the other sat casually in his pocket. His face was tanned, rugged, lined by the sun, and the breeze moved his long hair. He wasn't looking for anything in particular; he was just curious. He always had this inquisitiveness about everything. Where I merely saw the sea and hills covered with shrubs, Peter would study the age of the forest by looking at the vegetation. He'd notice the direction of the dominant wind by the shape of the trees, and the colour of the leaves told him something about the rainfall. To him, every stone, bird and drop of water revealed one of nature's many secrets.

He pulled a box of matches out of his pocket, took one match, split it in half with his nails, and used it to carefully clean his teeth. Slowly his gaze came back to me. With an almost surprised look in his eyes, he said, 'Matakitaki feels like another lifetime away, doesn't it?'

I nodded and smiled, then lay my head on my jumper to snooze.

'They're on a pig!' Without warning Mouse revved the boat so abruptly that I almost fell into the sea. We shot forward with a loud roar, swinging round with monstrous speed towards another part of the island.

'They're right here!' Mouse laughed as he steered the boat beneath a three-metre clay cliff with some roots sticking out. 'OK, one comes with me to hold the pig. The other holds the boat.'

'You go.' Peter and I pointed simultaneously at each other.

'You're the hunter,' said Peter.

Reluctantly, I scrambled off the boat and after Mouse up a slippery bank towards a loud squealing. There we found a big pig surrounded by Mouse's wildly barking dogs. I looked at the boar with a kind of appalled fascination, for I had never seen a living one before—and certainly not one that was being held by its ears, balls and back leg by a pack of growling dogs.

We were perched near the edge of the cliff. If the boar pushed the dogs, they would crash into me and I would be the first one to fall into the sea below.

'Can you grab the back legs?' Mouse was digging in his pack.

'How?' I asked, displeased with the unfamiliar responsibility.

Mouse went over and grabbed the boar's hind legs with surprising speed, and handed them to me. Then, instead of ending the pig's misery, he produced a small camera to film the scene. The boar was squealing its guts out but I didn't want to smile for the camera; I just wanted this whole episode to end. Half a minute later, Mouse finally stabbed the suffering boar straight in the heart with a knife.

As I slowly let the strong back legs go, I realised my hands were shaking. I slumped against a tree, while Mouse gutted the pig. He didn't need the meat; he would give the pig to someone else. He would hang the tusks next to the hundreds of others he had. I struggled to understand him.

Together we managed to haul the heavy dead weight to the boat.

'Quite a beast, isn't he?' Mouse said to Peter, pulling the long tusks with his fists. 'A good-size boar!'

We spent a wonderfully convivial weekend in the Sounds with Mouse at his bach, which was set amid a patch of forest with its own private beach. I enjoyed the warm air, summer sun and clear skies. The moody sea, the islands and the Sounds themselves were such a contrast to the mountains. We gathered seafood and fished, and Mouse caught another pig to give away.

On our journey back, Mouse said I could steer the boat. He stood up and I sat down on his seat. The boat was easy to steer, as the sea was very calm.

After a while Mouse saw something that looked like a log in the water and he came to my side to take over. I motioned to him to sit on my lap, and he did. I held Mouse with one arm round his waist. The months in the wilderness had made me more spontaneous, less hesitant, I realised. We had only two days with Mouse, and I wouldn't see him for a long time to come. What could possibly be wrong with affection? I smiled happily at Peter, and he grinned back at me.

Mouse was looking at the sea, and I was sheltered from the wind by his body. I looked at the boar lying dead at my feet, its coarse black hair matted with mud and blood. How could Mouse kill an animal so laconically? I wondered. He saw introduced animals as pests, a threat to New Zealand's ecosystem, and used that as justification for taking life without a second thought.

And as for me? I despised his killing, yet I hunted too. I detested his actions, yet I liked Mouse very much. I wasn't sure what was right and what was wrong.

Peter lifted the boar's head a little, by pulling on one of the tusks. 'There are no rules,' he said to me, as though reading my thoughts with his elf-ears. 'Humans can take life or not take life.'

'What's that?' Mouse turned round.

'Pork. We'll enjoy the pork tonight.' I buried my nose in his jumper, which smelled of lavender washing powder.

'It's only ten kilometres.' Peter was looking at the map, calculating the distance to our first camping spot. We were back in the mountains.

'Ooooh,' I exclaimed in a rather exaggerated manner. 'That's only a few hours, and we have sixteen hours' daylight!'

'We do have to climb nearly a thousand metres up the side of the mountain though,' Peter pointed out.

After walking for a leisurely hour along a stony riverbed, we arrived at a particularly beautiful spot in the sun and Peter suggested a cup of tea. Grateful for a break, I unpacked everything we needed to make tea while Peter lit a fire with wood from the riverbed. I sat on the smooth grey boulders, which had been warmed by the sun, and looked at the flames. They were almost invisible in the bright sunshine. As we drank our tea, we chatted and laughed as though we weren't about to climb 10 kilometres through West Coast jungle without a track up the side of a mountain. When we finished our tea, we decided we might as well have some lunch, too, since everything was already unpacked. So we ate some crackers with cheese, tomato, cucumber and Marmite . . . and then we had a couple of oranges each, so we wouldn't have to carry them. At last, we reluctantly packed our bags.

'Do you want some raisins?' I grabbed a handful myself, then handed the bag to Peter.

'Isn't that supposed to be for the hike up the mountain?'

'Well, we're hiking now, aren't we?' I said with my mouth full.

'I think we'll just walk up the creek.' Peter took the bag from me. 'Rather than getting lost on the spurs.'

This sounded very rational and reasonable to me.

Ten minutes later, the devilishly difficult part began. We entered the thick undergrowth of a dimly lit forest. There were vines and lianas everywhere, as if we had walked into a tropical jungle. The stream wasn't a bright little creek; it was an impenetrably dense, horrible gully. The water at the bottom was covered with half a metre of dark brown rotten leaves, slippery stones, ankle-breaking branches and knee-twisting logs. The big trees on the side were no help either, because a thick layer of wet, sooty fungus made everything in the surrounding area a frightening, slippery mess.

Paul had said that this area received three to six metres of rain each year. It was my first time in the West Coast ranges of the South Island, and I gloomily wondered whether we had chosen the right part of the country to spend the whole summer in. This did not seem a suitable place to live in a tent. But, since we were already committed, I pushed onwards.

We wrestled through knee-high vegetation, while slipping and sliding up the incredibly steep creek. At frequent intervals, webs of vines halted our progress. We had to crawl and jump to get through the jumbled tangle, often getting hooked by our packs the moment we thought we had escaped. The light was already fading when we finally found a grassy space near the water that was suitable for camping.

The next day we continued our journey to Paul's Paradise. At one point I sat down to rest while Peter slowly made his way towards me. As though in slow motion, I watched him step on an old, moss-covered log, then suddenly his leg disappeared into the rotten tree, and his heavy pack pulled him sideways. His knee remained stuck in the middle. It looked so absurd that I couldn't help laughing at his bug-eyed face and comical wheeling arms. When he finally came to a standstill, he grunted in pain and hugged his knee. We didn't realise then just how serious it was, but this knee injury would go on to bother Peter for years to come. That day he was able to continue, but his knee gave him real pain.

We entered a dragon-tree forest. Their slender trunks, most around 10 metres high, were covered in little sheets of brown paper-bark and their green palm-like leaves swayed in the breeze. The ancestors of these extraordinary trees hail back to the time of the dinosaurs, and it wasn't difficult to imagine a different time and climate when looking at them.

We emerged at last into the open space of the saddle, with views of the long forest-covered ranges to the west and the Southern Alps to the east: an experience not to be forgotten. I felt very relieved to be out of the dense, dark forest.

'Are we going to camp on this saddle? This high up?' I asked Peter, my hair flying about in the wind.

'Yes, this is going to be our spot. There's a creek close by for water. I think Paul said there's good hunting down there.' He pointed at the valley.

We gazed out at the expansive virgin forest where people had hardly ever set foot—now understandably, to us. I counted seven mountain ranges to the south, each covered in forest and some of the high peaks still under snow. Here and there puffs of mist swirled through the valley. It was such an astonishingly wild and untouched place.

A few days after we set up our camp, Paul arrived with our supplies. 'How do you like the place?' he called as soon as he was out of his helicopter.

'It's pretty good!' Peter said cheerfully. 'Come and have a look at our camp.'

We walked from the open saddle down into the surrounding beech trees, where our tent was pitched on a soft bed of moss and tussock that we had gathered. We had tied our tarpaulins and fly sheet between the stunted old trees, which were magnificent pieces of living art. Their trunks, with their furrowed bark, were deeply embedded in the earth, solid and indestructible; their branches were long and curvy, almost touching the ground. These trees had survived incredibly harsh conditions at an altitude of 1000 metres. Some were perhaps more than 300 years old.

'I'd like to build the hut around here,' Paul said. 'So that the campfire smoke won't chase away all the animals that are living down the valley. What do you reckon?'

'Yeah, this is a good spot,' I said enthusiastically. 'Tell us what we can do to make a start.'

'Well, we need to dig holes one metre apart for piles.' Paul handed me his plan and a measuring tape.

'What piles?' I wasn't sure what a 'pile' was, or what it was made out of.

'I'll fly the piles in later, dummy.' Paul laughed. 'Do I see some blonde hair?' He lifted my hat.

I grunted a laugh.

'Hey.' He jabbed me on the shoulder and pointed down the valley. 'I saw a mob of goats when I flew over just now. The more you shoot, the better! Otherwise, DOC will drop poison in the forest. Goats are considered a pest here,' he explained, as though we had never heard of the conservation issues with introduced animals. 'So you're doing the country a favour, OK?'

I just nodded.

'Good luck with the hunting!' were his last words to us before he flew away in his chopper, waving. We didn't see him again for over two months.

The longer we lived in our new campsite, the more we realised how extraordinarily remote it was—an almost forgotten place. Many wild things lived here in the alpine forests and clearings. One day a stoat appeared from behind an old tree with an enormous rat in its mouth.

It scuttled over the tree's massive roots, jumped over the stones in the creek and disappeared again on the other side. Night-time brought the sound of rare native frogs piping from the alpine bogs; their call sounded almost like a whistle, and they lived in small moss-covered ponds on the saddle. Sometimes we would hear a possum barking in the darkness, and often the strange, drawn-out screeching of long-tailed cuckoos broke the silence of the deep night. At dawn, small colourful parrots flitted through the evergreen forest. Overhead, falcons fiercely defended their territory from incoming harrier hawks. The longer we stayed, the more creatures we saw.

I often thought of Sofie, my great, tall, beautiful sister, who I loved so dearly. As children, we had shared everything and were still each other's best friend. When I declared that I was going to New Zealand, it broke her tender heart—and mine, too. All we had now were the letters that flew across the earth to reach each other. On the longest day of the year I wrote to her.

Dearest Sofie,

Can you imagine a way of life so quiet, so timeless, so abundant and full that watching a single leaf fluttering from the trees, lifted into the air by a little breeze, turning silver in the sunshine is meaningful? To be rich enough to live without working and to live in the midst of such astounding beauty is truly a privilege.

It is now around midsummer; the days feel as if they will never end! Since we don't have a clock, I think we only cook dinner at about nine. We most certainly sleep a lot less than we did during the long winter nights, but we still have plenty of energy.

You asked me once why I choose to live in nature. Well, you know, when I was in Zimbabwe and India I met women who were born in extreme poverty. They (understandably) wanted to get out of the hellholes they were living in and find some physical security by earning money to buy or rent a house. Compared to them, I realised that you and I were born rich.

To us, the promise of becoming wealthy isn't so exciting any more. I know what it is like to have the security of a job and of living in a house. I know the competitive world, where people fight themselves up the ladder for power and status. I know the world where pleasure becomes the meaning of life. What I don't know, though—and I think I should—is the natural world we were all born in.

I think it is difficult for a mind that has evolved with human civilisation to reconnect with nature. In 'The Epic of Gilgamesh', the city wall of Uruk symbolised the loss of connection with the greater rhythms of nature, and when we live in cities and towns we, too, lose this connection with the natural world, I think.

You might ask why we should reconnect with nature. I think it would make us a lot healthier, both mentally and physically, and our planet might also tolerate us for a bit longer. What do you think?

Much love, Miriam

Now that there was a real prospect of goats for food, I was determined to find one. I strolled off across the mossy flat and down into the valley. After about a hundred metres, the impenetrable vegetation started. As I crawled through the small holes made in the thickets by possums, I realised it would take all day just to reach the first goat, so I reluctantly went back to camp. The next day I returned, this time with a knife, a saw and a hatchet, and made a start on cutting myself a small track. Several days later, I set out for a second time with my bow and arrows.

My path led through the dense scrub into a stand of old beech trees. The yellow spots of bright sunlight dotted among the dark shadows formed a colourful carpet on the moss. I walked through a warm meadow of thick, soft grass. As I stepped into the cool water of a stony creek, small fish shot away from my feet. It was almost silent in the valley, with just the soft murmuring of the creek, which I followed downstream for a while. When I climbed up on to a grassy bank, I found myself quite unexpectedly face-to-face with a small group of wild goats.

I was so surprised that it took me a moment to find an arrow. By the time I drew my bow, the goats had already walked halfway up a nearby hill covered in trees and big black boulders. I considered running after them, but even though they seemed to move slowly they were soon out of reach.

Well, I thought, *at least they exist.*

I waited for a while, but the goats never returned. I turned and walked back to camp.

While Peter was resting his injured knee, I went out on many more hunts, and every time I made mistakes. Sometimes I saw no animals at all; then at other times, when I did see them, they would run away while I was trying to crawl as close as possible. Often when I managed to fire a shot my arrow would sail right past my target and into a tree.

I always came back empty-handed—but with every hunt I was learning to become more patient, more careful and more alert. I was glad that my enthusiasm and perseverance never waned.

One afternoon I crept towards a clearing and saw seven goats quietly grazing. I hid for a long time behind a tree before sneaking as close as possible. Silently, I stood up, drew my bow and shot an arrow into a big goat. I couldn't believe it: the arrow was stuck into his ribs . . . but he immediately ran away.

I had read that bow-hunters are supposed to wait 20 minutes before following the trace of blood to the dead animal; if I ran after him now, the adrenaline would make the goat—and me—run for hours. So I sat down just long enough to lose sight of the wounded goat, but after a few minutes I grew anxious. I ran to the bushes where he had disappeared, and was reassured when I spotted fresh blood on the leaves. I followed the traces into the forest, feeling proud of myself as I crawled on my hands and knees over the ground—like a real bushman! When the distance between the specks of blood slowly increased to over five metres I became more nervous. The image of the goat suffering, an arrow stuck in his ribs, was in my mind the whole time.

Eventually I saw no more sign.

The trail was lost.

I stood up, then zigzagged up the steep slope hoping I might miraculously find him lying behind a log. But no.

I wondered how long it would take for him to die in pain. I searched for a long time, bleating in the hope that he would answer, but there was nothing—only a very sad silence.

Eventually I turned round and headed back up my track. I felt ashamed and angry with myself. *What am I doing? What the fuck am I doing?* I bashed my fist on a tree in frustration. Tears filled my eyes. *Wounding innocent wild animals with my bow and arrow? Letting them die a slow, miserable death? Playing little Robin Hood?*

I was contributing to the misery and suffering on this earth. *Contributing to it!* I was just as guilty as any other wrongdoer! I felt like smashing my bow against the next tree. *Let it be finished.* I bit my knuckles, and my teeth made a deep imprint in my hand.

Sometimes it didn't make any sense.

Sometimes I just wanted to be back in a house with a vegetable garden and be a vegetarian again. Forget about this primitive life of hunting and gathering. It was all too difficult, way too hard.

When I got back to camp I quietly discussed with Peter—for the hundredth time—my dilemma. Should we be killing animals to eat? Or should we be vegetarians, and kill vegetables from the garden to eat? Kill calves to have milk? Kill premature chickens to have eggs? Should we have our money in the bank? Is it not invested for us in animal farms, in the armament industry to kill people in wars? What about the clothes on our backs, which came from the destructive cotton industry?

Every topic was a new agony. I stared at the smoky fire and reached for some firewood to throw into the fire.

'Hey, there's some living moss on that piece!' Peter took the log from me and plucked the moss off the wood.

Christmas came and brought with it wintery rain and an unexpected cold snap, which kept me from more hunting. The temperature was so low that I thought wistfully of the festive season in the northern hemisphere, with my mother's home cooking and special cakes, and little candles flickering in the Christmas tree in my parents' cosy home. In striking contrast, here we were having spaghetti, dried peas and a tin of mackerel. I felt even colder and more miserable than I had during the winter in South Hut.

While we sat shivering on our buckets round the fire, which smoked continuously, Peter stared at the ground. He slowly put his blue enamel plate back on to the bucket we were using as a table, and said in a monotone voice, 'I'm not feeling so good. The malaria might be coming back.'

I had carefully hidden those nightmarish memories in the furthest corner of my mind, but it only took that small sentence to make them all tumble out again. The incredibly heavy, debilitating heat. The thick jungle drenched in humidity. The flimsy huts on stilts. The crying babies. Papua New Guinea, and the disease that had very nearly killed Peter: malaria.

He swayed towards the tent, his movements slow and thick. He stopped to hold on to a tree halfway. I silently washed the dishes then crawled into my sleeping bag next to him. After a quiet hour, I heard his breath quicken and his teeth start to chatter. Careful not to make any noise that would hurt his over-sensitive ears, I wriggled out of my sleeping bag and draped it over his shivering body. Drizzle was softly falling on the tent, and a long-tailed cuckoo was shrieking its strange cries nearby. I stared into the darkness, feeling cold and miserable and quite alone. Tears welled up in my eyes as the images of Papua New Guinea came flooding back to me, as clear as though it was yesterday.

We had been travelling for a year from India to northern Papua New Guinea, and had planned to go up the Sepik River and into the highlands, cross the 4000-metre-high mountains, then boat down the Fly River all the way to the south coast. We planned to enter Australia via Thursday Island in two months' time.

We had reached the beginning of the forest, and we were sitting in the back of an open pick-up truck with a dozen locals. Incredible lush jungle flashed past as we made our way to the Sepik River, which would be the starting point of our expedition. Suddenly we were forced to stop: three men with strong torsos, fierce faces and wooden hunting spears were blocking the road.

'Hunting pigs,' my neighbour whispered in my ear.

Pig-hunting with spears in the rainforest! It was a sight beyond my wildest dreams. (Little did I know then that one day I, too, would find myself hunting in a forest.)

One of the hunters started to yell, gripping his spear, his skin glimmering with sweat in the incredible, humid heat. Fearing an outburst of violence, I looked at the old lady next to me. She just closed her eyes and shook her head ever so slightly to indicate that there was no need to panic. She was right. The dispute soon ended and we drove on.

Some time later we reached the end of the road, and everybody jumped off the ute to walk the last kilometre to the village. Interminable rainforest stretched ahead of us.

'Do you have a knife?' The village teacher asked us when we arrived. He was the only one there who spoke any English.

'Yes!' I proudly held up the ceremonial knife I had bought in Indonesia. It suddenly looked rather flimsy.

'Yes, this is good,' he said.

'What do I need it for?' I asked, picturing myself harvesting coconuts.

'Enemies.' His deep-set hazel eyes were sombre.

'What enemies?'

'Robbers.' He was quiet for a moment. 'Rapists . . . maybe even cannibals.'

I swallowed nervously and looked at Peter, who just kept smiling.

'Good luck.' The teacher shook our hands before we set off into the jungle.

Peter led the way along a small trail.

'Are you not worried about these enemies?' I asked him, scanning the thick vegetation for leeches, snakes and spiders.

'No,' he replied. 'I simply refuse to believe that I'll fall victim to violence of that kind. I would have missed many magnificent places in the past if I believed otherwise.'

His confidence and courage had a remarkably positive effect on me, and I felt an exciting sense of entering a secret corner of the world.

We walked for three days, spending the nights in villages along the way, where we were greeted by bare-breasted women and skinny children. They had big bellies and flaky skin, and were suffering from malnutrition. They were friendly but a little shy, and lived in thatched huts on stilts made from small poles, with ladders for climbing inside.

One quiet morning, I looked out of the open door of our hut to see four men with bare feet and clothed only in shorts approaching. They strode in single file through the village, and didn't stop to speak to anyone. These highlanders moved in a rhythm that resonated with the jungle; gracious and strong, they were clearly connected to the earth on which they walked. I was suddenly aware that I was born in captivity compared to these men—raised in a town, educated in buildings, surrounded by so much comfort that I had lost my backbone. I felt like a budgie in a cage, while they were the eagles in the sky.

Then, one night, Peter became very sick with a high fever. The following day he could still talk and sit up, but on the day after that he could only lie down in the hut. On the third day, he tried to stumble to the long-drop toilet just outside the village, but collapsed on the ground. I found him lying semi-conscious in the grass. As I ran to him, the frenzied chirping of the insects and songbirds seemed to slow down to an eternal silence, and it was as though the heavy, moist air was trying to embrace him, smother him, swallow him up.

He opened his eyes slightly and groaned. 'Water.'

I ran to fetch water from the tank on the other side of the village, and when I returned I found about 20 people gathered round Peter. A priest loomed over him, evoking a prayer: 'Papa God, bai you lukim dis fella, waitman. Him he sik too muss. Suppose you no lukim, he dead-pinish.'

I felt numb. This was bad. Very bad. The priest thought Peter was going to be 'dead-finish'.

If only we had never come here, I thought. *If only we had never attempted to cross the jungle.*

That evening, Peter and I moved into the school building, as Peter could no longer climb the ladders into the thatched huts. Our mats were spread between the wooden benches and tables of the classroom, and the rain drummed on the corrugated-iron roof. Flashes of blue light lit up the sky every few seconds and the thunder was so loud it resonated in the ground. With every flash of lightning the classroom was illuminated, and I saw more and more water seeping in underneath the walls. Pools were forming on the floor.

'Can you find me the painkiller?' asked Peter.

What painkiller? I thought frantically, then I remembered the first-aid kit that some French people I'd met had given me when I was travelling alone in Pakistan two years before. Peter had kept the super-strong painkillers. In the flashes of light, I emptied my pack then crawled over to Peter with a pill and the water bottle.

'It stops the fever from cooking . . . my brain,' he sighed.

I felt such a sense of despair that I began to cry. I knew he was perilously ill, with a sky-high fever, but we were helpless here in the middle of the jungle without a doctor. We had no choice; we had to give up on our plan of crossing Papua New Guinea and somehow find a way back to the road and back to civilisation.

At dawn, Peter was able to stand up. I packed our bags, and supported him on the long return journey along the riverbed. Peter walked erratically and stumbled often, and we had to rest every hundred metres. Even though I was aware of what a dangerous situation we were in, I could do nothing besides urge him to drink and struggle onwards. I felt as if I couldn't breathe in the humid air.

After three agonising days like this we finally reached the end of the road. We lay down in the pounding heat and waited for a vehicle—any vehicle—to come by. There was no traffic at all. The chatter of the birds was drowned out by the noise of chainsaws and bulldozers, which were cutting down valuable rainforest timber. Hearing the destruction of such precious trees—the habitat of so many birds and animals—was heartbreaking.

We waited there for many hours before a lone yellow petrol tanker appeared, then pulled over. We couldn't go faster than 20 kilometres per hour and it was scorching in the old truck. Sweat dripped from my forehead into my lap, and my legs were glued to the hot metal box on which I sat. Peter's head hung forward.

In the afternoon, we reached the town of Vanimo on the northern coast, where it was even hotter than the jungle. Chinese ships sat in the harbour, waiting for their hardwood logs. We swayed into the small white hospital building.

'There is no doctor present,' the nurse told us. She could do nothing for us.

So we left, and stumbled to the home of a kind local man we had met when we first arrived in Vanimo. He had offered us a room if we ever needed it, and we gratefully took him up on this offer now.

Peter was deteriorating rapidly by the time we reached the house. Half-conscious, he lay down on a mattress. The smell coming from his body was nauseating. He looked as if he was not even there any more. Death was entering the room; I could smell it.

Peter opened his eyes slowly, and looked at me with desperation.

I handed him the very last painkiller and the grimy plastic water bottle.

He could barely lift his head to drink, sweat forming slowly on his forehead. I lay back down on my mat on the floor and listened to the bass of a stereo playing next door. I was overcome with a feeling of resignation. At the age of 23, I was solely responsible for the two of us, forced to be strong even though I didn't feel it.

Later, Peter told me that the fever had become so intense that he had felt his mind crumbling. A strange sensation had come over him and he couldn't sense his feet. This peculiar feeling advanced up his legs, towards his hips, stomach, chest and arms. It had just reached his neck when I had given him that last painkiller, and that had broken the fever and brought him back to life again.

I organised our visas to return to Indonesia, and with help from our local friends heaved Peter into a public-transport van. I was carrying both our bags—one on my back and one in the front. We had to get out of the van to walk over the border into West Papua, then on to another bus on the other side. Somehow we made it to the hospital.

'Sorry, sorry.' The Indonesian nurse kept pricking Peter's hand. His veins had collapsed and his blood tests revealed two strains of malaria: *P. falciparum* and *P. vivax*.

'He's very lucky,' the doctor said in broken English. '*Falciparum* kills many, many people here.'

At last, hooked up to a drip containing medicine and vitamins, Peter slowly opened his eyes and looked at me. He softly squeezed my hand and tried to smile. I took a deep breath.

Peter had recovered quickly once he was in hospital, and two weeks later he was out. But it took more than two years for him to recover completely, with several recurrences a year. We had travelled for years through countries where malaria was an issue, and we had never got it. We had become complacent and, as it turned out, over-confident. At the time, there was a drug that every local had told us you only needed to take if you got malaria—but when we realised that Peter had malaria, he took it and it didn't help.

Those weeks in Papua New Guinea had taught me a good lesson. The word 'security' has a different meaning to me now. In the eyes of death, there is actually no security at all. Life can end for any reason, at any time.

The days at Paul's Paradise after Peter's malaria recurrence were quiet. Peter lay in the tent and slowly began to feel better. Luckily he hadn't needed to take Lariam, the medicine he carried everywhere with him after Papua New Guinea. Although it was effective, it produced horrible psychotic side-effects. Now he was recovering, and was confident that the worst had passed. Compared to that first malaria attack in the jungle of Papua New Guinea, he looked more serene in the peaceful forest.

While he recovered, I completed chores like baking bread, cooking food, making tea and doing the dishes in the creek. I sat on top of the firewood, underneath the tarp, and looked out at the great misty stillness of the forest. Long white braids of lichen hung from the tree branches. The beams of sunlight that shone through the forest were unbelievably straight compared to everything else, which was curly and round. The effect was breathtaking.

'You know what, Peter?' I said.

'Yes?' he responded from inside the tent.

'It was in Papua New Guinea that I first thought of myself as a budgie in a cage. We're all born in captivity, conditioned to seek security instead of freedom, but actually we don't know what freedom is because we have never had it.'

'No indeed.'

'If we stop seeking psychological security,' I continued, 'there's a chance that we might find out what freedom is.'

'Hmm, yes.' Peter sounded thoughtful. 'What would happen if you touched insecurity?'

I considered this. 'Fear!' I said surprised. 'You'd feel fear. Fear is the wall between security and freedom.'

'You might be right, yes.'

'I'm not talking about the physical things,' I said. 'Like daredevilry—that's a different matter altogether.'

I looked at the drops of water sitting on top of the moss. They looked like tiny pearls.

'Quite interesting, eh,' said Peter. 'So every time we feel fear we now know we're reaching the boundaries of security—and that we should look further and see what will happen.'

'Yes! But you know what the difficulty is?' I said. 'Recognising fear!'

'What do you mean? Everybody knows what fear feels like.'

'But it has many faces. Sometimes there's only a slight feeling of discomfort. Sometimes there's numbness, or trembling with adrenaline, or anger, even tears . . . Jeez, the list is endless.'

Peter laughed. 'So many doors to freedom!'

In the afternoon, a weka suddenly appeared from behind some trees. The flightless native bird, with its orange and brown feathers, studied me with great interest before peering inside the tent to investigate Peter. It pecked at anything that wasn't tied down, running off with the soap and threatening to steal a spoon. I fed it pieces of bread, which it accepted with alacrity, but it was not to be completely tamed. On the third day it continued its journey over the saddle, marching off like a confident hiker without need of a map or compass.

The moment the weka had disappeared, a warm wind from the north turned up.

Peter peered intently at the clouds on the horizon. 'To feel this warm at a thousand metres means there's a big low-pressure system coming.'

The rain soon came down in torrents. The downpour sounded like a bottomless bucket being emptied over the tent and continued for 12 hours without respite. Our little creek became a river, and pools were forming all around us. I grew increasingly nervous about getting flooded. When the thundering rain lessened for a minute we scrambled outside to rescue our camp. While Peter attended to his beloved pile of firewood, I started scraping a narrow ditch round the tent. When we had done all we could, we returned to the tent and surrendered to whatever would come.

Finally, in the early morning, the big rainstorm abated and the sky cleared from the south. Cool, fresh air blew gently over the mountains and the next day I walked down the valley with renewed optimism. I had become more attuned as a hunter. I spotted hoof prints, and could sometimes smell an animal before I saw it. I had learned to use knowledge and experience, but also begun to develop an intuition for sensing the presence of an animal.

I sat down in the shade of a big tree overlooking the sunny riverbed. There was a small, grassy clearing nearby. My bow lay by my side. Any moment a goat could appear out of nowhere. I had to be ready for it. The creek murmured softly and a warm breeze came gently up the valley. A big hawk circled a few times overhead, before gliding off to the west. I watched the patches of sunlight move over the bushes and trees, transforming them from green to orange. At my feet were many little white flowers with yellow hearts. They looked so pretty among the ferns, and had a beautiful sweet fragrance.

Eventually I stood up and strolled between the trees along the bank of the creek. I crawled behind some bushes to spy on a beautiful clearing, and my heart jumped when I saw three goats: a billy, a nanny and their kid were quietly grazing in the shadow of two big beech trees. My hands shook as I nervously fitted an arrow to my bow, then I slowly moved out from where I had hidden behind a tree and fired an arrow at the kid.

It was a lucky shot. The arrow went straight into his heart. He staggered a few steps, then fell down, mortally wounded. The nanny bleated. She was very upset and walked a few paces towards her kid. The billy moved a few steps away, and snorted to the nanny as to say, 'Come on, let's go. He's dead.'

My heart was beating in my throat. The nanny walked over to her kid to sniff him, then she eventually joined the billy goat. She stood and looked back at me for a long time before at last disappearing into the forest; it was as though she wasn't willing to let her kid go. There was a terrible sadness in the air.

With tears in my eyes, I went and sat down next to the dead goat. He had distant blue eyes and little horns, and his pelt was still warm. I cried for this beautiful creature, and for its poor parents, who were now walking without their kid.

I wished I had a way to thank the little goat for its life. I wished I could believe in a god or a deity who would allow me to take life if I said a prayer. It would make a difference, if I could believe in it; I felt it might make taking a life easier in a strange way.

Eventually, I took out my knife and opened his body. I removed all the intestines, which we wouldn't eat, and placed them on a big stone in the clearing, so that hawks flying in the sky above would see their share. I felt it was my duty to let nothing go to waste.

I carefully laid the kid across my shoulders then began the hike back to our camp. I sighed, feeling sad. I was surprised by how I could love this little goat so dearly while, at the same time, its warm body lay dead across my neck. The further I walked, the more at peace I felt.

This is how humankind once lived and survived, I thought. This was an ancient legacy. With my bow and arrow, I was walking the path of our ancestors.

When I climbed that last kilometre, I began to feel elated too. *I shot a goat with my bow! Finally, finally, finally!* After so much practice and countless failed hunts, I had at last accomplished something truly remarkable! I was ecstatically proud and laughing with joy. I danced to the ancient rhythm of life and death.

Peter was waiting for me at the edge of the forest. He had sensed my arrival. 'You got one!' he called out. 'You got one, Miriam!' He sounded as euphoric as I felt.

'I got one!' I lifted my bow in triumph.

I sawed off one of the little goat's horns, bored a hole in it then threaded it on to a piece of string, which Peter knotted round my neck. I wore the necklace in memory of the young kid. It was a symbol of the sacrifice that lies at the heart of life's cycles and flows. The little goat had become part of me.

Peter took out the heart, liver and kidneys and fried them in ghee over the fire. To eat meat from an animal I had found, shot, butchered and carried myself was incredibly rewarding. The healthiest meat in the world: a young wild goat in the remotest wilderness. The nourishment was more than protein and calories; it gave energy beyond words.

We had wrapped the carcass in a special cloth and hung it from a branch over the stream to keep it cool, but the summer temperatures were quite high even at this altitude. On the second evening I uncovered the meat only to find something white crawling on it.

'Maggots!' I cried out, with big eyes.

Peter came running fast.

'Oh god, look at this!' I said despairingly.

'We'll go through it carefully,' Peter said sternly. 'We'll pick them out one by one.'

We spent hours looking for maggots, all the while fighting off a cloud of blowflies. In the end we declared the meat clean, but knew full well that there were probably more maggots hiding in there. Once

Peter had cooked it, we ate it hesitantly—suddenly everything looked like maggots, even the rice.

'The word "maggot" is definitely more revolting than actually eating them,' Peter said. 'Maggots eat meat. It's all protein. You can't even taste them.' Then, after a moment of silence, he added, 'I've read books about the war, about guys surviving on maggots and much worse . . .'

'Yes,' I said despondently. I was trying not to think about the 'much worse'.

A few weeks later, Paul reappeared with the wooden piles and sheets of corrugated iron strapped underneath his helicopter. We placed the piles into the holes that we had dug and reinforced them with rocks. It was a tedious job and took longer than expected. In the evening, we sat round our campfire enjoying a satisfactory slice of camp-oven bread.

'If you don't mind me asking, how do you actually live without having a job?' Paul said, as he shifted a log into the flames.

'Well,' Peter replied, 'we're not on a government benefit of any kind. We're living off our savings and the accumulated interest. If we keep our spending down, we can survive without working.'

'But if we wanted to buy property or rent a place, we would have to find a job to pay the bills,' I added.

Paul nodded and looked at the fire.

'We're living on less than most so-called poor people do.' Peter paused for moment. 'There's nothing more terrible than poverty, but if living simply is a choice it's quite good fun really.' He looked at me with a smile.

'I think of myself as rather rich, actually!' I laughed joyfully. 'If time is money, we are millionaires!' I went on in a more serious tone. 'Our food is basic, but I would eat anything and sleep anywhere to avoid being stuck inside a building surrounded by an ugly, dead town and imprisoned in a job with its blinding, monotonous routine. To me that is a kind of prison.' I blew on the smouldering fire to get the flames going again.

'Yeah, I know what you mean,' Paul said. 'I've spent years on building sites, working every day, spending all the money I earn without thinking. I'd like to make a living with this helicopter, but I fear I'll have to go back to labouring to pay the bills and the mortgage.'

We sat in silence for a while, each of us occupied with our own thoughts.

Then Peter said, 'After years of studying such interesting things for my PhD, I was rather disappointed with my job as a lecturer. I felt I was caught in university politics and occupied with trivial things. One day during a long, boring staff meeting I looked out of the window and thought, *I'd really rather not be here*. That was when I started planning to leave New Zealand for India.'

'You just left?' Paul's voice held a whiff of excitement.

'Well, it took a while to plan everything—but yes, in the end I resigned, sold my belongings and my house, and left with my wife at the time for India. I can't tell you how exhilarating it was to finally throw the house keys in the letterbox and walk away to the airport with just one small bag.'

'Maybe one day I'll do the same,' Paul said, sipping his tea.

When Paul had flown home again, we hiked up to the steep, rocky mountaintops. Without a heavy pack, the pain in Peter's knee was tolerable. We scrambled on our hands and feet up the vertical rocks, which had been warmed by the sun, while the fresh breeze cooled our backs.

On the tops, we sat on a cushion-like, cream-coloured plant called a vegetable sheep, which has tightly curled leaves that are so densely packed it looks like wool. While we were enjoying the view in every direction of stunning, forbidding mountain ranges, we spotted a big group of chamois running over the brown rocks—they looked like a type of goat, but are actually members of the antelope family. Young and old leaped and hopped from rock to rock, seemingly unaware of the yawning crevasse to one side of them. We watched these fearless animals with great admiration.

'Remember the Gaddi shepherds we saw in the Himalayas?'
Peter said.

'Of course,' I replied, watching the chamois disappear into the
distance.

'They had just as little fear as those chamois. They simply never
learned to be afraid of heights. I asked some of them once whether
they ever got vertigo, but they didn't even know what I was talking
about. I've seen them strolling up near-vertical faces without a trace
of fear. Absolutely astonishing.'

One evening when we were sitting round the fire, Peter slowly stood
up and ambled off barefoot through the thick sphagnum moss. There
was something about his determined footsteps that made me follow
him. He stepped elegantly over fallen branches, between clumps of
tussock, and arrived at the clearing on the saddle. The sun had just set
behind the distant blue-grey ridges. The trees, grass and moss were
bathed in a reddish glow.

As I stood there barefoot in the soft moss, I looked into the valley
below. As subtly and gently as a scented breeze, I became aware of
a vast body of silence and eternity, a clear presence of something
unknown—almost another dimension. It was such a presence that
I was compelled to stop thinking and begin listening. I listened in
complete quietness and with total attention. Effortlessly.

For a moment everything was whole, innocent and holy.

The next morning, the sky was clear, with a light breeze from the east.
Since it was good drying weather, I washed my jumper in the creek
with a bar of soap. I noticed the birds stop singing, then soon after I
heard the faint sound of an engine. I hung my jumper over a branch,
then walked to the open clearing as Paul landed his helicopter.

'Right,' said Paul. 'Here's the plan.' He pressed his lips together to
emphasise the importance of the piece of paper he was holding, and
showed us a drawing of the whole hut.

'Let's have a look,' said Peter.

We were standing at the hut site. There were 12 piles sticking out of the ground, and Paul had brought more materials for the hut with him.

'Can you give me a hand with this, Peter?' Paul was motioning at the sheets of ply. 'Miriam, can you get me a hammer, a pair of pliers and a crescent from my toolbox over there?'

I ran to the toolbox, but when I opened it I realised I didn't know the English names for half of the tools in there. I took a hammer and ran back.

'Where are the pliers?' Paul sounded slightly annoyed.

'I don't know . . .' I stammered.

'Goddammit!' he said irritably.

He strode across to the toolbox, as if we were in a hurry. I followed him like an anxious dog.

'This is a crescent,' he said curtly, as if he had already explained it a hundred times. 'And these are pliers.' He held them up. Then he smiled.

I smiled back, pretending I was in a very good mood. When we were walking back, though, I felt angry because I didn't like the reaction the incident had triggered; I felt like a pathetic, whimpering dog, waiting to be patted. I hated this feeling even more than Paul's grumpiness or ill-chosen jokes.

I somehow couldn't quite understand Paul. He was very good to me—he had spent many hours sharpening all of my arrows, and brought us apples from town—but I don't think he ever realised that I didn't like his jokes about my Dutch accent. 'Speaka da English!' he'd often snicker. I always tried to laugh his comments away, but each time I felt more uneasy.

Nonetheless, I did enjoy building the hut with Paul. Although he had grumpy moments, he was quickly cheerful again. He taught me how to plan carefully, measure precisely and fit the poles together so that everything was exactly right.

While Peter tacked the boards on to the sides of the hut, I sat on the top beams to nail the corrugated-iron sheets into a roof. It was fantastic to see a little house being erected in the forest. I tried to remember the entire process carefully, in case I ever needed to build another hut by myself.

When it was finished—complete with a firebox—Paul asked how often we planned to visit.

'Well, it depends. Maybe never,' Peter answered casually.

When I saw Paul's face, I quickly explained that this would be our backup hut.

'Backup for what?' asked Paul.

'Anything—a deadly, contagious disease, for example. Then you'd want to be as far away as possible,' Peter said.

'Sometimes I imagine myself in a fatal situation,' I said. 'And just before dying I would think, *If only I had done this or that, I would still be alive.*'

Paul raised his eyebrows. 'Yeah, imagine if I struggled up here through the snow in midwinter to get away from a plague that had killed everybody except me, only to make it to this hut and find my matches were wet! I'd die of hypothermia on the first night.'

'Exactly!' Peter laughed. 'You'd wish you'd brought some waterproof matches, wouldn't you?'

'You'd sure wish you had learned how to make a fire using flint stones or sticks!' I said.

We imagined many more disastrous futures. When we were confident we had covered all possible scenarios, we looked at the hut in front of us with great satisfaction.

'Well, this hut might save our lives one day,' said Paul. 'Then we'll be bloody glad we built it.'

I smiled. 'I bet the one thing we haven't thought of—'

'Will be the very thing that will actually happen!' Peter laughed.

Regrettably, we didn't stay very long in the hut, because we finished up all of our supplies soon after it was completed and had to make our way out again. When we described our struggle on the way in to Paul, he exclaimed that he had seen a much better route from his helicopter. Pointing it out on the map, he showed us how we could go up the ridge then drop down into the great river to our west.

We packed up and hiked down my hunting track into the valley. It was a hot morning, and some pigeons cooed throatily as we walked through the trees. We waded through the warm, muddy swamp water, where two paradise ducks started honking and continued to do so until we were out of sight. The creek we followed slowly became a little river that flowed into a cool, shadowy gorge with big grey walls. Eventually we found ourselves out in the open again and came to a green meadow. With big trees surrounding it, the place had an enchanting, secretive atmosphere. There was a tree fuchsia nearby, with gnarly branches and bark that looked like curly strips of paper, ready to fall off. It had very tasty purple berries. We took off our packs, built a fire and cooked our dinner.

This valley was one of the most beautiful places we had ever camped. At twilight I took Peter to a spot where I had seen a hind and her fawn some weeks earlier. The deer were there again, peacefully grazing against the backdrop of a loamy hill with a luxuriant growth of maidenhair fern. We sat down behind a fallen tree, our chins resting on the log, and watched them. They watched us.

The next day we climbed on to the ridge.

'So much for the easy ridge!' Peter fumed. He tried to push the leatherwood scrub aside, but the branches were so tough that he couldn't make a big enough opening for his body and his bulky pack. He swore and tried walking on top of the scrub. When that didn't work either, he angrily threw his pack on to the ground, then dragged it wildly behind him. The tree daisies looked nice and soft, but endless exposure to the wind had made the plants extremely tough and wiry. They formed an almost impenetrable barrier—but going down the sides of the dangerously steep ridge was not an option either.

'Where are we?' Peter had reached a small clearing surrounded by small trees that obstructed his view. He was massaging his injured knee.

'Look on your map,' I called, pushing through the scrub in a crab-like crouch.

'I am!' he yelled back. 'We have to turn off at some point, but I can't see where.'

While he studied the map, I listened to a skylark. Its rolling, chirruping song with whistling notes was very clear and bright, even though the bird was so high that I couldn't spot it. From its position far above, the skylark would be able to see all the ranges in the area, I thought.

I wasn't concerned, because I knew we couldn't get lost. All we needed to do was make our way down into the valley about 500 metres below. I was just hoping we wouldn't run into unexpected cliffs or crevasses. I put down my heavy pack and clambered up a big tree, but the view was restricted—I could see nothing more than from the ground.

In the end, Peter led us intuitively down a spur and into the big valley. With every hundred metres that we descended, the temperature increased, the trees became larger and greener, and the first sandflies appeared. After three days of bushwhacking, it was so liberating to arrive at the open riverbed. Here, we also witnessed the effect of the great rainstorm after Christmas: bushes and trees had been completely wiped out and swept down the valley. There was a big strip of grey mud on each side of the river.

Then we saw a footprint in the sand. We stared at it disbelievingly for some seconds.

'Somebody has been here,' said Peter.

I felt as if we had landed on the moon and discovered somebody had been there before us. This was the first sign of another human in our remote wilderness home. It was a strange feeling to be so impressed by a few footprints. We studied the print for some time, speculating about what kind of person had made it.

After many hours of walking down the big river, we came upon an orange triangle indicating a public pathway. The track had originally been well maintained, but the flood had washed it out. We followed the markers to a farm track, which slowly turned into a muddy, potholed road. At first I was glad to be able to walk without examining the ground for hidden perils, but after a while I noticed that, with the comfort of a track and especially the road, we had lost something else. The forest had been pushed away and was now at a distance. *Untouchable*. Now there was a separation between us and the wilderness, and with that separation the world of mental constructs began to reassert itself.

We saw a figure approaching with a dog, and soon realised it was a woman. We had not seen another woman for three months. When she came closer, we said hello. I marvelled at her gentle smile and her kind face, with a dawning understanding of the attraction to female energy. I suddenly felt that at the core of primal female energy lies a great strength. This woman was unaware of this quality, as is most of modern society, but I recognised the gentle, receptive, yielding power in her—and, by extension, in all women, including myself.

I smiled. It felt as though something in my heart had matured, sprouted, started to grow.

A red ute came towards us, with two little dogs running at its side. Just as I was wondering where I had seen those dogs before, Paul wound down the window and said, 'I thought I might find you guys round here.'

CHAPTER 5

AUTUMN

We were standing barefoot in a big sphagnum swamp, holding hayforks. There was hardly any breeze and the sun, high above, was swelteringly hot. Nearby a grey-green fernbird, with its long tail and reddish head, was sitting in the rushes, uttering, 'Uu-tick.'

I answered, 'Uu-tick.'

It fluttered away to another clump of reeds.

'There's a good bit over here!' Peter called.

We were heaving the light green moss into wool packs, which Paul would pick up in his helicopter then sell to a man who shipped it overseas. We were working to pay Paul for the costs of transporting us and our supplies in his helicopter. A hundred wool packs was our aim; it would take us one week. At the end of every working day, we were tired and had no energy for gathering wood, cooking slow meals over the fire, collecting buckets of water or baking bread. I experienced why many hardworking people choose comfort as soon as the opportunity arises.

'So, where are you going to go for autumn?' Paul asked. We were back at his house, and I was hunched up behind a computer, immersed in the digital world.

'We'd like go up the Arawhata River in South Westland,' Peter answered, flicking through a newspaper on the table.

'Oh, I wouldn't go there if I were you,' Paul said. 'Every man and his dog will be out in that valley during the roar. The way you guys go walking off track all the time, you could get shot by a deer hunter.'

I looked up from my emails into Peter's concerned eyes.

'Why don't you go into the Mōkihinui Valley instead?' Paul suggested after a moment of silence. 'Much quieter than the Arawhata.'

'Where's the Mōkihinui?' I asked.

'Just north of here, on the West Coast. It's quiet and full of goats. There's even a bivouac called Goat Creek Hut.' He looked at me with an excited grin. 'It's not far from here, in a straight line. I can fly your supplies in, if you like.'

I smiled at Peter. 'Goat Creek Hut sounds good!'

While Paul flew our supplies to Goat Creek Hut, we started hiking from the old gold-mining town of Lyell. In its heyday in the late 1800s, it'd had a population of more than 2000 people, complete with a police station, courthouse, banks and hotels. That was hard to believe now—it was completely overgrown with lush forest. Apart from some rusty iron and machinery parts, there was barely any sign of the town left. It was astonishing that, in less than 70 years, the living forest had completely erased it.

We marched all day up an old cart track and camped on top of a pass. That was where the easy trail ended. From our vantage point we could see for the first time the great, forested river valley down below: beautifully wild and inviting. We could see ridges and spurs, all covered in dense forest. Each kind of tree had its own distinct colour.

After breaking camp the next morning, we spent many hours sliding down an incredibly steep path to the river. I had to brake every few steps against a tree to stop myself from tumbling all the way down. The trail markers finished altogether when we finally reached the river.

We had to crisscross the river many times, which was easy as the water was low and quite warm. It was late afternoon when we found a beautiful spot to camp in, just before a gorge. We lit a fire and sat down with our tea. While looking at the river, which flowed through a ravine ahead of us, I remembered Lao-tzu.

'Nothing is softer or weaker than water,' I said, 'and yet it can change the hardest rocks. The weak conquers the strong. The soft conquers the hard.'

'It's actually not just water that cuts a canyon,' said Peter. 'It's also time. If you poured a million litres of water on a mountain, little would change. But a gentle trickle for a million years? That will cut through rocks. It's perseverance and endurance that counts. That which is most powerful is subtle—almost invisible. Nobody notices me throwing seeds all over the place, for instance, but by the time I'm dead many trees will be growing.'

'Literally or figuratively?' I smiled.

'Both.' He stood up to fish some seedpods from the yellow-flowered kōwhai tree out of his pocket.

'This is a seed, and you are a seed.' He smiled, kissed me and threw the seedpods in a sunny spot where they might easily grow.

While the sky slowly turned pink and orange, we sat in silence. Our minds started to slow down and fall in tune with the rhythms of nature again. My body felt relaxed, and with this came a feeling of joy. There was no cause for stress or reason to worry. It was as if the forest and the river absorbed all anxious thoughts, and we were only relating to the environment directly around us. Our life was once again pleasantly simple.

In the last light we saw two small goats strolling up the valley. They lay down in the grass underneath a shapely tree on the other side of the river and looked at us. One was brown, the other black and white. To see these beautiful wild goats brought me so much joy; they were very trusting and peaceful. I felt no need to hunt them, for the simple reason that I didn't have my bow in my hand. When I set out with my bow and arrows, I seemed to change into a hunter; without the bow, I very much delighted in seeing wild creatures.

———

After a long, restful night, we woke to a morning that had the making of a flawless day. The warm air had a sweet, soft summer smell. I packed our bags cheerfully, while Peter studied the map.

'Do you want to walk through the gorge here—' he pointed at a terrace—'or go all the way up there to get round it?'

I looked at the thick jungle above us and answered casually, 'Oh, the river looks easier.'

So we walked into the gorge, marvelling at the 60-metre-high cliffs on both sides. The water was mostly low, but sometimes it reached our hips and we had to carry our packs above our heads. Our shorts got a little wet, but dried again quickly in the summer sun. It was all in the spirit of adventure, and I enjoyed it very much.

Then we came to a pool that was too deep to wade through. Peter pointed to a spot where we could climb out of the gorge and enter the thick forest. It was a steep slope covered in leaf litter and dense undergrowth, and we struggled for at least an hour through the slippery forest until Peter got tangled in prickly, barbed vines.

'Not this way!' he called out.

I spotted a way to finally get back to the river, and climbed over a big, rotten log. I did see a couple of wasps, but I didn't give them much thought—until Peter, who was just behind me, yelled, 'Wasp nest!'

I raced down the gully, and reached the open riverbed embarrassingly quickly compared to poor Peter, who was still trying to climb down the steep slope and was now under attack from the furious wasps. When he finally arrived, I laughed, relieved, as I knew that he was quite resistant to wasp stings. If I had been the victim of a wasp attack, I would have collapsed in pain.

'I've been stung a dozen times!'

'Really! Are you all right?' I was getting my water bottle out of my pack to refill it.

'I'm OK, but one stung me repeatedly on my throat.' Peter sat down on a big stone. 'It could be quite dangerous—my throat might swell up and, if that happens, I won't be able to breathe. That happened to my brother once when he was a kid.'

'Then what?' I had suddenly jolted to attention.

'You'd have to do a tracheotomy on me.'

'A tracky on-to-me?' I had never heard the word.

'You'd have to make a hole in my windpipe.' Peter sighed.

I frowned.

'A hole.' He sounded weary. 'So that my lungs can get air, even if my windpipe is blocked by the swelling.'

I glanced at the dense forest and the fast-flowing river, suddenly acutely aware that we were two days of tough hiking from the nearest road. 'Do I cut with a knife, or a pin, or . . . what?' I asked lamely. I was trying to sound coherent, to take in the vital information, but my legs had started to tremble slightly.

'Use the smallest knife and sharpest blade we've got,' Peter said.

Why had I never been taught about this during my outdoor first-aid courses? I wondered.

'I *am* feeling a bit dizzy and headachy . . .' He clasped his head with his hands. His voice started to sound drowsy. 'I'll lie down on my back. You put a jumper underneath my neck. The moment you cut, blood will flow into my throat, so you have to insert a tube that will serve independently as an airway.'

'A *tube*?'

'Yes, like a straw.'

A straw? I thought. *For god's sake. Who takes a straw into the bush?* I'd never seen a straw in a first-aid kit. 'I don't have a straw,' I croaked, starting to feel dizzy myself.

'You have to find something that is *like* a straw.'

I thought feverishly about making something out of branches, rushes or reeds. Maybe something in our packs? None of it looked like a plastic tube. I pictured the worst-case scenario: he would die, the police would find us (somehow), Peter would be lying there with his throat cut, and I would be the only suspect, because by that time there would be no sign of wasp venom . . . I felt so nauseous with the weight of responsibility that I almost threw up.

We sat on the stones for a while. I felt very sorry for myself, there in the middle of the wilderness in such a precarious situation, responsible for Peter's life. I watched him anxiously. He reached for the water bottle, and I quickly put it in his hand. When I took the bottle from him to drink some water myself, he moved his neck around, touched his throat lightly and said suddenly in a normal voice, 'I think I'm going to be OK after all.'

'What?' I laughed.

'There's no sign of an allergic reaction,' he said, looking at the bumps on his legs and arms.

I was so relieved, but there was also a nagging worry that I wouldn't have been able to save his life had I needed to. 'Jeez,' I exclaimed, 'I wonder if I could have cut a hole in your windpipe, sweetie.'

'Of course you could have. Extraordinary things can be done in emergencies.' Peter sounded confident, but I wasn't so sure at all.

Once Peter had recovered, we hiked down the valley, stopping to rest in beautiful places. We didn't sit around in shorts for too long at this lower altitude; if we did, the sandflies soon found us. These relentless biting bugs went for any exposed skin, but especially liked feet and ankles. Peter called them 'the guardians of the wilderness'—if it wasn't for them, wild places like this would be much more visited. The first time I had encountered big clouds of sandflies, they had nearly driven me mad, and their bites had itched for days. I had gradually grown used to them, though; I still felt them biting, but I hardly ever scratched. They were too small to bite through clothing and too slow to bite when we were moving so, unless we were walking, we mostly covered up.

In the afternoon we walked on a narrow strip of grey rock, between the swift river and a tall cliff. As we came round a corner, we surprised a shag. The grey bird had just caught a trout but when it saw us, it dropped the fish back in the river. The fish floated helplessly on the surface of the water.

'Quick!' Peter waded in and grabbed the fish before it could drift downstream.

I clapped my hands with joy. What luck! We took our packs off, collected some wood, speared the fish on a stick and roasted it over a fire on the riverbed.

'I can't believe our luck!' I kept saying, and every time Peter laughed. 'Everything is provided!'

'Nature provides all living beings with everything we need to exist in this world,' Peter said. 'Air, water, gravity, light, ground, soil, food— everything. Even well-being is provided by nature and beauty.'

'Well, if you dumped me out here naked, I'd soon die. Humans are the weakest, most inadequate of all animals without our tools like this pot.' I lifted the billy in the air.

'Yes, but we have a brain to work things out,' Peter replied. 'That's our key to survival.' He blew into the fire to bring it back to life. 'It's amazing how nature provides everything, without asking for anything in return.'

'Until we die,' I said. 'Then we give our bodies back to the earth. Our bodies will decompose and become soil. In a way, mortality is the price we pay for life.'

After three days of walking, we reached the supplies that Paul had stashed near Goat Creek Hut, a somewhat dilapidated and very small white shelter with a red door. The hut was situated about a hundred metres from the big river, but close to Goat Creek. We never made any attempt to sleep inside it; instead we camped between the big old trees nearby. We lit a big fire to bake bread, and while we were waiting for the dough to rise Peter pulled something out of his pocket. It looked like an envelope.

'Guess what this is.' He smiled as if he had outfoxed me.

I laughed. 'Give it here.'

'No, no, no. You have to guess!' He grinned and held his hands behind his back. I jumped up and playfully tried to take it, but he locked my head under his arm.

'A letter?' I tried.

'No.' He tightened his arm round my head, making me shriek with laughter.

I gave in. 'Don't know! Don't know!'

He shook the envelope and I heard it rattle. 'Seeds!' I yelled. I was very pleased with myself for having guessed it correctly.

He released me from the headlock. 'Well, no need to shout,' he teased good-naturedly. He smiled, proud to have come up with such a clever idea, and walked over to the bank of the creek. 'If I put seeds in the soil now, we'll have fresh radishes, bok choy, spinach, beetroot and silver beet in a month.'

We made our garden in a little flat space among some big, rough granite boulders and clumps of toetoe grass with tall white plumes that waved graciously in the wind.

'The fertile soil from the tops gets washed down with the creek.' Peter gathered a handful of silt and let it slip through his fingers. 'This is the best soil. It's like a miniature version of Holland. Let's hope our dikes are high enough and the river won't flood our garden.'

I filled the billy with water and Peter poured it carefully over the soil to help the seeds germinate. It was quite wonderful to see, a few days later, the first tiny green blades poking out of the silt. Each day, we tended our little garden with much joy, and after a few weeks we ate the salad greens that we had missed so much in the previous seasons.

We were blessed with the most brilliant weather imaginable. The dry autumn conditions were so pleasant that we soon forgot the misery of the cold, wet spring and summer. Autumn was the season of abundance! Almost every day, we set out to search for berries. Peter showed me where to find the fruit, and pointed out the edible ones and the poisonous ones. We found white, blue and purple berries, and they all tasted wonderful. Our favourites were the big patches of blackberries, which we ate and ate until our tongues were stained deep purple. Picking them took a long time, but that was of no concern to us. Time seemed to have slowed down. Two weeks felt like two months. We had been living for three seasons in the mountains, but it already felt like three years. The person I had been last year had long gone.

Warm breezes often came down the valley. When I went hunting, I usually walked up the river. My feet had grown accustomed to the big granite boulders and I no longer stumbled over them. The riverbed was the only open space in the valley, a highway compared to the nearly impenetrable forest on either side.

Whenever I spotted a big tree in the distance, I would carefully approach it, as goats enjoy sitting underneath such trees to re-chew their grass.

One time, I spotted a side-creek that looked promising. After about a hundred metres, the banks became steeper and steeper, and I found myself in a narrow gorge. The water had carved a silky tunnel through the grey mudstone. I walked up this natural slide and came to a deep pool. The clear, blue-green water was quite warm, so I undressed. Then, holding my bow in one hand and a bundle of clothes in the other, I swam to the other side then climbed back up on to the smooth, grey rock. It felt warm underneath my bare feet. The water had shaped the rock into the most magnificent forms. I ventured on through the canyon until I came to a small waterfall, which tumbled a few metres before landing in another pool. Mist rose into the air. It was a wonder that all the beauty around me existed. I waded through the pool, then climbed around the rocks above the waterfall. I felt like an explorer from centuries earlier, discovering an empty, unknown world.

When I came back to camp I wrote a letter to Sofie, hoping that I might meet someone who would post it in town one day in the future.

Dear Sofie,

Do you remember how we always used to talk about having children at the same time, so that they could grow up together? Well, I'm not so sure any more whether I actually want children. I used to think it would be possible to raise them in the wilderness, but in the last 10 months I've become much more realistic. I think it would be very difficult indeed to live a nomadic life in a tent in the mountains (not to mention without a tribe) with a baby or small child.

There is also something else I've been thinking about, and I wonder if it makes any sense to you: I feel as though my life is a train on a fixed railway line. At the end of the line I'll find death, but that is far beyond the horizon yet (I hope). As the train of my life has travelled forward, I've noticed the signposts flashing past: age five means school, 18 means university, 23 find a job, and 27 find a husband. Now that I am nearly 30, I see pregnancy coming up.

We aren't really encouraged to consider when we should do what, because society has already created 'The Perfect Template', which we are expected to follow. Now that I am aware of the signposts, though, I am suddenly questioning things. I'm not saying that we shouldn't have a partner or children—but should we, perhaps, try to find a way to jump off the train and walk in a direction of our own choosing?

Do you understand what I mean?

Much love, Miriam

One day we were visited by a formidable weka. We didn't know whether this one was male or female, but Peter called it Wilma. Wilma was so big and strong that she was doubtless a reincarnation of Napoleon. She could open anything solid with her sharp beak, which she used as a jackhammer, and she could run faster than me with her big strong legs. Her eyes could spot a tiny beetle in the leaves from metres away. And she didn't beg for food; she demanded it.

The show really began when another weka family turned up, and we made the mistake of sharing our leftover rice and rolled oats with the newcomers. That innocent act sent Wilma into a fury. She was outraged at the prospect of having to share *her* food. She fought the parents and the children as if her life depended on it. Then, after she had bullied them to a safe distance, she started patrolling the area night and day—she never seemed to sleep. Every two hours, she would check her boundaries for intruders, screeching incredibly loudly along the way. The forest at night is normally very silent—every little noise sounds peculiarly clear and articulated—but not so when Wilma was patrolling. Peter would sigh, 'Wilma.' Then, after two seconds: 'Shut. Up.'

Wilma never did shut up. She liked possum fried rice, and she wasn't going to share her humans without a fight.

Over the weeks and months, we befriended Wilma. Her intelligent ruby eyes watched us all the time; I had the impression that she was studying our sounds, habits and patterns, as if she was some kind of weka anthropologist studying human-ape behaviour.

After nearly two months in our quiet, dry valley, the first rain came. It poured down in torrents all night. When it stopped the next morning, I crawled out of the tent. 'Have a look at this!' I yelled excitedly, for I had never seen anything like it. 'Come out, Peter!' I impatiently shook the tent to encourage him.

Muddy grey river water was slowly sloshing towards the tent, which was luckily pitched on a mound. The previous night I had crossed the knee-deep Mōkihinui River; now it was a 100-metre wide, foaming torrent with huge waves running down the middle. The murky flood had uprooted living trees and was hurling them towards the sea. We could hear boulders rolling along the riverbed in turmoil. The flood had thundered over our little garden and wild water was rushing through the big trees.

Feeling quite safe, we were so wildly excited that we jumped up and down like a pair of kids, calling to each other and pointing at the wonders of nature's power.

It was 10 days before we could cross the river again, and that meant that we were temporarily forced to remain in our camp and read books. I wrote a lot in my diary.

> I have been thinking about Krishnamurti's statement 'Your dependence and attachments have prepared the soil for your sorrow'. If I look closely at myself, I can see a great psychological dependence on Peter. He said the other day that he has the feeling I cling to him too much because of my fear of being alone. I think he might be right.
>
> I can walk quite happily on my own for a day, or even a week, but I know the fear of being totally alone has not gone away. Over the years I have, in fact, built an affectionate cocoon for the two of us—that's what I call 'love', and I feel very safe inside it. It is my version of security, without having a job or a house. I would like to find another way to love, without the fear of being alone or losing Peter. We discuss it quite a lot, but these matters are not so

easy. It is much easier to just leave them, to bury them in the ground until a
flood comes and uproots everything . . .

The river slowly returned to lower levels, and straight away the first grasses and little plants emerged through the mud and sand left on the riverbed.

'Isn't it amazing that nature is ready for any disaster and opportunity,' said Peter when we were walking one warm, sunny morning to collect firewood. 'Millions of seeds are waiting in this soil for a chance to grow, to secure life's survival.'

'Yes,' I agreed. 'No matter what happens, life will succeed. It doesn't care in what form.'

'It's extremely versatile and adaptable!' Peter laughed. 'Even if the planet was bombed to barren nothingness, it would just wait a million years and life would eventually come back out of the sea.'

That cheered me considerably. 'Indeed! Life cannot die.'

Peter picked up some branches that had been washed downstream in the flood and put them in a pile. He stretched out his arms, and I loaded him up with firewood. I collected another pile of wood, tied a piece of string round it, and carried it back to camp. We lit a fire, toasted some bread on hot coals and, after two cups of tea, I stood up and took my bow.

'I won't be back before dark,' I said, tying my knife belt around my waist. I had been out hunting over many weeks and seen some animals, but for various reasons I had not been successful.

The afternoon was hot, so I set off in a bikini top and shorts. I had a piece of string tied round my wrist and my bow in my hand. If someone had seen me, I would have been quite an unusual sight, but there was nobody else around for miles.

I walked fast enough to evade the sandflies, but slow enough to pick up the slightest scent in the air. After a few hours, I caught the scent of some goats. For most people, the smell of goats is repulsive, but for me it meant food, so it smelled good.

I cocked an arrow and looked for a goat that stood side on, but all

I could see were 12 noses—the worst position for an 'intuitive' bow-hunter. I knelt behind a small bush, hoping one of them would turn side on. Unfortunately, they all strolled straight towards me. I was forced to lie down completely. They came so close that they were actually looking at me through the bush, so I pretended to be dead, drowned and tossed in the grass by the flood. To my amusement, they believed my performance and kept casually grazing. Then a small kid came very close to me, and I couldn't resist trying to peek. It was nibbling just a metre away and, when it spotted my moving eyes, it knew it had been tricked. It ran away in panic, and the rest of the mob followed it within seconds.

I cursed myself, and had to circle round for a long time to find them again. When I spotted a big goat in a perfect position and at an ideal distance, I did not hesitate: I shot all my six arrows, one after the other. Two arrows hit—one punctured a lung, while the other caught its foot, but the goat was soon running out of sight.

I searched for my arrows, but could not find any in the long grass. I stood perplexed for a minute; I didn't know what to do without my arrows, but I had no choice. My only solution was to find the wounded goat and kill it with my knife. I wasn't going back to camp without arrows or goat. So I left my bow on a big stone and searched for specks of blood. I followed a path into the dense bushes until I almost crawled into a spiderweb, which made me realise the goat couldn't have come that way.

Where would a wounded goat go? It wouldn't struggle into the dense forest; it would go up the side creek, of course! About a hundred metres up the boulder-strewn creek I found, to my relief, the wounded billy goat. He was resting behind a big washed-up log. I backtracked silently and sneaked through the bushes to come out on the other side of the log, right behind him.

Grab his horns with your left hand and cut his throat with your right, I thought. My heart was beating wildly as I hesitantly moved my hand towards his horns . . . but, the moment my hand hovered over his head, he smelled me and shot off with surprising speed. I had to be less hesitant next time—if there was a next time.

As he ran off over the big grey stones in the riverbed, foam was coming out of his mouth. His lungs were punctured, and he looked so weak that I decided to outrun him. I jumped from stone to stone with my knife in my hand. After 50 metres, I tired and slowed to walking pace. The goat stopped too, waiting until I got close before it moved off again. In this manner, we travelled a long way up the valley.

You're the most important thing for me, right now, I thought. *And I'm the most important thing for you.* This goat and I were, in a strange way, completely connected.

Then he suddenly disappeared from sight.

I edged around a steep cliff and found him in a small cave. We stood face-to-face for a moment. I walked closer to the goat, preventing him from escaping. When he tried to run past me, I thrust my knife between his ribs. His heavy body sank awkwardly on to my feet. I moved backwards and sat, dazed, on the stones. It was done. Finished. My legs were shaking, and I was panting from running, the adrenaline and the abrupt end.

What now? I thought. The lifeless goat looked very big lying next to me.

I dragged the heavy carcass over the big boulders to the nearest tree in the forest. It took all of my strength to lift it into the air, while simultaneously tying it to a branch with my rope. I removed the intestines, and put them out in the open for the hawks.

The horned head, I placed on a tree stump.

Rest in peace, billy goat, I thought.

The birds were singing their last songs for the day. I looked anxiously at the sky. Dusk was slowly creeping over the forested mountains, cold air rolling down from the tops. It was a long way back to camp. I hurriedly tied the front legs to the back legs with my rope and strapped the animal to my back, the way that Mouse had explained to me. The goat was still warm, and its fur prickled my bare skin.

The carcass swayed awkwardly from left to right as I walked. It was a long, tiring journey, but the last light in the west guided me through the swift river crossings. I smelled the smoke of our campfire from a long way off; the wind had turned again.

Peter was sitting beside the small fire when I finally arrived. Exhausted, I squatted down while he untied the goat and lifted it off my back. We sat round the dancing flames and I quietly told him every detail of the hunt, while the silver moon rose over the tall mountaintops.

I waded into a dark pool in the river to wash all the blood off my body and out of my hair. Looking up at the moon in the clear night sky, I thought of the long chase and the killing. It had been quite savage. I realised I had become the very person I would have loathed in my youth—when I was a good vegetarian with the higher moral ground. I had come down so far, so to speak, that I was touching the lower ground. The earth.

It was just a year earlier that I had explained to Virginia on my last day at the school how I wanted to live without any barrier between the naked earth and myself. *Well, this is it,* I thought now, surprised. *Here I am. There is no barrier any more.*

We spent the following days cooking the goat. The meat was tough and had to be boiled for a long time. We squatted round the fire to eat the meat. Since a lot of it was still on the bones, we ate it with our hands. When the bones were picked clean, I cracked them open with a stone to get to the marrow: the most delicious part of the animal. Our faces smeared with fat, we chewed the bones and smiled at each other. Apart from our modern clothes, we could have been living in the Stone Age. It brought a surprising amount of fulfillment and contentment to be leading such a simple and practical life.

The only other creatures that demanded a share of the meat— besides Wilma, of course—were the wasps. The population in the valley was mind-boggling. As long as we didn't disturb them, they were not really aggressive and never stung us. When we were eating our goat meat, however, at least five wasps would crawl on to our plates. They would also land on our legs and eat the sandflies off our ankles. As the days became shorter and the nights colder, the wasps grew even hungrier and, desperate to survive, they started to eat each other. We witnessed this wasp cannibalism with some fascination: two wasps would pick on a weaker one, bite its body in half and eat it up.

In the warm evenings, we ate curries and played chess on a big flat stone near the river. While Peter studied the game, I would watch his face, with his bushy eyebrows above his blue eyes—just as I had done the evening we had first met in South India.

We had come across each other in a quiet local restaurant surrounded by lush green rice paddies. It was a still, warm evening, with crickets calling in the distance. I had been travelling for five months all over India with my chess set, and Peter was the first serious player I had met. We had played a game and afterwards we drank sweet chai out of small glasses and talked about trekking in the Himalayas, until the restaurant closed.

He walked me back to my guesthouse. It was just outside the village, past a mob of street dogs, which Peter was not afraid of. We hugged goodbye.

'I'll take a shortcut through the rice paddies,' he told me. 'It's only a few kilometres.'

I watched him disappear into the darkness without a torch. His wavy hair lit up in the moonlight. He was like a wolf that could never be tamed. I decided then and there that I would go wherever he went.

At dawn, I packed my bags and walked to the small nature reserve that he looked after. Snakes, lizards, squirrels and monkeys had found refuge in between the big, round rocks that were as old as the earth. Even a shy crocodile lived in a pond near Peter's hut. It was a quiet oasis in the midst of the busy villages.

'Nini slept outside on those rocks over there last year,' said Peter. Nini was a friend of Peter's who had also stayed at the reserve.

'I will sleep outside on the rocks too,' I replied.

Peter nodded approvingly.

So, that night, I lay peacefully outside on a big, flat, warm rock. Looking up at the stars, I felt free and strong.

The next morning, Peter said to me, 'I heard a monkey screaming last week. It was so awful, it gave me the shivers. It went on for ten minutes or more. A goatherd told me it was a leopard catching the monkey . . . but you shouldn't worry. That was last week. The leopard is gone now.'

I felt uneasy, but since I had slept outside the previous night I knew it was possible to do it again. I did, however, move from the rock to the verandah, right next to Peter's door. *If I hear a leopard*, I told myself, *I'll stand up, open the door and go in.* I lay down on my little mat and stared into the darkness. Any fear I had felt during the day multiplied at night. I was terrified. I didn't want to go to sleep, in case I didn't hear the leopard's paws approaching. *How often does a leopard need to eat?* I wondered. I would be an easy target in my sleeping bag.

I wanted Peter to take me on a journey into the Himalayas, but I knew it would require a lot of courage. I was determined to show him I was brave enough. I hardly slept, kept awake by many fearful thoughts, but I didn't see a leopard.

The next morning I asked shyly if I could sleep in the hut.

'Of course,' Peter had replied with a big smile.

'Do you remember how I slept outside your hut crying all night for fear of leopards?' I asked him over one of our fireside games of chess.

'Yes.'

'Weren't you afraid I would be snatched by a leopard?'

'No. I knew the leopard had gone,' he said. 'I just didn't know how else to get you into my hut.' He grinned. 'Your move.'

We lived for more than two months in total peace at our camp near Goat Creek Hut, almost forgetting that the outside world even existed. Our only visitors were birds and animals. Sometimes a warm front came from the north, or a cold snap from the south. We lived so quietly that we stopped counting the days, weeks and months. Our only measure of the passing of time was the waxing and waning moon.

Then one morning, after what felt like an eternity of silence, we awoke to the sound of a helicopter. We hurried to the hut to watch the machine land daintily on the grass. The pilot jumped out and walked over to us, while his passengers—two men—pulled boxes and bags out of the helicopter.

'How're you doing?' he yelled over the sound of the engine. 'I'm Wayne!' He shook our hands. 'You guys fly fishing?'

'No, we're actually just living here!' I shouted.

'Living! For how long?'

Peter raised three fingers. 'Three months!'

Wayne looked very surprised. 'That's incredible!' He then gestured apologetically to indicate that he had to hurry back to his chopper, since the costly engine was still running. I smiled to show we understood, and Peter waved. The pilot jumped back into his helicopter and flew away over the forested ranges.

We approached the two men. They were both in their late thirties, and were carrying the last of their gear into the hut. One of them was slim, with long blond ringlets that came to his shoulders, a narrow, handsome face and light blue eyes. We learned his name was Daniel. He wore jeans with a black shearer's shirt and high boots, and round his neck hung two handmade necklaces: one with a piece of pounamu, and the other made from deer teeth. He had casually slung a rifle over his shoulder, and he made a living trapping possums and turning the skins into blankets.

The other man, Carl, was also lean and wiry, and spent most of his days on offshore islands saving albatrosses and other endangered species. It looked like he hadn't shaved that morning and his hair seemed as though it had grown longish by accident. He wore a brown woollen jumper with holes in it, and jeans. He was good-looking in his own way, with his strong, broad shoulders. The first thing he did was take out some tobacco and roll a smoke. He gave a very relaxed and confident impression.

These were men from the wild West Coast of New Zealand's South Island, where you have to be tough to survive, where appearance doesn't matter, where you need an attitude of self-sufficiency to enjoy your life. There was something intriguing and appealing about them.

'The government and energy companies are eyeing up the Mōkihinui River for a dam,' Carl told us, when Peter asked the purpose of their visit. 'In order to offset any possible damage to the environment, they plan to protect birds and animals in the upper reaches of the valley. They need a bird survey done for their proposal, and they hired us to do it.' Carl stamped out his cigarette.

'So what does that mean you do?' I asked.

'We sit in designated spots in the forest and write down the names of the birds we hear,' said Daniel. He pulled out his machete and chopped a piece of flax off a bush with one stroke.

'Do you think the dam is a good idea?' Peter asked.

'Well, they reckon it'll create jobs for West Coasters,' said Daniel. 'But this is one of the last rivers in the country that is untouched from source to sea.' He tied the piece of flax round his ringlets like a hair-tie. 'We should protect it.'

'The dam is pointless anyway, if you ask me,' said Carl. 'This mighty river has a habit of grinding these stones up.' He tapped the rocks around him. 'That lake behind the dam'll be filled with gravel and sand in less than a hundred years.'

'The real question is why we even need so much electricity in the first place,' said Daniel. 'They'll have to flood a big part of the valley floor, which will drown birds, insects and snails. All so that people can just waste more power.'

Later on, while we were all sitting round the fire, Peter mentioned our hut on the saddle at Paul's Paradise.

'Schooling for the apocalypse, eh?' Daniel quipped. He always had a smile playing on his lips, as if he was both surprised and amused.

'What skills do *you* have?' I asked.

He told us he had mastered hunting, tanning skins and sewing them into clothes, building huts, boats and houses, gardening, welding, and making fishing nets, eel traps, possum traps and gunpowder. He could even make his own knives and guns.

When Daniel had finished his long list, I could scarcely believe he was for real. He spoke modestly about his experiences, as if everything was really quite simple and he had just learned it by accident. He told us stories about his expeditions in the Amazon jungle and how, when he was 25, he had wanted to marry a Bolivian 'jungle chick'. Though he never found his chick, he still owned some land on the edge of the rainforest. I got the impression that Daniel lived alone, somewhere on the coast, scheming one solo expedition after another, too free-spirited to even be interested in women, but I was quite wrong: he was married with two daughters. He did live in a wooden hut on the coast, but they were thinking of moving to town.

When we had a quiet moment the next day, I decided I'd better learn as much as possible from Daniel. He started explaining in precise detail how to treat and tan possum skins, and described various sewing techniques which I wrote down in my diary.

I thought I'd tell him, light-heartedly, our wasp-nest story. When I arrived at the bit about cutting Peter's throat, Daniel casually commented, 'Oh, the old tracheotomy.'

'Um, yes. The old tracheotomy,' I repeated, wondering if I was the only one who had never heard of the operation. Then I carried on. 'So we were there in the gorge, and Peter asked me to make a straw. Can you imagine such a ludicrous demand? A *straw*! I was thinking of reeds or—'

'You're holding one right now,' Daniel cut in. 'Your pen!' He smiled.

I laughed sleepily. I felt I was starting to look a touch imbecilic next to my survival hero.

After four very interesting days, it was time for Daniel and Carl to leave again. We promised to keep in touch, and Daniel wrote down—in surprisingly tidy handwriting—his name, cell phone number and postal address. He then drew a map on the other side of the piece of paper that showed how to find his hut on the coast. I gave them my letter for Sofie, and hugged them both before they climbed back into Wayne's helicopter, and lumbered off into the clouds.

In the weeks after their departure, the days grew noticeably shorter. The shadows became darker, and the nights cooler and longer. It had been an unusually long, warm, dry autumn, but the first frost eventually came, and with it stags started roaring. The hidden deer that we had only ever seen the hoof prints of now gave away their secret whereabouts. Each stag was defending his patch and trying to attract hinds. To hear a big stag—some weigh as much as 200 kilograms—calling in the quiet night was magic. It was as if their roars came out of a hidden canyon below the earth, so deep was the sound that resonated through the silent mountains.

After three months in this quiet valley our food supplies had diminished, and we were getting ready to pack our bags and make the journey out. We didn't go back the way we had come in; instead, we followed the river down the valley. The river was gradually increasing in size. Most times we were able to find a shallow place to cross it, but sometimes we had to ford through swift channels. One time we arrived at a deep pool in which long, flat eels floated between submerged brown logs.

'Look. Eels!' I said affectionately, as if they were harmless goldfish.

Peter slowly backed out of the water. 'Those eels are waiting for victims,' he said, climbing up a difficult bank that nearly collapsed on him. 'Imagine you were swept away in that big flood last month and got trapped underneath that log.'

I grunted a laugh.

'You'd get eaten by your mates there. They would start at your stomach—which is the softest part—and they'd gradually devour you, right down to the bone.' He was now standing above the river. 'And, what's more, they've got backwards-facing teeth. Once they bite, they can't let go—even if they want to.'

I started to move, my eyes fixed on the creatures, which now looked to me like lurking crocodiles. As I hurried over the big slippery logs, I imagined falling over and being grabbed by my legs. For the rest of the day, I avoided all pools.

We spent the last half hour struggling through shoulder-height horsetail grass. At last we climbed a hill and reached Forks Hut.

'If they build the dam, this will all become a lake,' said Peter, looking over the southern and northern branches of the river. It was a very large area. I hoped they wouldn't build the dam.

We rested a couple of days at Forks Hut and baked our last lot of bread. Just as we were shouldering our packs and reaching for our walking sticks to continue the last leg of our journey, a big helicopter turned up. I immediately recognised the pilot: it was Wayne.

'Still out here?' he yelled over the engine noise, as two hunters jumped from the helicopter.

'Yes, but we're about to walk out!' I shouted.

Wayne pointed back down the river, and I nodded.

'Why don't you come out with me?' Wayne yelled, smiling.

We accepted the offer without a second thought and jumped in. The helicopter slowly lifted us away from the valley that had been our home for the autumn. We left the river, with its glistening stones, where I had done the dishes every night. We flew away from our fireplace, where the last wasps were still eating each other. Our camp with our little pathways disappeared into the distance. Wilma would still be patrolling. My goat head would still be resting on the tree trunk, in a valley that was almost devoid of human beings. We flew in our big dragonfly over the dancing treetops and the silent mountains. The gentle early-winter sun threw deep, dark shadows across the forest.

As we flew over the last range, we saw the blue sky meeting the vast ocean, the horizon a straight line in between the two. Cumulus clouds were resting in the north, white billowing shapes. The forest clearings became paddocks with roads. The first houses appeared, dotted in the isolated, treeless farmland. The contrast with the chaotic, ever-changing river and forest was almost dispiriting.

'Let's have a coffee,' said Wayne, when we had landed, just outside the town of Karamea. We were blinking at the suddenness with which our circumstances had changed. One moment we had been in the heart of the wilderness, facing a two-day hike back to civilisation; now we found ourselves at the Last Resort cafe, situated at the end of a winding, 100-kilometre-long road.

While Wayne ordered coffees, I went inside to find a bathroom. A young woman stood behind the bar, cleaning wine glasses with a tea towel.

'Hello!' I called out, and waved jubilantly.

The way the young woman laughed made me realise that my greeting must have seemed overly enthusiastic, but I just felt very happy and excited.

When I walked past the long mirrors I caught sight of myself. My face was very tanned, and my hair had grown quite long and was bleached by the sun. I was surprised to see my soft green T-shirt looking so shabby and shapeless. My shorts were faded and my sandals, which I had worn every day, looked very scruffy and were covered with dried-up mud.

When I came back outside, I found Wayne and Peter talking amicably.

'So, your total weekly expenditure for food is about the same as my weekly bill for coffees,' Wayne said incredulously. They were laughing merrily. I noticed Peter's calm posture and vibe, earned by surviving four long seasons in the wilderness. One arm lay carelessly over the chair next to him; in the other hand he held an empty sugar sachet between his fingers, as if it was a cigarette. He looked strong and confident.

I took a sip from my small cup and put one foot on my seat, before remembering that it might look indecent. Very slowly I recomposed myself. I was suddenly aware of the code of conduct—ways you should talk, look, laugh and walk. There are rules about every inch of human existence. In the past, I had always functioned seamlessly; it was only now that it struck me as strange.

When we had finished our coffees, Wayne invited us to stay the night at his house. Once we got there, he asked me, 'You want to check your email, tell your mum you're alive?'

I opened up my inbox and, after emailing my parents, found a message that had been sent two months earlier:

Dear Miriam and Peter,

We would be honoured if you'd be willing to live in our hut in Abel Tasman National Park. It's 20 minutes' walk from the sea, where there are golden sand beaches, and is situated beneath big mountains. The place is unused and the

rats are trying to move in. It's yours, if you want it.
  Greetings,
  Terry and Rachel

After dinner that night, Wayne asked us, 'So, what is it like to spend a year in the wild?'

We were sitting round the table with his wife, Julie, and their 12-year-old daughter, a cup of tea in our hands and a bowl of mandarins between us.

'For the mind that is focused and runs at high speed,' I said, 'living in nature is extremely boring, as there's hardly anything to do. But, if you take the time to slow down, it's a world of incredible wonder. Living round a fire amidst the beauty of ancient trees, the rhythm of a flowing river, weather that is coming and going . . .'

'I'd like to do that,' said Julie.

Wayne looked at his wife. 'It's pretty tough living out there, you know!' he said, then he added, 'Know what I find most amazing?'

'No, what?' I smiled.

'That we can have such a good evening without touching any alcohol!'

I had never even thought of alcohol. We all talked tirelessly until one in the morning. Peter and I were bouncing with energy and so elated by this spontaneous meeting that we could have talked all night.

While everyone was getting ready for bed, I walked outside. The air was quite cool. The smell of the approaching winter was in the air. I looked into the darkness all around me and wondered what the future would bring. A breeze moved the leaves in a nearby birch tree and, for a brief moment, the whole tree seemed to rustle. When it turned silent again, a sickle-shaped moon slowly appeared over the mountains in the east.

The best skill in the world is to feel at home wherever I am, I thought.

CHAPTER 6

ABEL TASMAN NATIONAL PARK

We met Rachel at a little market in the town of Takaka. Tourists sat on benches sipping organic coffee from paper cups, while dreadlocked backpackers were dotted on the grass weaving flax baskets. A musician was playing an Indian sitar on a small stage. I looked around the stalls, which were selling goat's cheese, pickles, paintings and free-range eggs. All the organic products looked healthy and beautiful, but the prices were too high for our budget.

'Oh hi, Peter and Miriam!' I recognised Rachel's joyous voice from a distance. She was waving her right hand, and clutching a small white poodle with the other. Rachel was tall and pretty, with brown eyes, a haircut straight from the hairdresser and clothes from designer shops. Lovely perfume, too. She was Peter's cousin and her partner, Terry, owned the hut in Abel Tasman National Park that they had mentioned in their email.

'Hi, guys!' Terry was there too. Stocky and strong, with a charming smile, he was a builder by trade and had built the hut himself. After we had hugged and exchanged formalities, Peter asked how it was possible to own a piece of land in the middle of a famous national park.

'I knew the right people at the right time,' Terry said. 'It was jolly cheap back then, too. The land's probably worth a fortune now.'

'Do you often stay in the hut?' I asked Rachel, petting her fluffy dog.

'Me? No.' She smiled brightly. 'I like to visit. It's lovely there, but I don't think I would be comfortable sleeping over. It is, quite frankly, totally rat-infested.' She laughed merrily.

I liked her very much, even though we could not have been more different.

'How long do you think you'll stay out there?' She put her poodle on the ground.

'Maybe one year,' I answered. 'I'd like to learn how to grow vegetables in every season.'

'Hey, in the summer . . .' Terry paused, searching for the hut keys in his bag. 'In summer you might see some campervans motoring to the end of the road, but in winter it should be pretty quiet for you guys. You've only got one neighbour—an old lady called Elisabeth, who still lives in the old homestead a few kilometres away.'

We left Takaka—and the last shop—with three months' worth of food in the boot of our car, which Mouse had taken care of for us, and drove for an hour over a sealed road among the hills. We passed deserted golden-sand beaches and stunning bays. When we entered Abel Tasman National Park, the asphalt ended and the dirt road began.

'Listen to the birds!' I wound down the window and reached out my arm to feel the cool, moist air. I could have almost touched the thick lianas hanging from the branches in the big trees. The forest at sea level was so different from the vegetation in the mountains; it felt as if we had entered another country. The big nīkau palms on the side of the road looked a bit like coconut palms, giving me the impression that we were in a tropical jungle.

'Look at those huge tree ferns. Aren't they amazing?' said Peter, pointing to a big green fern, which must have been at least 12 metres high with three-metre-long fronds hanging elegantly over the road. Peter was smiling, and looked as excited as I felt. We were both so energised by being in a new place.

Round a sharp corner, the road suddenly went into a gully with a small river running through the middle. I held my breath as Peter drove through the water, because the car was made for town and was low to the ground. When the bottom scraped noisily over the rocks, I worried we had damaged something—we were a very long way from any mechanical help—but fortunately the car survived the ford.

After a long journey, we finally drove over a very narrow bridge without railings and on to Terry and Rachel's land. Once on the bridge, Peter could only guess where the planks were, and I was impressed by how calmly he kept the wheels on the wood. The long driveway passed through a forest of tall native kahikatea trees, and after a few hundred metres we entered a big grass clearing surrounded by hills. Round the corner, we found the wooden hut, which was built on the sunny side of a narrow valley.

Peter switched off the engine and we stepped out of the car. The silence came almost as a surprise. The place felt very peaceful.

'Our new house, Miriam!' Peter exclaimed and gave me a joyous hug. 'We can unpack our stuff, sit in a chair and relax. Nobody is going to turn up on us.' Peter stepped on to the spacious verandah. 'Look at this old shop door!' The wooden door had a big glass window with the word STORE etched into it. 'This is all seventies style. It's like an old hippie hang-out.'

I walked inside and saw on my left a kitchen area. I opened the windows above the sink and looked into the green-and-blue cabinets. The heart of the cottage was a firebox, which we could cook on. In the corner was a big bed. The cosy sleeping area was separated from the rest of the cottage by batik cloths.

To us, the hut was luxurious. It was private and it had running water—cold water only, but very handy nonetheless. The water was carried by a long pipe all the way down the hill from a little clear stream. Outside on the edge of the forest was a long-drop toilet. It had a very deep hole—no possibility of backsplash. In the mumbling creek near the hut, I found a deep pool where we would be able to wash our clothes and ourselves.

The next day, Peter found a suitable place for a garden, and we started turning over the soil with shovels.

'Hey, look at this! Full of worms.' He sounded very cheerful.

'What do worms do?' I asked. I wanted to learn everything about gardening.

'Worms are our little helpers, Miriam,' he said with an infectious laugh. 'They turn hard, unworkable soil into nice soft humus. Be careful not to chop them up!'

Peter was in his element. He had cultivated many large vegetable gardens in the past. To see him content always made me feel happy.

'See what you're digging?' he said.

'The soil, you mean?'

'Yes. Notice how it's sand? The sea used to come here. This was once a beach.'

I looked around and I could envision the tide coming in. The valley floor was very flat and the surrounding forested hills quite steep. When we had finished our work in the garden, we walked back to the hut.

We mostly lived on the verandah, which was furnished with a big round table and four chairs. The roof kept us dry and when it was cold we put on an extra jumper. We never really moved into the cottage, except after dark. After living outside for a year, we were reluctant to go back inside a building.

One day when we were outside on the verandah playing chess, we saw a lady who looked to be well into her seventies walking up the track to the hut.

'Good afternoon,' I called out cheerfully.

'Oh, hello. I'm awfully sorry to disturb you,' she stammered, taking off her brown slouch hat and revealing her short white hair.

'I'm Elisabeth.' Her pale blue eyes flashed shyly. She was barely five foot tall, and had a round face with soft skin.

I introduced myself and Peter, trying my best to speak gently so as not to scare her more than she already seemed.

'We're neighbours,' she said, then pointed to where she had come from. 'I'm living over there.' She looked puzzled for a second. 'Well,

I suppose it's there actually.' She gestured behind the hut. Her accent sounded almost British, like the old people's voices I had heard on the radio.

'Come and have a seat,' Peter, who was always softly spoken, said. 'Would you like a cup of tea?'

'Well, actually—' she laughed nervously— 'I was wondering whether you'd have some matches?' She fumbled in her pocket. 'I will pay you for it.' She wanted to give me a 20-dollar note. I almost laughed; 12 boxes of matches wouldn't cost more than a few dollars.

She moved unsteadily up the steps, and her posture gave an impression of frailty. Once on the verandah, she stood still for a moment, unsure where she was supposed to sit. I pulled a chair into a more welcoming position. When the tea was poured, she took a sip from the enamel cup and seemed to burn her lips.

'So have you lived here all your life?' asked Peter.

'Well, yes. My grandfather broke in the land, and my father farmed it all his life. I grew up here in the homestead.' She slowly put her cup back down on the wooden tabletop, which had been bent by the sun. Her hands were small and narrow—more suitable for knitting than farming sheep, I thought. In a voice so soft that I had to strain to hear her, she told us how everything had had to be transported by boat. Her grandfather and his brothers had eventually built the road with picks and shovels. I asked how she organised her food now. She had a friend, she said, who brought her supplies every fortnight. She invited us to come to her place if we had time, then she hesitantly stood up.

'How long have you been without matches?' I asked, giving her several boxes.

'Three days,' she said, then looked embarrassed.

'Have you been sitting in the cold for that long?' I knew she lived without electricity. This fragile but tough old lady intrigued me.

'Oh, well, I made sure the fire didn't die, but this morning when I got up it was out. I remembered hearing from a friend of Terry's that you were here. Lucky for me.'

She took her hat and bade us farewell.

———

The warm autumn weather was dwindling, days were drawing in and the nights becoming colder and longer. We lived very quietly and very simply. We worked in our garden during the day, and in the afternoon we often walked to the sea. After dinner, we would go inside. I would sit at the table, softly singing and playing the guitar. A candle illuminated my lyrics and melodies, which I had scribbled on scattered pieces of paper. I had written about the wilderness and the world. Many of my songs were about freedom, but most of all I liked to sing love songs for Peter, who would lie listening in bed just behind me.

'I love a wild man, he lives with me. He dares to live a life without security . . .' I sang one evening.

'Very nice, sweetie,' he said when I had finished. I blew out the candle and, wearing two layers of clothing, crawled under the blankets beside him. I lifted his arm and rested my head on his chest. *Pa-dum . . . pa-dum . . . pa-dum . . .* His heart was beating slowly. My head felt lighter in his arms. I wanted to lie on his heart forever, in this quiet forest, in a deserted bay, in a faraway corner of the Pacific Ocean.

We lay there peacefully in our warm bed, until I heard a sudden sound: *D-r-r-r-r-r.*

'What's that?'

'Rats!' hissed Peter in a tone that suggested that the Grim Reaper was knocking at the door. We could hear one rat running in the ceiling. Then another came up inside the wall. The first one—or maybe a third—started to chew loudly on the wood. It sounded as though they would soon gnaw right through the ceiling and land on our bed.

'What shall we do?' I whispered.

'You sound afraid,' Peter said. 'Why? Didn't you have a rat as a kid?'

'That was a pet rat! A nice little white one. Not a big wild rat that wants to eat people's fingers!'

After a disturbed sleep, I woke again at dawn. When I saw a mouse darting through the kitchen, I hurried to the bucket of rat poison and pitilessly nailed the round pieces of bait on to the rafters.

The rodents started to die slowly and miserably between the walls of the hut, and left us with an unbearable stench. Our war against the rats went on for the whole winter.

'I want to get rid of them as fast as possible,' I declared. 'I dislike them with a passion.'

'Aha!' Peter laughed. 'Now you know how New Zealanders see possums, stoats, ferrets, goats and all the rest of the animals that have been declared pests!'

One afternoon, when we were busy in the garden, we heard the growl of an approaching engine. Peter put down his shovel and looked first at me, then at the driveway. A white pick-up truck appeared.

'Mouse!' I threw the poles in the dirt and ran barefoot to the road.

Mouse tooted when he saw me coming, then jumped out and lifted me almost off the ground. Grinning, he hugged Peter. He was wearing a dark green jumper, which made his green eyes stand out. His skinny legs poked out of the bottom of his shorts, which looked funny above his gumboots. He was now 39, but he had still a very youthful appearance. He opened the dog boxes and his four dogs leaped out and ran all over the freshly dug soil.

Mouse had brought food supplies, newspapers and many stories. Over numerous cups of tea, we filled him in on everything that had happened since we had last seen him.

That evening, Mouse took his rifle out of its bag and looked at me. 'You wanna shoot a possum for dinner?' He was already searching for an extra jumper and his torch. We stepped out of the cosy hut into the cold, moonless night.

'Quiet,' he whispered to the whining dogs in their boxes; they sensed we were going out for a hunt and wanted to come with us, but we left them behind. Mouse shone his spotlight into the trees and the bright circle of light wheeled up and down, from tree to tree. He was looking for possum eyes, which would glint like little mirrors. We slowly ambled up the forested driveway. The call of an owl sounded in a nearby tree. The luminous beam of the torch trailed through the darkness, but the rest of the world was totally black. Another owl hooted from a different direction, and the first one answered.

'Jeez, my hand is freezing.' Mouse's hand with the spotlight had been in the cold air for a while.

'Give it to me,' I whispered.

He passed me the torch, but I also took his hand. I rubbed it and blew warm air on it. His palms felt like mine: broad, calloused, rough and strong. Then, quite spontaneously, I pressed my lips on the back of his hand. I smelled a faint, sweet scent. We suddenly grew quiet and slowed our pace until we stood still. I switched off the light and smiled. The silent darkness covered us like the wings of a bat.

'Oh, really?' He laughed softly.

When I kissed his hand again, he stepped a little closer. I leaned forward and, with my lips, felt the shape of his face. My mouth hovered over his cool nose and warm cheeks. The night was so quiet, I could hear him breathing. Then I found his lips, and kissed. He had a soft, moist mouth. He kissed back—a little hastily, as if he was nervous.

I gently pulled at his woollen jersey, and he moved closer. I made him kiss more slowly. It felt as if only his mouth existed in the whole world, and everything else had vanished into the darkness. He brought a finger to my face and touched my cheek very tenderly, following the contour of my cheekbone. His mouth found mine again. I closed my eyes and felt only his touch: the most intimate communion. He kissed slowly now. Time itself seemed to slow down.

I heard something rustling in a nearby kahikatea tree. I switched on the light and saw a possum climbing on to a branch. It looked into the beam and froze. Mouse handed me the gun while taking the torch.

'You shoot,' he whispered. 'Look through the scope, put the cross on its head, pull the trigger.'

I hesitantly took the gun. The cross in the scope kept swaying from side to side. I pulled the trigger. The bullet hit the possum in the head, and it fell dead on the ground. The loud crack of the gun destroyed the magic of just moments earlier, and quickly sobered us up.

'Good shot! He never knew what hit him,' said Mouse. His voice sounded suddenly loud in the stillness.

'This is a hundred times easier than the bow!' I handed the rifle back to Mouse, who unloaded the bullets. 'It's as easy as pressing a button to destroy monsters in the computer games I played as a kid.'

'Yeah.' He laughed, picking up the possum by its tail. 'You see why everybody else has moved on from bows and arrows.'

When we came near to the hut, Mouse switched off the spotlight. We could see Peter reading a book by the flickering light of a candle. Mouse crawled silently with the possum in his hand over to the verandah, then scratched at the hut door with its claws. When it remained quiet inside, he slowly opened the door a few centimetres. With his hand behind the possum, he made the animal shuffle into the hut. Peter was silent for a second, before bursting into laughter. 'Good evening, Mr Possum!'

It had been quite an absurd hour: I had walked in the pitch-black night, kissed a friend and shot a possum for dinner. But it was real at least. It was not just some fantasy; this was actually happening.

Life is too short to dream, I thought with a smile as I stepped back into the warmth of the hut.

'It's strange for couples not to feel jealous,' said Mouse after dinner.

We were sitting around the firebox, with the door open so that we could watch the flames.

'Well, I think jealousy is very destructive,' said Peter. 'A lot of people act as if they own each other.'

'You're right. No one owns anyone, really.' Mouse was silent for a while. 'I know all this, but somehow I can't stand the thought of Debbie touching another guy. That would drive me insane!'

'But for yourself you don't mind?' I said, patting his feet, which were clad in big woollen socks and resting on my lap.

'No, no, course not!' He laughed heartily and wiggled his toes.

'But why?' asked Peter.

'I guess I'd be afraid she'd like that other guy more than me.'

I nodded. 'You'd have to trust that she wouldn't run away.'

Peter looked thoughtful. 'Well, if Miriam fell in love with you, wanted to marry you and have children—which is very unlikely—I couldn't really prevent that, could I?' He laughed. 'Miriam is young and attractive.

She has many choices. I can't control her, even if I wanted to.'

'I'll never get married again,' Mouse said.

'But, Mouse, you are married,' I replied.

'I know.' He sighed. 'But she seems to be angry all the time. People change, over the years. I don't know . . . She hates her job, comes back tired and watches TV. We hardly ever do anything together these days.'

He admitted that he and Debbie weren't very happy any more. When he left after four days with us, we wished him well and he promised to come back, whenever work allowed.

I was curious to see where Elisabeth lived so, one morning soon after Mouse had left, I made my way to her house. I walked through the forest and out to the dirt road, where I was met with a cool breeze. In the far distance, I could see an old homestead on a small rise. The big clearing between the road and the house had once been a sheep farm. The long grass was pale, as if it was getting ready for frost. In some wet areas, grass had made space for reeds. In the distance, wisps of mist hung between the sharp ridges and gullies of the forested mountains. The wind sang on the nearby hilltops, and long, streaked clouds hurried northwards.

I got a fright when I walked past a gorse bush and heard a sudden explosion of rapid wing beats: *Trrrrrrrrrrrr!*

'Chi-car-go! Chi-car-go!' two round quails called emphatically. They flew two metres, then ran along the trail before disappearing into the reeds. The track wound into a swamp, where the water came up to my calves. It amazed me that Elisabeth had to go through this every time she came out. Maybe she didn't go anywhere for this reason.

I followed the path for about two kilometres. Eventually two big oaks indicated human settlement. On the grass beneath the trees lay many acorns and brown leaves. There was a tumbledown barn near the gate, with loose sheets of iron that squeaked in the wind—an eerie tune, which made the whole scene feel like a spooky old fairytale. A thick layer of moss and lichen formed a velvet coating over the old gate, which I had to push quite hard to open, since it was sagging on its hinges. Smoke was coming out of the chimney of the wooden house. The white paint was peeling in places and would have made the house look deserted, if it wasn't for the mowed lawn.

'Hello?' I called out. 'Anybody home?'

Elisabeth appeared in the doorway. 'Hello! I'm just baking some muffins in the oven,' she said quite cheerfully, as I stepped on to the verandah. Her face had some colour and she seemed more confident here in her own place.

Inside, the house was filled with the pleasant smell of fresh baking and smoke from the fire. It felt as if I had walked into a living museum of a forgotten world. Bright sunlight streamed through the windows and lit up the house, which was not much bigger than our hut—yet Elisabeth used to live here with her parents and five siblings. A dusty sofa sat underneath an oval painting of her grandparents. It was clear that Elisabeth lived mostly in the kitchen, where her half-finished embroidery lay on the table next to an old-fashioned biscuit tin with a picture of a young queen of England on it. Behind her chair was an old coal range—something I had never seen before. It had a big heavy door, behind which was the oven; behind another, smaller door burned a coal fire, which also warmed up water for the house.

We went out and sat on wooden chairs in the sun on the weather-beaten verandah and drank tea from little porcelain cups.

'Don't you feel lonely out here?' I asked.

She looked startled for a moment, as if she was not used to answering questions.

'No, no. Well, everybody feels lonely sometimes, I suppose.'

She put her fork down on her plate and smiled without looking at me. She had only just started on her muffin, while I had finished mine 10 minutes ago. I looked out over the great clearing in front of us. In the far distance we could see the blue sea.

'There is so much to do here. Look, I still have to tidy up all these garments and papers.' She pointed with a soft open hand to five different piles of rubbish scattered over the green lawn. She had segregated everything as if the recycling truck from town would soon come to pick it up.

'And I have Midnight.'

'Midnight?'

'He's a possum that lives in the portico. Every day at dusk I put his supper out for him. I love the wild birds, too. Dad used to scare them away from the muscatel grapes, but I reckon there's plenty for everyone. Do you hear that warning call?' She looked at me with wonder in her eyes. 'That could be a stoat walking past the birds, don't you think?'

I had never paid much attention to birds and their calls, and I vowed at once to listen from now on to the birds' messages.

'When Dad's dog died a few years back, I never got another one,' Elisabeth went on. 'I like wild animals. They are so much easier to keep, because they're not dependent.'

She told me how her mother had died quite young, and she had looked after her father, who lived to be well into his nineties. She told me about her brothers and sister and the farm. Eventually I heard the big clock inside strike 12 times. It was time for me to leave, but I promised Elisabeth I would return.

I walked back over the acorn path, where I now knew Elisabeth had run as a child. Underneath the oaks rested an old rusty plough, mostly covered by long grass. Once horses had walked here with hay carts and ploughs. Sheepdogs had run barking behind flocks of sheep. Unlike the Mōkihinui, where everything lived in the present, this place was held in the past. For Elisabeth it was the old; for me it was the new.

I found it fascinating to visit her in her smoky kitchen with the coal range and the old clock striking the hours. It occurred to me that one day I, too, would be old and appreciate some company.

So, my life was now enriched by Elisabeth. She was my strange, beautiful, fragile friend. I had been longing for a female friend over the last months, and now I had one. Smiling, I promised myself that I would look after her and make her happy.

Tap, tap, tap . . .

'Who's there?' Peter looked at me with a smile. It was dawn.

'Coming! Coming!' I called. I stepped out of bed and went and laid a handful of oats on the planks of the verandah.

William was a very clever weka who knocked every morning at the hut door. He appeared and disappeared mysteriously, and he knew how to be wild without being afraid. William had recently found himself a weka-wife—Wanda—who I now saw running over the crisp white frost and up the steps to get her share of oats, too.

I lit the fire to thaw out the hut, and a little later on we sat outside with a cup of tea. Dressed in many woollen jumpers, we admired the arrival of a new day.

'Look at the hoar frost on that tree.' Peter pointed at an old kōwhai tree on the shadowy side of the clearing. The air was so cold that I could see his breath. We were living in a frost pocket. Cool air came rolling down the still mountains and settled in the gully. The condensation under the roof had frozen overnight and, when the morning sun hit the corrugated iron, drops of water started to fall down all around us. One big drip landed in my cup and some tea splashed out. Slowly the sun reached the valley floor. The ice melted and the grass turned green. The air was still, and everything silently enjoyed the sunshine.

Food and warmth were a constant focus for us at the hut. After going spotlighting with Mouse, I realised how many possums there were living in the area. During the quiet nights we heard them barking at each other in the forest. I set traps to catch them. By observing their patterns and behaviour, I learned what they liked and disliked. It was easy to spot their narrow, well-trodden trails underneath the low vegetation and up the big trees. I was afraid of trapping Wanda and William, so I spent a lot of time building traps into the trees. Whenever I caught a possum, I would skin it, give the body to Peter to cook, and pin the pelt on to a wooden frame I had built for this purpose.

I tanned my skins the way that Daniel had explained to me in the Mōkihinui Valley. First I applied a thick layer of salt, which I would scrape off the following day. I repeated this several times. Then I smeared a mixture of baking powder and kerosene on to the skin and left it overnight before rubbing it clean again. Every now and then, I would scrape the skin too much, so that it turned brittle and broke in half; at other times, residual salt would attract moisture and cause the skin to rot. When I finally managed to tan some skins properly, I began to sew them into blankets and hats. I found this whole process very enjoyable. The women in my mother's family had all been good at sewing, and my sister Sofie studied fashion design, so it felt quite natural for me to try sewing myself.

Elisabeth had mentioned to me that her brothers used to collect big mussels from the rocks out at sea, so one day we set out in search of the tasty shellfish. To get to the surf, we had to walk for more than an hour through the estuary at low tide, which included fording a river. On our way we saw hundreds of birds on a sandbank. 'Keria, keria!' the oystercatchers called. They had long red beaks, black backs and white bellies, and were walking only a short distance from a group of terns.

The inlet was mostly golden sand, but some parts were covered in deep mud. When the tide was too high, we had to climb up the side of a sandy cliff to get round the inlet. Upon reaching the open sea, we followed the empty beach until we stood on a ledge, looking down at the waves crashing on to the rocks below. One moment I could see the mussel beds; the next, all the rocks were completely submerged. I was reluctant to go near to the water, because I was afraid of being swept away and sucked out into the ocean by a rip. Peter showed me how to read the rhythm of the waves, and we counted together: every fifth or seventh wave was bigger than the others.

The sea was something dangerously wild and new to me. I had learned to read the weather in the mountains, and I could cross rivers and climb over rocks and trees with a bow in my hand, but I knew nothing about reading the surf. To begin with, I tugged at the mussels on the high rocks, but these little ones were densely packed and very hard to pull out. I spotted bigger mussels on the rocks down in the surf, so I gathered my courage and jumped swiftly in between the waves on to the brown rocks. It was like jumping into a turning skipping rope, and every few minutes a giant wave would crash wildly over the rugged rocks. Keeping watch over my shoulder for approaching breakers,

I yanked the big green mussels off. With one hand I hurriedly filled my flimsy plastic bag, which I held in my other hand—the same hand that was also keeping me perched on the rocks.

Sometimes a breaker would splash right over me, but the water was never cold and I would grin excitedly in the face of the wind and the waves. My fear faded, and I slowly started to appreciate the wild, unforgiving ocean. We would boil our mussels in a big pot, then burn all the shells in the fire and use the ashes to fertilise our garden.

Gradually, the spring days became longer and warmer, and the garden grew more abundant by the week. Peter explained seasonality, pH values, soil and trace elements, and I did my best to remember everything. I drew diagrams in my notebook and wrote a glossary at the back; the whole experience felt a bit like an official apprenticeship. I also had two books about herbal medicine that I studied diligently. It was good knowledge, but I had no opportunity to test any of it, because we never fell ill.

I was determined to learn about the garden, but I had to force myself to be enthusiastic. I didn't find it easy to always be the one who was learning, the one who was 'under instruction'. Sometimes I'd forget details and, when I asked something for the second or third time, Peter would sigh and say, 'I've already told you this!' Then I felt hurt and stupid. In those moments, I wanted to throw the shovel in the dirt, walk away and have nothing to do with gardening.

But my hurt feelings never lasted long. The natural beauty around me had an extraordinary ability to dissolve any negative thoughts and feelings. To see the beauty of the sunshine through the branches of a tree, and to listen to the birds—who were not worried about anything—helped to bring things into perspective, and lifted my mood. Living in such wild beauty was very good for my mind.

I would watch Peter in the garden, when he would take off his sandals and carefully step between the beds, watching the plants so intently that it looked as if he had forgotten the rest of the world. He would tread slowly over to the beans, then squat down, pick off some dead leaves and pull out some grass. He would touch my shoulder ever so slightly, when I was about to step on a pumpkin tendril. 'Careful, they are very sensitive,' he would say.

Without noticing it, I became more watchful and alert. Peter never told me to listen, but over the months he taught me to sense the plants. I discovered for myself that tomatoes didn't like to be touched. Other plants disliked water on their leaves or grass around their roots. Every plant had preferences that could not be learned through study, only through instinct. By living around our plants, I slowly started to become aware of their characters—the plant-beings.

We grew more vegetables than we could eat, and I took our extras to Elisabeth, whose spring lawn was dotted with yellow daffodils and jonquils. She had tried to grow some vegetables, but Midnight stole the food before she could get to it. Every time I visited her, I fixed parts of her homestead; it was slowly falling down around her. While I was busy with my hammer and nails, Elisabeth would knit or work on her crochet, making woollen squares for a quilt. My errands were merely an excuse to see her. It felt as if we were in a play set in 1930, in which she was the landlady and I was the handyman. In this faraway corner of the world we could be whatever we wished. When my chores were completed, we would sit on the verandah sipping tea served on a decorative tray.

Elisabeth enjoyed her old homestead, living without electricity and cooking on her smoky coal range. She loved all she knew, but I had the impression that the burden of the past weighed on her. She wasn't a stubborn, strong or eccentric woman; she was as gentle as an alpine flower. So fragile that an unobservant person could trample on her without realising it. I liked my friend very much, for there was something genuine and innocent about her.

The garden was in full bloom. We had everything we could think of: possums for meat, fresh seafood, and every day we ate our own vegetables. Then one day it started to rain. The drumming on the roof was so loud that we could hardly hear each other talking. It rained continuously for three days, and on the fourth night the thundering downpour reached unbelievable proportions. The clouds had burst above Golden Bay.

When the rain finally became a drizzle on the fifth morning, we ran outside. The little creek had turned into a powerful, murky river that had carried tons of sand off the mountains. It had left its original bed and was now flowing rampant over the driveway. The grass clearing had become a lake with a metre of sand on the bottom. Everywhere were scattered logs and trees, which had been pulled out of the ground in the upper valley. The exposed mud turned into quicksand the moment we tried walking across it. The damage was unbelievable.

We looked at the mudflat that had been our garden. Not just a garden—it had been our life. We had spent many months working, fertilising and cultivating the soil. That quarter-hectare had given us all the vegetables we needed, and it was devastating to find it all gone.

Peter looked up the valley in despair. 'I bet the road is completely destroyed. We'll never be able to get our car out. What are we going to do for food?'

'Can we plant it again, in a different spot?'

'It will take ages!' He squatted down on a muddy log.

'We'll have to walk with a pack to Takaka for supplies,' I said.

He looked up at me, his face troubled. 'How much food do we have?'

'Two, maybe three weeks.' I shrugged. 'I'll walk out and hitch-hike. It's not a problem.'

Luckily our hut had been built high enough to avoid the flood. The little building was still intact, but the pipe supplying our water had been totally washed out, so we had to collect water in buckets from the creek.

Later we learned that a metre of rain had fallen in less than two days. It was referred to as a 'once in 500 years' flood. There were roadblocks manned by Civil Defence officials. Farmland had been covered in sand, mud and logs. Gigantic landslides had flattened houses. There had sadly even been casualties, and Abel Tasman National Park was temporarily closed to visitors. Hikers were no longer permitted to walk the famous coastal trail, as all the bridges were washed out and big landslides had made the track impassable.

Elisabeth's house had only just been spared. The river had dumped broken trees and bushes, gigantic stones and tons of sand behind her house. When we visited her, she said she had never seen anything like it in her life. The whole valley had become an enormous kilometre-wide sandpit. She said she had heard the thundering of the earth and felt very scared.

Peter and I walked along the dirt road to see the damage. Huge slips had washed the road away. Big scars of bare rock were interspersed with wide bands of fallen trees. Gorges more than a hundred metres deep suddenly yawned in front of us. The streams were stained with brown mud. We had to clamber over ancient trees that had been ripped out of the forest. After a few hours we could go no further, because the road had vanished all together: there was just one big, golden-sand ravine.

As soon as we were able to, we made a start on a new garden in a higher place. During the summer, the plants grew quickly and we were soon eating the first fast-growing vegetables—but all plants that had needed a long growing season were forever lost, including our potatoes. Since we could not drive in or out, we were now completely isolated. The removal of the road had a surprising effect: we suddenly felt a wonderful sense of quietness, as though we were back in the untouched wilderness. All contact with the outside world had vanished. The only way in or out was via the sea, just like the days when Elisabeth was a child, or by helicopter.

Summer brought with it cicadas—hundreds of them, perhaps even thousands. The whole forest vibrated with their song. Standing among the trees, the clapping of the insects was almost deafening. The nymphs spend years under the ground, until they crawl up and anchor themselves to the bark of a tree. Their skin splits open and a cicada flies out, leaving behind its dry brown jacket. There were empty cases on every tree. Sometimes a big cicada would accidentally fly on to my arm and I would study its green back that looked as if an artist had painted it. With its red eyes and hooked claws, it would have been a scary creature had it been bigger.

One hot day we tried following a river up into the mountains. The valley was a long way from any walking track and we found ourselves looking at beauty that had possibly not been viewed by anyone for a very long time. At one point, we were stopped by a gigantic, smooth rock. We clambered up it, our fingers holding on to the narrow ledges. Once we reached the top, we saw a wild waterfall. It seemed to be pulsing in a rhythm; it was incredible to watch the heartbeat of the fall.

After lunch we climbed on to a ridge and found ourselves among ancient rimu trees. One native conifer was embraced by a northern rata. The vine had beautiful red blossoms, and the ground was covered with a carpet of petals.

'Will this rata kill the tree eventually?' I asked, touching the vine, which had grown as big as my thighs.

'Well, ecologists say that a rata will out-compete a rimu, that it'll strangle the tree to death,' Peter said. 'The Darwinist view is focused on competition and survival of the fittest, which has become a cultural construct. In reality, I reckon there's a lot more symbiosis going on than meets the eye. A rata vine will only germinate in mature trees, and the rimu allows a rata's embrace until it dies. As the old tree decomposes, it provides food for the rata. It's an extraordinary cycle of life.'

I followed Peter on to the vine; it was almost as easy as climbing a ladder. After about 10 metres the ground appeared very far away, and I was afraid of falling down, but Peter kept climbing. I hesitantly went after him. The rimu was so gigantic that we soon found ourselves high above the rest of the forest. I hooked one leg into the rata vine, and looked out at the great vista of soft treetops. We were at the same height as two bellbirds. They were very surprised to see us in their tree. The canopy below us moved gently with the breeze, and patches of bright red flowers stood out among the green leaves. I could see tall tree ferns below us, their fronds a perfect parasol. The rimu we were sitting in swung softly from left to right, and the air was heavy and taut, ringing with the sound of cicadas. I felt a strange sensation, as if my whole body was resonating with the sound of the clapping insects. It was amazing to be up so high above the forest.

Eventually we made our way back down to earth, and in the late afternoon we walked home. We were just about to turn into our driveway when we spotted a stooped man with a few dogs walking over the road.

Peter grabbed my arm. 'Just wait a minute. That guy looks dodgy, like he's snooping around, looking for something to steal. It's better he doesn't see us walking into our driveway.'

We hid behind a tree until he was out of sight.

Back at the hut, we were on the verandah drinking tea when we saw somebody walking towards us. My mouth fell open. I now realised that the man we had seen with the dogs was Mouse. His shoulders were slumped; he looked lost and defeated.

I ran over to him. 'Mouse!' It felt as if the last of his strength ebbed away when he sank into my arms.

'Debbie left me,' he said.

All that remained of him was a shell, a sad forlorn skeleton with tears in his hollow eyes. His usually brave face, happy smile and boundless energy had disappeared. The change was so enormous that I was immediately very worried for him.

We sat down and Mouse told his story. They had become increasingly angry and frustrated with each other, he said, and had grown apart. Last week, she had told him she wanted a divorce. He had screamed in anguish and thrown their wedding pictures across the room and his ring at the wall. As Mouse talked, he began to cry and said that he would do anything to get her back.

It wasn't a surprise to me that they had finally separated. What was so astonishing, though—almost scary—was how devastating it clearly was for Mouse.

The next morning, we walked to Mouse's boat. He had heard on the news that the road had been destroyed and so he had brought boxes of food supplies for us in his boat. Over the next few days, he gradually became calmer. While we baked bread on the fire outside, he would sit quietly looking at the forest and at our garden. We witnessed a peacefulness settle in him that we had not seen before.

'The more you live in beauty, the more you start to see beauty,' he said once, totally out of the blue.

Slowly he began to make sense of what had happened. He had grown up in a violent and poverty-stricken world, and all he had wanted was a middle-class lifestyle that would give him a sense of stability. With the divorce, he would lose half of everything, and his property would have to be sold. With his land and animals gone, his security and status would vanish too.

After a week, he began to be more cheerful and smiled more often. One warm day we dragged Terry's kayaks to the river and paddled out to sea. We followed the coastline until we found a beautiful, untouched little beach with golden sand. We collected driftwood and lit a fire to make tea. Mouse spotted some mussels on the rocks. He knotted the sleeves of his T-shirt and we used it to collect the shellfish, then boiled them in the billy for lunch. While we were eating, we watched the blue ocean and two red-billed gulls dropped out of the clear sky. With their red legs, and perfect white and grey feathers, they looked like businessmen in smart waistcoats. They had spotted us from far away and, in return for a mussel, one of the business-birds gave us a show. He stood on his toes to make himself look big and tall, then started screeching at the second business-bird, who was cowering and pulling his wings down in a comical manner. When our food was gone, they lost interest.

On other days, we went for long walks or worked in the garden. We often sat together in the warm sunshine and chatted. I would sit cross-legged in the long grass while Mouse plaited my hair and talked to Peter. Mouse never ceased to amuse and surprise me, and he was more affectionate and gentle than I had seen him before.

All three of us were just so happy. I was struck with genuine delight that it was possible to have such perfect harmony between people. There was no jealousy, competition or complications; we were just together, in the heart of the wilderness, surrounded by untouched forest. There were no prying eyes of a judgemental society, with its silent rules of who should love whom. It was a most free and pure form of friendship.

One evening we talked about Mouse's future.

'You know, Mouse,' said Peter, 'I was in a similar position to you when I sold my property. It was fantastic. I felt so free.'

'Yes, but you chose to get rid of everything. I was forced to.' Mouse smiled. He thought for a moment. 'You guys don't own anything, but you have each other. You don't worry about losing your property, but you worry about losing each other.' He looked at me. 'If something happens to Peter, you'll collapse!'

I felt stunned. 'Yes,' I admitted. I knew he was right. I paused for a moment before I spoke again. 'I feel very secure with Peter. I can live anywhere, in any new place, as long as I have Peter with me. He is my anchor and security.' I looked at the fire. 'But, of course, with that security comes the fear of losing Peter. I'm so afraid I'll lose him that I wrap him up in a cocoon.' I tried to laugh.

'And that's the worst thing you can do,' Peter answered with a wry smile.

'Hey,' said Mouse, 'why did you choose a man who is thirty years older than you and might die of old age while you're still young, then?'

'I fell in love.' I smiled broadly at Peter. 'But, if I ever find myself alone, hopefully I'll be strong enough to stand on my own feet.' I sounded more confident than I really felt.

'And who's to say that I'll die first, anyway?' said Peter. 'You could die in an accident or from some disease, and then it will be me who's left alone.'

'And what would you do, Pete, if you were alone?' asked Mouse.

'It would be extremely difficult. This way of living is only suitable for the two of us, so I'd have to do something totally different.' Peter leaned forward and readjusted his sock. 'But I have lived alone in the past, so I know I can do it.'

———

After two weeks with us, Mouse had to return to appointments at home. The weather had changed and a strong easterly wind was blowing. When we walked him back to the inlet, we saw whitecaps on the waves in the distance. Before stepping on to his boat, Mouse promised to turn round if the ocean was too dangerous. Peter and I pushed the boat out to deeper water. 'Don't get lost out there,' said Peter. But Mouse didn't hear, for the wind was blowing noisily. He waved and smiled. We waved back.

'Don't get lost out there!' Peter yelled again, and this time Mouse lifted his thumb in the air. Then he turned and bravely motored out of the estuary. Dark clouds were slowly gathering on the horizon. We sat and watched him slowly head out into the open sea.

'Is he turning back?' asked Peter. The boat was just about to hit the white caps.

'No,' I said. 'He is going on.'

One beautiful summer's day, I decided to hike the quiet trail through the mountains just above the hut. Peter's knee had still not recovered enough to march up steep trails with a heavy backpack, so I kissed him goodbye and headed off alone with enough food for six days in my pack. The call of kaka, the red mountain parrot, welcomed me to the mountains. The higher I climbed, the closer I came to the realms of heaven. I liked living in our hut, but there was something about the mountains that I couldn't leave. Walking over the hostile, hard ridges, where storm and wind were playing freely, gave me a feeling of insignificance that was strangely liberating. Only the present counted. It had a purifying effect and gently took away all the nonsense that didn't really matter in the eyes of nature.

Living in one place for a year had beautiful aspects. I saw the seasons coming and going, the plants growing, and my friendship with Elisabeth flourishing. But, in the summer months in particular, I felt a pull to the mountains and an urge to start wandering again.

I followed the ridge track and spent the night in my tent in the quiet forest. I thought of Mouse's comment that if something happened to

Peter I would collapse. I envisioned Peter's death, and tears filled my eyes; the idea alone was crippling. I stared into the darkness for some time, until I realised I was more afraid of my own thoughts—that something might happen to Peter in the future—than of what was happening right now.

I felt like a child who was terrified of the shadow of a wolf on a wall, only to discover the shadow was actually made by my own two hands before a light. A lot of fears were based on abstract thoughts, I saw.

I enjoyed hiking during the day. The track was easy to follow, the forest was beautifully diverse and the views over the bay were breathtaking. One evening, I pitched my tent on the soft grass beneath a big beech tree. I lit a fire and ate my dinner. When the light started to fade, the sky turned pale blue in the east and pink in the west. The silhouettes of the trees became sharp and distinct. I strolled a little way into the forest, with no particular purpose. As I walked without aim or goal, I suddenly felt the world expanding. Everything was beautiful and made sense. It occurred to me that the meaning of life lies in aimlessness: when there is no focus at all, the world opens up.

I thought of the village I had grown up in. The quiet, small roads lined with willows, along which I had rode so often on my yellow bicycle. I had liked to cycle to a small reserve and climb into a willow to watch the birds in a lagoon. As a child, the world had always been new and beautiful, but when I grew up that feeling had vanished. By living in nature and walking in beauty, the enchanted world was slowly revealing itself to me again.

Most days during the quiet summer, Peter and I would walk to the coast. The huge estuary looked different every time. There was a small, picturesque island in the middle of the inlet, and a stunning bay, with extraordinarily clear water. At low tide, the mudflats were rippled with beautiful patterns, and the inlet was alive with crabs and shellfish that hid in the mud until the tide returned. Stingrays rested in the many ponds.

One day, Peter and I followed the rocky shore at low tide and collected a bag of rock oysters. On the way back we found a warm pool. My head rested on Peter's lap, while his feet swung in the water. We discussed the idea of buying a piece of land for ourselves one day. We fantasised about the fruit and nut trees we could plant, the design of the hut we would build, and the goats we would keep for milking and making cheese.

'The only problem is,' said Peter, 'I'd never want to get a mortgage again. I had to take one out when I had an orchard. It's a constant stress, having to pay off debt.'

I remembered a few pictures I had seen of him as a 30-year-old, smiling wryly between neat rows of orange and avocado trees, with a black cat in his arms.

'The mort-gauge: the measurer of your death.' He smiled, tapping the rock with a small stone.

'We need to find a piece of land that we can buy debt-free,' I said.

'Land with fertile soil to grow a good garden is often more expensive.' Peter carefully laid his warm little stone on my forehead.

The soft afternoon light created an orange glow around us. The old beech trees hung tirelessly on to the rocks, their big, strong roots exposed and eaten away in storms. I smelled the sweet scent of mānuka flowers mixed with the salty coastal air. The tide was rising so fast that we could watch the water flowing in, the sea gradually covering the sandy estuary.

As we sauntered back to the dirt road, we came across a young woman with curly hair. She greeted us cheerfully with a French accent. Her face was heart-shaped, and she had brown eyes and dark hair. She was slim and fit-looking and wore loose shorts, a tight top and pink sports shoes. She had a tiny backpack, and every few minutes she sucked some liquid from a tube that came out the side of it. She told us casually that she was out running, and showed us the 30-kilometre route on her smartphone, explaining that now she just needed to cross the estuary to get back to her rented chalet on the other side.

'That'll be difficult. You might have to swim,' said Peter, with a laugh.

'My parents are waiting for me.' She pointed across the bay. 'They've come here for a holiday to see me. My mum will get anxious. I'll have to go round the edges.'

I tried to tell her that the inlet was much bigger than it looked and wasn't easy to walk round, as the cliffs and rocks were very steep and rugged in places, but she was very determined and had already started taking off her shoes. Since I knew it would take her hours to walk round the bay, I suggested instead that she come with us, take our kayak and paddle down the river.

'How will you get the kayak back?' she asked, slowly standing upright again.

'You can hide it on the other side, and I'll come and collect it tomorrow at low tide.'

She was persuaded, and we walked home over the long sandy track. We learned her name was Celine and that she was a surgeon specialising in cancer at a public hospital. She was only four years older than me, yet the world she inhabited could not have been more different from mine. She spent most days indoors, operating with the latest technology to save people's lives. She was smart and direct. She had so much energy that when she was talking she seemed to be almost bouncing in the air, as if she was constantly jerked by a small electric charge. I had the impression that she saw life as a string of obstacles which could be very easily tackled so long as you were strong-minded.

'As a medic, what are your thoughts, your concerns about the future?' asked Peter, who never missed a chance to learn something new.

'A pandemic,' she said without pausing to think. 'It's not if but when it will happen. A fatal virus or bacteria can travel all over the world in air-conditioned planes in a matter of days. There's an increasing number of antibiotic-resistant diseases, too. People think we are progressing because we have a higher life-expectancy, but human immune systems have never been weaker than they are today.'

I told her about our 'prepping for the apocalypse' and our backup hut, and she listened with interest. 'What will you do when a pandemic strikes?' I asked.

'Me? I'll go down with the ship,' she replied. 'I'm a city girl, not a trained survivor.'

'You should come to us!' I laughed. 'Your medical skills might save our lives, and we might save yours.'

While we were showing her our vegetable garden, William and Wanda turned up with their four chickens.

'These are our weka,' I said proudly. 'They discovered we were a good source of food, and Wanda has hatched Westie, Wimpie, Wicky and Woolly.' I laughed.

'Are these wild?' Celine asked.

'Oh yes,' said Peter. 'They live somewhere in the forest. A lot of native birds are quite tame, because they didn't evolve with ground predators. Weka are not really afraid of people, but they always look anxiously at the sky if an aeroplane flies over. They're used to airborne predators.'

After some camp-oven bread and possum stew, Celine and I carried the kayak to the river. I took the front, and Celine held the back.

'So, what is it like to be a French surgeon in New Zealand?' I asked.

She didn't respond for a few seconds, and I almost thought that she hadn't heard my question at all. Then she said, 'I've worked in several different hospitals and found that my level of happiness is directly related to the general atmosphere of my unit. When other doctors and nurses are supportive and responsible, my life is good. If there is friction or conflict, my life becomes quickly unbalanced and stressful.'

We walked in silence for a moment.

'Don't you miss a hot shower, a new set of clothes, a good restaurant, or a bit of culture?' she asked.

'Um, no.' I looked behind me to meet her eyes and I smiled. 'I know that, in exchange for comfort or pleasure, I get to live in this.' I pointed at the mountains in the distance, and the waving raupō reeds on the side of the track. Their cigar-like heads stood firmly on their two-metre-long stalks.

'Nature's beauty,' she said. 'One thing you can't buy.'

When we arrived at the bridge, I lowered the kayak into the flowing river. The water was so clear that the stones on the bottom looked just as bright as the pebbles at the edge.

'Do you have a postal address?' she asked. 'I've got a book on survival in the wilderness that I don't need.' She paused. 'Well, I might need it, but I don't have time to study it, so I'll send it to you instead.'

I gave her Terry and Rachel's address, and she tapped it into her phone. She scribbled hers on the bottom part of an old receipt, before stepping into the kayak. When she was sitting comfortably on the water, she said with a smile, 'I certainly admire your free life!'

I laughed. 'Don't forget to visit nature. It heals the mind.'

When she had disappeared, I turned over the receipt. I saw she had bought a piece of organic cheese and a bottle of wine and paid $87 for them. We truly lived in different worlds.

One afternoon at the end of the long summer, I walked to Elisabeth's homestead. I climbed over the fallen tree, stopped by the last berries of the season and calmly made my way to her house.

When I entered the mossy gate, there was a peculiar silence. A rabbit hopped over the lawn. The squeaking poles and wires made a grave and persistent sound in the still air. No smoke came out of the chimney and Elisabeth was not in her chair on the verandah.

'Elisabeth?' I tried to open the old wooden door, but it was locked. Through the window I saw her embroidery on the table. My eyes fell on the wooden-handled hammer and tin of nails that I had left on the verandah on my previous visit, when I had repaired a hole I had spotted in the roof. Elisabeth had found a bit of iron for me to seal it with, and we had laughed when she had insisted on holding the rickety old ladder, made by her grandfather from native timber, while I had hammered at the roof.

There was clearly no one home, and when I returned again two days later the house was still empty. Elisabeth's life in the wilderness seemed to have come to an abrupt end. Whatever had happened, she had not had time to tell me that she had to leave. The piles of papers, blankets and clothes remained on the lawn. She had never managed to bring order to her family belongings; everything would have blown away in the first autumn storm. I put it all in wooden trunks riddled with little borer holes, next to the long scythes in the shed. I returned to the verandah to sit one last time in the warm sun. So many feet walking over the wood had created a smooth dent. I noticed the window wasn't locked, so used the hammer to nail it closed to keep out burglars and clever possums.

I felt very sad that Elisabeth was gone. We had enjoyed each other's company, and I had great admiration for her courage to live in this place, in such a primitive manner, at her age. I looked at the withered grass and at the ocean in the distance. Dark clouds were gathering in the north, and the smell of rain was in the air.

Eventually, I stood up and walked to the gate. A little breeze lifted the first yellow oak leaf out of the tree. It slowly drifted down into the long grass, where the first acorns had already fallen. The leaf was beautiful—surprisingly colourful. It was the first of many that would, yet again, cover the earth. I closed the gate behind me. The past had passed on, to make space for a new beginning.

After many weeks of shifting logs and rocks to divert the river from the driveway, we were finally able to drive our car to the end of the road, where some bach owners had organised a barge to pick up stranded vehicles. We sailed past empty coves and inlets, and I was once more astounded by all this beauty. Clouds hung in the mountaintops, and the dense forest in the distance seemed wild and impenetrable.

Once we drove off the barge, we went to town to see Terry and Rachel. While Peter was helping Terry outside and Rachel was preparing some salad and salmon for dinner, I found Elisabeth's brother in the phone book. He told me that Elisabeth's family and her doctor had declared her unfit to live alone in an isolated, broken-down homestead without a road to bring in supplies and care so they had sent a helicopter to pick her up. Her brother assured me that she was in a safe place in town.

I imagined Elisabeth would have stepped into that helicopter without resistance. She wouldn't have known that she might not come back. She would never have had the courage to tell the doctor about how the sea view from the verandah, baking muffins in the coal range, her wild birds and Midnight had all made her so happy.

Rachel interrupted my chain of thoughts. 'Oh! Before I forget, Miriam,' she said, 'we received some mail for you.' She handed me a package. Inside was an orange book, with a note.

Here's the book on survival I promised you. I hope it will be of interest and benefit to you. I look forward to a reunion. I will come to visit you—wherever you are—if you can let me know your whereabouts.

Bisous, Celine

When I opened my email inbox, I found a message from Daniel. He had moved with his wife and children to town and his wooden cottage on the West Coast was going to be empty for a year. If we were interested, he wrote, we could stay in it for free.

'Have you got many emails?' Rachel asked, flicking through the weekend edition of the newspaper.

'Well . . . we might be moving to the West Coast,' I replied.

She looked surprised. 'Oh. Whereabouts?'

'I'm not sure, but I have a little map somewhere.' I laughed with the excitement of moving on, of exploring a new place and giving the hut back to the elements, just as Elisabeth had done with her homestead.

Rachel looked bemused. 'It's incredible,' she said, 'the way you two move through the country, seemingly without effort!'

'Yes, maybe it is,' I said, smiling. 'Well, we only go through open doors.'

— CHAPTER 7 —

THE WEST COAST

BEWARE OF CHILDREN said the rusty iron sign. It showed a picture of
a child holding a knife in its hand. We had turned off the coast road
into an overgrown driveway amid mānuka bushes, and after a few
kilometres we saw a shed where a vehicle was parked. There was
no sign of a house, so we hesitantly followed a narrow walking path
down into a thicket. After a couple of hundred metres, we came out
in a clearing with a breathtaking view of the ocean. We were very
high above the sea and it felt as if we could see the end of the world.

In front of us was a small cottage with dark red windowsills made
from recycled timber.

Daniel had heard us coming. 'Hey, you made it!' he called. 'How're
you doing?' He jumped off the verandah rather than taking the steps.
He wore the same black woollen shearer's shirt that he had in the
Mōkihinui Valley, but he had grown a short beard since then, which
looked surprisingly dark compared to his curly blond hair. He hugged
us quickly, then turned to show us his home, which he had built with
his own hands. Every piece of wood and iron, he had carried down in
a wheelbarrow. Inside the octagonal cottage, light shone in through
the many windows. In a corner stood a blue sofa and a coffee table—it
looked as if Daniel had cut a plank with a handsaw from a big tree
to make this table. The atmosphere created by the simple furniture,

beautiful wooden cabinets above the sink and shining planks on the floor made me feel immediately at home.

Behind the cottage was a big bathtub; we could have hot baths outside while it was storming and raining, because the firebox heated the water cylinder. Next to the tub was a giant plant with dark leaves. It caught Peter's eye, and he felt its thick leaves. 'This is a very healthy Chatham Island forget-me-not, Miriam,' he said in a grave voice.

I looked at him and waited for an explanation.

'It means never forget the rain.'

We looked at the sea. A band of dark clouds was approaching fast from the west.

Buttercups had conquered the vegetable garden, which was waiting to be dug over again. Twelve cackling hens and a rooster welcomed us eagerly. One large hen, 'Old Chook', had bright orange feathers and scuttled towards Peter. When he carefully picked her up, she turned to look at him with her old orange eyes. Her big strong legs were sticking out stiffly between his fingers.

'The water supply comes from the carport,' said Daniel, as we were walking down the track. 'The roof collects the rain in a big tank, which is piped to the kitchen.'

'Has that tank ever been empty?' asked Peter.

'Never.' Daniel smiled. 'This is the land of rain.'

We continued our tour and arrived at a small shack 50 metres in front of the house.

'And this is the toilet. I'm afraid it's a bit primitive.'

The structure had no door, and if rain came from the west you'd get wet. Underneath the wooden seat was a big black bucket.

'If I were you, I'd empty that bucket often.'

'Um, whereabouts should we empty it?' I envisioned dragging a sloshing shit-bucket behind me through muddy humps and hollows.

'Give it to something that will benefit from it.' Daniel shrugged. 'Like a tree.' He pointed out some good shit-dumping places while we walked back to the house.

'Well, that's all there is to know. I guess I'd better keep going,' he said, as the first drops of rain fell from the dark clouds above.

'When will it stop raining?' I asked.

'These are only a few winter showers.' He laughed. 'The real monsoon starts in September. It usually dries out in November, but sometimes it doesn't.' Even when he talked, it seemed that Daniel was smiling, as the corners of his mouth were always turned up.

We walked back to his car with him, and Peter asked, 'Daniel, how come you're letting us live here? You could rent it out, couldn't you?'

Daniel stood still. 'Well, I can't live on the wild side myself any more. I used to think that I could live in the wilderness with kids, but that turned out to be much more difficult than I expected. It takes the girls two hours to get to school and back every day, and they miss seeing their friends. Everything has just become a hassle. At the moment, I'm caught in a web of responsibility and need to provide an income.' He looked at us. 'If you're living here, I can live through you guys. In a sense.'

After he left, we carted our belongings in a wheelbarrow down to our new cottage, then sat on a bench on the verandah. There was no fence or marker, but in front of Daniel's land a forest reserve began. The trackless wilderness stretched a couple of hundred metres down a steep slope to the sea. The view over the ocean gave an amazing sense of space.

It felt as if we were alone in the whole world. We gazed in wonder at the beautiful sunset. The last of the light shone through a dark, eye-shaped cloud. Bright orange radiated from its centre. As the sun disappeared below the horizon, red, pink and even green spread throughout the sky. Streaks of vivid indigo reflected on the ocean. The light show increased in brightness above the turquoise water, until it slowly faded. The day was over.

We felt like the children of a sky god while we stayed in Daniel's wooden cottage overlooking the sea. The heavens brought rain and sun, thunder and light, wind and warmth. We were living with the weather and its moving beauty, with the delight and wonder of the sunsets. Behind us was the rugged, untouched Paparoa Range with its towering peaks and spikes, rocks and ravines. It was a land of moss and rain, ferns and caves, palms and beauty. The West Coast was the living soul of the wilderness.

After a week Daniel came back to pick up the last of his belongings. Some 50 metres from the cottage, he had a built a target against a bank. It looked like a *Muppet Show* theatre with empty wine bottles. When he took out his gun, I blocked my ears. 'Can you hit those bottles from here?' I asked.

'Most of the time.' He lifted his gun and fired. The sound of broken glass falling backwards into the bin behind was strangely satisfying. 'Recycling,' he said, reloading his gun. He looked like a cowboy from the Wild West with his worn blue jeans and leather belt, and the way he aimed at the bottles. 'Come have a look at the rest of my artillery.' He grinned as he unlocked an iron door that was set into a massive cement box behind the cottage. The gun safe was filled with antique pistols, shotguns, revolvers and rifles.

'Sure, the bow and arrow go back the furthest,' he said. 'But the simple mechanism of a gun has been around for centuries too.' He had sensed my resistance towards using guns, and my idealistic preference for hunting the original way. 'These old ones have a character of their own,' he said. 'Some of them have been used in wars, others for hunting. They have seen magnificent places, done extraordinary things. If you hold one, you can feel its character. Here, try it.'

He handed me a pistol with flowers and other elegant patterns carved into its side. It was heavier than it looked, but I didn't feel any history in it.

'God, yeah.' I smiled and handed it back to Daniel.

'Now, you should use this rifle while you're here.' He pointed to a very light, slim model, the wood and metal beautifully carved. 'This one is a hundred-year-old Winchester. It has travelled across the world, and been handled by many adventurous young men—and perhaps even some women,' he added with a smile. 'This rifle is almost as basic as a bow. It doesn't even have a scope, so nothing can break or go wrong.'

I held it hesitantly.

'With a bow, you're wounding animals,' Daniel went on. 'With a gun, you'll kill them with the first hit, which is much more humane. Plus, you won't have to buy expensive arrows any more.'

He handed me a box of bullets and taught me how to shoot the bottles at the *Muppet Show* target theatre. Although I had obtained a firearms licence two years earlier, with the intention of learning how to shoot, I had very little experience with firing. In fact, I felt anxious just looking at firearms. I disliked the noise, and after hearing about many hunting accidents I didn't trust any gun or its owner. As a kid, I used to play soccer with the boys in the village, but I had never joined in their pistol games. Like the adults around me, I thought that guns were the symbol of evil.

Every time Daniel visited us in the cottage, he taught me more about firearms. He was so enthusiastic that I cautiously accepted his rifle. I was grateful to have a teacher; without him, I would never have learned how to hunt with a gun. He taught me how to shoot at a target; how to breathe and relax the body before pulling the trigger. He explained the different methods of cleaning the barrel and chamber. He also taught me how to sharpen a hunting knife by holding it loosely and listening to the swishing sound on the stone. If the sound altered, the angle had changed and the knife would not be so sharp. For Daniel, everything was an art form, and I slowly began to appreciate his view of the world.

I started hunting in the green forest in the foothills of the mountains. I walked up the rivers and ventured into side streams where the water had carved tunnels through the mudstone. I roamed the stunningly wild places, and discovered hidden limestone caves and magnificent cliffs in which mosses and small shrubs had made a home in the cracks.

One dangerous aspect particular to this wilderness area were natural tomos—limestone holes in the ground. A tomo looked like a deep well, and when branches and vegetation covered the surface you could be unlucky and fall 10, 20, even 30 metres into the dark hole and die screaming. I knew both animals and the occasional hunter had suffered such a fate in the past.

One day I followed a high limestone cliff into the deep forest. When

I noticed a narrow ledge, I climbed up and came out on an overhang 30 metres above the ground. The platform was quite big and had a fantastic view over the forested gully. I dragged big stones into this cave to make a table and chair, and often sat there to listen. The white walls behind me worked like a big ear: if any goat called in the distance, I could easily hear it. I learned to effectively imitate the bleating, and that sometimes attracted billy goats to my cave.

Over the weeks and months, I got to know my way around every stream, gully, cliff and tomo. It felt very different to hunt with a rifle. As long as I held the gun in my hands, I felt a strange sense of power, which abolished all kinds of fear. I wasn't afraid of falling into a tomo, getting lost, wet or cold, or meeting a person with bad intentions. It gave a false sense of security, and I could see how this sense of power could be addictive. I could understand how a country where everyone owned a pistol could become a nation with an illusion of confidence.

The act of killing was also different with a rifle. I was separated from the animal by the machine; it felt as if I was merely an observer, while Mr Winchester did the job. But the effectiveness of a bullet was undeniable. It killed a goat instantly, and it provided a lot of meat. Most times I went hunting, I came back with a goat.

To keep the meat fresh, I had made a big cylinder with chicken wire that we hung from a beam in the shade behind our cottage. I had sewed an old lace curtain round its frame to stop the flies from getting to it, through which the wind could blow so that it functioned successfully as a fridge.

We lead a satisfyingly self-sufficient life: as well as the meat that I hunted, we had chickens to give us eggs, and the garden gave us greens. We didn't spend much money to live, but one day I decided to try to earn some.

I stood forlorn on the silent coastal road. Without a watch, I had no idea what the time was, but it must have been very early, for there were no vehicles. Dark clouds were coming from the sea and soon it started to drizzle. I was miserable and wet. Who would want a wet hitchhiker in their car? After what seemed a long time, I finally heard the faint sound of an engine, and some minutes later a campervan came over the hill. It stopped, a blond man opened the door and said, '*Nederlands?*'

I burst out laughing. It was amazing that this Dutchman could see just from my face that I was born in the same part of the world as he was from. He and his wife were touring the country and were happy to give me a lift into town. It was nice to be able to speak my mother tongue again. They asked me why I had immigrated to New Zealand to live in the wild. I answered that the beauty of the wilderness—which, I thought, was really the energy of the uncontrolled—gave me a sense of vitality that I had not experienced in Holland. After a lot of friendly chatter, they dropped me off at the supermarket.

I hesitantly walked inside and bought a scone. When the girl at the checkout gave me my receipt, I asked, 'Excuse me, but can I see your manager?'

She looked terrified—so much so, in fact, that her wide-eyed expression froze in icy silence. It had an odd effect on me: I too was muted. Fortunately, the girl next to her, who was putting my scone into a plastic bag, looked with surprise at her colleague then said to me, 'Yes, the manager is upstairs.'

'Thank you. I just wanted to ask if I am allowed to busk here.' I lifted my guitar in the air.

The manager was friendly enough, and said I could sing at the entrance to the supermarket. I had my folk songs in a folder, a tambourine round my ankle and a clicking instrument under my foot. I had grown up in a house of music and theatre, and my sister Hanna was a professional singer—she used to encourage me to sing while she played the piano, so the idea of performing in public wasn't so alien to me, but I still felt nervous. I began my first song in a high quavering voice, but nobody took any notice. They walked past me as if I did not exist.

It took some courage to continue, but I reminded myself that I should not be afraid since I wasn't in any danger. I wasn't going to fall off a mountain, drown in a river or freeze in the snow. I was very safe. All I was going to do was sing some harmless songs.

It was only after my third song that my voice warmed up and I dared to look up from my folder. The people in this small West Coast town seemed somewhat isolated. I decided to make an effort to look every passer-by in the eyes, so as to acknowledge his or her existence. Each time I succeeded, the person smiled back. After an hour, people became very friendly and I received many compliments—a few people even mentioned Joan Baez or Judy Collins. Some stood and listened, and one woman asked whether I was available to sing at a wedding. One kind old man pushing a bicycle turned up from the other side of the car park and pointed at the words on my guitar. 'What does that mean, freedom is for free?'

'Well,' I said cheerfully, 'freedom is a gift. It's free! A lot of people work for years to save their money for later, but by the time they have enough to do something different they don't have the courage for it. Then, later is too late. You don't have to be a millionaire to find another way of living, is what I mean.'

The old man smiled and nodded. 'I worked all my life. As soon as I retired, I wished I had stopped working earlier.' He looked at the distant mountains for a while. 'But I didn't have a choice. I had four kids to feed, bills to pay, a mortgage to work off. The whole nine yards.'

I nodded sympathetically. 'What kind of job did you have?'

'Teaching. Here at the boys' college.' He pointed to his left without looking, then fished a five-dollar note from his pocket and carefully placed it underneath some coins in my guitar case. 'Good on you, my dear. You've got a nice, clear voice. I could hear you singing from the other side of the car park.' He waved goodbye and walked away with his bicycle.

With all the encouragement, I started to smile and enjoy myself. I discovered that this was a very good way to pay for groceries. I sang for six or seven hours, then, at the end of the day, I did my shopping and hitchhiked back to the cottage.

'So, how much money did you make?' asked Peter, when I returned with a big smile.

'I made a mince!' I held up a big bag of coins.

Peter laughed. 'You mean a mint.'

'Oh yes, a mint.' I grinned. 'I made enough to live on for the rest of the month.'

'I know how you make your fortune.' Peter picked up a $20 note. 'They're paying for ten seconds of happiness!'

'Well, that's a sufficient contribution to society, don't you think?' I smiled.

Daniel had given me an old Swanndri jacket. The dark green wool was so thick that it protected me from even the worst prickles, and it was so warm that I would never die of hypothermia if I had to spend a night out in the forest. It was so heavy that I would never forget that I was wearing the New Zealand symbol of wilderness. Unfortunately, it was also partially moth-eaten and it took me a week to patch up all the holes. At the same time, I sewed in pockets with zips for bullets, string and a first-aid kit.

Daniel had left some old books about deer hunters who set off by themselves with a billy, a bag of salt and a gun slung over their shoulder to roam the mountains for long periods of time. They slept in their Swanndris and ate what they shot; they had 'gone bush'. This idea delighted me no end, so when the midwinter sun broke through I proudly declared that I, too, was going bush.

I told Daniel, who was visiting, that I was going on a deer-hunting trip by myself for a week.

'Really?' He smiled, and I was pleased to see he looked impressed. 'Let me give you a decent gun for the occasion.' He unlocked his treasure chamber, and passed me a big hunting rifle. 'Here, take this one. It's my favourite,' he said.

The next day the sky was clear and the air crisp. I set off proudly in my new Swanndri, with my gun in hand, my knife on my belt, and a tent, sleeping bag, spices and a billy. I thought I looked exactly like the men in Daniel's books (aside from the obvious fact that I'm not a man, of course). The only food I took was a bit of bread for the first day; once that was finished, I would eat venison or, failing that, goat meat. Deer are alert, sharp, very clever and difficult to find—and I really knew nothing about them. But I would learn, I told myself, with my usual optimism.

I walked through a beautiful canyon. Colossal white limestone walls towered 250 metres up on either side of the clear, flowing water. In some places, ferns and mosses clung to the cliffs, but mostly they were so steep that nothing could grow. Trickles of water had left artful black and grey lines down the limestone. I carefully checked the water level when I forded the river, as I knew that if it rained the water would rise and I could get trapped in the upper valley.

After walking for many hours, I found the gorge gave way to forested mountains. I spotted an animal track going up into the trees. At the top of the slope was a smooth, grassy flat beneath two big trees. It was obviously a resting place for deer, as I could see their droppings. It was also an excellent spot to camp, so I pitched my tent, but I didn't make a fire, as deer can smell smoke from miles away.

In the evening I lay on my stomach beneath the trees, with the gun under my chin. While the birds sang, I watched the grazing spots in the broad river valley below me. Eventually the light faded and darkness fell. There was not a sound to be heard, until the first owl began to call. By five or maybe six o'clock, it was already pitch black, and I suddenly became aware of the cold. I crawled into my sleeping bag in my tent, and watched the dark shadows outside for a while. Finally, I zipped the tent closed and tried to sleep.

I dozed, my mind caught up in irrelevant thoughts of things a world away, when a very large animal suddenly crashed into one of the tent's guy ropes. I got such a shock! My heart boomed in my throat until I realised it must have been—obviously—a deer. *I shouldn't be so terrified*, I thought, listening to the deer crash off through the forest. I was, after all, supposed to hunt this deer with the gun that lay idle at the tent entrance.

I woke up well before dawn and crawled outside into the cold morning. Wrapped in many warm layers, I once again took up my position beneath the tree. The grass on the riverbed below was white with frost.

The lilting and joyful trills of the birds rang through the crisp early morning air. A bellbird sat on a branch near me, hopping about and straining its little body to produce notes. In between its husky, yearning hums, I could hear its wonderful clicking, rasping percussion. *Birds are the earth's first musicians*, I thought. All about me, high-pitched tunes lifted into the air like a fountain and were then replaced by a tapping similar to water dripping on rocks. As the day broke, the music grew fainter and the river sounded louder.

I lay there silently, watching the grass slowly turn green again in the warm sun. Then I stood up and collected wood to light a fire. I picked the tips off a mānuka sapling, and used the tiny leaves to make tea, which is said to contain vitamin C. The smoke drifted slowly up the valley and I knew that no deer would come close again. I actually felt quite relieved not to have seen a deer: they were such beautiful big animals, it seemed ridiculous to shoot one dead. I decided I would rather shoot a goat—though also very beautiful, they were more abundant in this area, and easier to find, shoot, transport and keep.

After toasting the last of my bread, I walked into the forest with my gun. There was no marked trail of any kind and I meandered silently between the trees. I came across many grassy flats, rocky chasms and ancient trees. I sat for hours on spurs, looking out over the riverbed and listening intently for any sound of bleating goats. Everything was at peace on that clear midwinter day. I felt quite comfortable alone in the forest, and I thought of how uneasy I had been walking off into the mountains by myself during our first winter in the wilderness. I realised that I had overcome my fear of being alone. The will to be free of fear had been stronger than the fear itself.

When I stopped for a rest around midday, I wrote Sofie a letter.

Dear Sofie,

It is the middle of winter here, but the trees are evergreen and the days are as warm as a Dutch summer. It is only during the long, frosty nights that I am reminded that it is winter.

I am the only person in this valley, but I have recently discovered that I am actually never really alone. Wherever I go, I have a very cheerful little

companion: Thought! It chatters tirelessly about an incredible range of
topics. Sometimes I get sick of listening to old memories, and would prefer to
have some peace and quiet—especially when I'm trying to get to sleep—but
Thought keeps talking away like a radio. It is mostly quite optimistic, but
also repeatedly reminds me of all the things I have done and said wrong in the
past. Sometimes a second Thought will jump into existence to tell the first one
to shut up, and then the matter gets quite complicated. Am I the only person
with a chattering companion? I imagine you probably have a very similar
friend to mine . . .

   Love, Miriam

Late in the afternoon, I saw a goat and fired. The gun, which was
capable of shooting a moose, blasted my ears like a cannon. I could
hear nothing but a loud *peeeeeep*. For a moment it felt as if I had gone
blind, too. I couldn't hear where the goat had run, but when I walked
closer I saw that it had not gone anywhere: the billy goat lay quite dead.
When I dragged it back to my camp, I suddenly missed Peter. He was
always so overjoyed to see me arrive with a goat, and without him the
hunting felt a lot less rewarding.

   I held the big liver in my hand and wondered how to cut it into
pieces. Peter always brought some sort of chopping board, but I didn't
have one. I used my knife to remove the bark from a fallen log, and cut
the liver on the wood. It got dirty, but I fried it anyway. The taste was
strong and I didn't enjoy it much; I was dreaming of toast with peanut
butter—which I didn't have.

   I had kidneys for breakfast the next morning. They tasted slightly
better than the liver. At lunchtime I stared at the carcass in the tree.
Where were the tender eye fillets that I was supposed to eat first? I was
suddenly aware of my inability to even cut up the meat; Peter always did
all the butchering. Eventually I managed to roughly cut out the fillets.
I opened my jar containing the little bags of spices, but I had no idea
how much of each spice I should use. This, too, was Peter's department.

   In the evening I cooked the back steaks. They tasted all right, but
had the texture of rubber. What had I done wrong? As I sat silently

beside my fire, chewing the rubbery meat, I realised that the long-horned animal had been so old that the meat was terribly sinewy and almost inedible without being cooked for a week. But I was determined to eat the goat for another four days, because that's what I had come out here for.

The next day I wondered what those 'gone-bush' hunters actually did after they had shot themselves something to eat. Once the excitement of hunting and cooking was over, a great sense of boredom came over me and I reached for Celine's book on survival.

The boredom seemed to come and go. It helped to look at the fire, as it had a purifying effect. I thought about my great journey with Peter in the Himalayas the year that we met. We had spent two months walking over many mountain ranges. One day, I had stopped to rest on a big stone, while Peter kept climbing towards a higher pass. I looked down into a great valley: gigantic, barren ranges stretched in every direction, and the wind had shaped the rocks into magnificent pillars. It was there that I had understood that if I led a very simple life my mind would become clearer, and that would lead to a healthy, unpolluted body . . . and maybe even to a pure life, whatever that might mean. *Simplicity, clarity, purity.* This was a vision I had always kept with me, as it seemed the natural course of things in the world.

After four long days, the weather changed on the fifth morning. I could smell rain coming. The air was heavy and moist and smelled almost sweet. I walked back to the cottage with the meat in my pack. I didn't care that the goat had been geriatric and the meat was as tough as a bootlace; I simply felt proud that I had shot and eaten an animal. As I walked, it occurred to me that my trip could also be seen as a failure—after all, I hadn't even seen a deer on my deer-hunting trip. *One can bend any failure into a success, and any success into a failure*, I realised with a smile. *It's all a matter of perspective.*

The cold rain increased in the days after my return from the bush. It never seemed to stop. The sky was always grey. We could see bands of rain coming and going over the ocean. In between showers, we ran outside to feed the chickens, which were pecking around in the mud. It was horribly dreary, and we wondered why we had ever come to the wet West Coast. It started to feel like a redo of spring in Downie's Hut, but this time at least I had a distraction: Daniel had given me some boxes of professionally tanned possum skins and tails. I kept myself occupied for weeks cutting the fur pieces into little squares then sewing them into a big blanket. With a lot of effort, I flattened out the possum tails and sewed them together; they were so tough and thick that I broke numerous needles. I made one possum-tail mat for Peter—which used 200 tails and took two weeks—then I made another one for myself. The mats were a warm replacement for the yoga mats we had been sleeping on.

I also had my guitar. 'It's the love that counts, my sweet one. It's the love that counts, my lovely one . . .' I sang for Peter one night. He was lying on his possum-tail mat, with a book in his hands. 'Did you like my song?' I asked when I had finished.

'Yes, very nice.' He put his book down. 'But what *is* this love that you are singing about?' He smiled, and reached for a toothpick.

'It's my love for you!' I laughed.

'Me, or an image of me?' he asked. 'Love is a whole world of its own,' he went on. 'If you love somebody you have to do this, say that, act this way and look that way.' He moved his head from left to right as he spoke. 'It's linked with obligations, rituals and endless, meaningless words.'

I suddenly felt a knot in my stomach. I just wanted to sing sweet love songs. I wanted him to take me in his arms and be very happy, forever. 'Do you think that's what we have been doing?' I muttered.

'Yes. We talked about it last year. Your cocoon, in which you feel so safe, is what we all call love. But if you privilege safety and security, you'll end up with a meaningless routine,' he said. 'A bit like a prison.'

I stared out of the window. I didn't like where this conversation was going. The rain was streaming down. The mānuka bushes were moving about in the wind like a thick fur coat.

'I wonder if two people can live together without staleness?' Peter went on. 'Keep it alive, spontaneous and new?'

'Yes, but how?' I croaked. My voice sounded as if I was going to cry.

'Well, I don't know. Maybe by seeing what the ritual does? Right now it gives you a satisfactory but false sense of security, but after some years you'll hate the staleness, the fixed habits and the lifeless rituals. This is what—'

'How do you know?' I felt suddenly irritated at Peter speaking to me as if I was always the ignorant one.

'I've been through all this several times,' he said gently. 'I've been married before. After many years you think you know each other, and the curiosity, the inquiry stops. The relationship becomes "the known", which is the past, not the present.'

We grew quiet. I looked at his serious eyes.

'It's only you and me, here in the wilderness,' he said. 'All our eggs are in one basket. We have to be so careful.'

I simply nodded. I knew that if I tried to talk I would have cried.

That night as I lay in bed his words echoed in my head. What was this love and our relationship, really? Was I merely caught up in perpetuating a perfect image of it? Was I simply playing a role in a play full of endlessly repeated words and gestures? Was I tricking myself?

'Is this all a fantasy?' I asked Peter in the morning, while we ate our toast with butter and Marmite.

'What—our life?' he asked, chuckling.

'Yes, and our relationship. I guess any image is always false,' I said. 'An image—or an idea—is fixed, but reality is always changing.'

'Yeah.' Peter reached for his cup of tea. 'All the rules about how you ought to behave with one another in a relationship are arbitrary, really.'

'Spontaneous action is more truthful,' I said.

'Yes, if you can see the idea, the image, you can drop it. Just be affectionate when you feel like it. Say what you feel instead of forced rituals. If you see what I mean.' Peter cut another slice of bread. 'But this is not a mathematical equation with one correct solution. It's an ongoing thing, I think. Like a fire, you have to keep watching it all the time—not just sometimes.'

———

That afternoon, I sat on the wooden floor sewing a body-warmer from my pieces of possum fur. It was quite a puzzle to fit them all together. I looked out of the window. Peter had cleaned the windows just a few days ago, and already they were covered in salt again. Dark clouds were forming in the distance above the ocean: more rain was coming.

I heard a voice and, to my amazement, I saw Celine walking down the track to the cottage. I was very surprised, as I had not expected her—we had given her our address weeks ago, but hadn't heard back. I jumped up and ran to greet her. It was nice to see her. Celine explained that she had wanted to escape the city for a weekend and had decided—quite spontaneously—to visit us.

That night there was a storm—as usual. The cottage shook, the windows flexed and the rain drummed on the roof. Mānuka trees bashed the walls and pieces of iron were flapping about nearby. We had grown accustomed to these night-time noises, but the next morning Celine didn't look very well rested at all. I wondered whether she regretted her holiday destination and, in an attempt to make her wilderness experience worthwhile, I offered to take her hunting.

We waited for the rain to stop then set off into the forest. After ten minutes, it began to rain again. I apologised for the bad weather, but Celine assured me that, for her, any day outside the hospital was a good day. We marched on through the soggy forest. There were fern branches and mānuka bushes leaning over the narrow track, and within seconds we were soaked to the skin, but it was all part of the adventure. When we came across a patch of mud and clay, I showed Celine some hoof prints in the soil: a big goat had been past, and a very small goat had, too. In the rain, I explained, any mark washed away quickly, so these goats had probably been here just a few hours earlier. Next to the river was a small meadow, and I pointed out how the short grass had been munched on. When we walked past a big cliff, we stopped and found goat droppings beneath the white walls, and I explained that goats like to sleep in dry places.

Then I smelled a goat. I pointed at my nose, and looked at Celine. She gestured, with a slightly panicked expression, that she couldn't smell anything. I nodded swiftly and tiptoed into the dense vegetation.

I beckoned to her to follow me into the thicket, and she did so hesitantly.

'It is quite interesting,' Celine whispered. 'Normally I'm in charge. I know where I am and where to go. But now I have to trust you. I hope you know what you're doing, because I've got absolutely no idea!'

'We haven't gone far,' I assured her. 'The way out is easy.' I pointed to my right.

After I had concluded that the goat had long gone, we returned to the track and walked for some time, then Celine suddenly asked, 'What are we looking for?'

'A goat!' I almost burst out laughing.

'Yes, but I mean what colour? White, like they have in Switzerland?'

'Oh, no. Here the wild goats are mostly black and white, and sometimes brown.'

As we carried on, I placed my feet carefully and walked silently, avoiding branches and stepping on big stones. I saw Celine doing the same thing.

We kept walking. Nothing happened.

Then, quite suddenly, we spotted a big goat standing beneath a nīkau palm. I positioned myself quickly and fired. It ran away wounded, and I chased after it. When I reached the goat, it had collapsed between two big ferns. Their fronds hung over it like a parasol. A few moments later, Celine joined me. She looked shocked. I remembered my first kill; I didn't want this to be a nightmare for her. I said we would do things slowly and explained the gutting and skinning process. Although she looked a little uncertain, she said that she wanted to try butchering the goat.

As I hung my Swanndri in a tree, I said that we might get dirty. 'It's best to take off as much as possible. It's much easier to wash your body than bloodstained clothes,' I said. 'Afterwards we will just wash in the river over there.'

Celine looked to where I was pointing; in the dense forest it was easy to miss the quiet river. Then she took off her raincoat and her T-shirt, and stood there in just a bra and shorts. She had taken my advice quite literally.

'OK, let's hang it up,' I said.

'Hang it up?' Celine asked. To her, this must have all been quite strange.

I pointed to a solid branch in a black beech tree nearby, and she helped me to drag the goat over to it. We tied it into the tree with a rope.

'I have to cut with this?' Celine gasped when I handed her my hunter's knife. 'I usually use scissors and an electric scalpel to operate. I might puncture the intestines with this thing!'

We both stared at the big knife. It suddenly seemed huge in her small, fine hands.

I showed her how to use one hand to protect the bowels. I said that we wanted to separate the heart, liver and kidneys, which we would eat for dinner. She started off hesitantly, but soon warmed up to the job.

'Aha! Interesting. Here's the diaphragm, which separates the abdominal and thoracic cavities,' she murmured as she worked. 'It's all slightly different from humans. The blood smells different from our blood, don't you think?'

I replied that I wasn't too familiar with human blood.

'This space here,' she went on, 'between the lungs is the mediastinum, and here is the trachea and aorta. This here is the inferior vena cava. Can I have the hatchet?' Without looking up from the goat, she stretched her hand out in my direction. At first I thought it was peculiar that she should call out all these medical names, but then it occurred to me that naming the body parts gave her a sense of normality. It was her way of dealing with this otherwise totally abnormal situation.

'Without retractors I don't have a good view of what I am doing,' she said. 'Where is the oesophagus? Ah . . . can I have the knife again?'

She was so focused, she appeared to have forgotten that she was standing in a mossy, dripping forest, operating on a dead goat.

'It sort of feels wrong to have blood on my hands,' she said suddenly. 'Normally I have two pairs of sterile gloves *and* a reinforced gown on. Doing this barehanded and in my bra is somewhat odd.'

When she was finished, we lowered the butchered parts into my pack. The rain had eased by now, and the sun was shining through the trees. We walked to the river and washed. I used sand to scrub off all the dark red stains, and Celine hesitantly followed my example. I found some dry branches below an overhanging rock and, with a bit of dry newspaper that I had brought, I managed to light a fire and made mānuka-leaf tea. While we toasted our camp-oven bread, I asked Celine how it felt to be away from computers and cell phones for a weekend.

'Ah, it's very peaceful,' she admitted. 'But I'll have a mountain of emails and messages on Monday morning, and Thomas might wonder why I haven't texted him back yet.'

Thomas was an Irishman she had been going out with for a few months, but she wasn't too sure about him. Something was missing, she said. 'He's intelligent and bright and reasonably handsome, but I get the impression that he's quite content to just settle for "average". His dreams are small and dreary to me. I'm afraid I'll get bored with his stable life.' She smiled and pulled some moss from a branch to clean the mud off her boots. 'As my father always says, why not aim for the best?'

We talked about relationships, and I described how it seems that often we'll have an idea about how a relationship should be, while the reality can be quite different—basically, what Peter had been trying to explain to me just the day before.

'Doesn't it bother you that Peter always explains things to you?' Celine asked. 'As if you're the student and he's the teacher?'

'Yes, sometimes. Yesterday I felt a little annoyed,' I said. 'But, actually, I think two people in a relationship will always have different qualities. I'm stronger and fitter; Peter cannot compete with me physically. He is twice my age and has a lot of knowledge and experience that I cannot possibly have, so I am destined to learn from him.'

'True,' she said. 'Even without an age difference, two people will always be different.'

When Celine and I returned to the cottage, we sat on the possum mats and recounted—in great detail—our hunting story, while Peter cooked the goat. As we ate our curry, I noted that, apart from the spices and rice, we had grown and hunted the whole meal.

'It tastes very wholesome,' Celine said. 'Not a bit like a watery chicken from the supermarket!' She laughed. 'Hey, on the way up here, I saw some coastal land for sale. Some of it was quite reasonably priced,' she said. 'I was considering buying some land for myself, perhaps for a holiday house. Do you ever think of buying your own land?'

'We did think about it,' I said. 'But, after seeing this rain, I'm not sure I want to live on the West Coast for the rest of my life.'

'Maybe if we see a place for the right price, we might consider it,' said Peter.

'Wouldn't you like to have children?' asked Celine. 'This seems such a good place for them. They would grow up in nature, they could be home-schooled . . .'

I told her about Daniel, who'd had exactly the same ideas for this place and how different it had been in reality for him.

'I don't think I want to have children,' said Peter. 'I might be too old for it.'

'And you, Miriam?' Celine asked.

'I certainly wouldn't want to have them right now. Also, if Peter doesn't want them, it would be rather difficult, wouldn't it?'

'You could find another partner,' said Peter, with his mouth full of food.

'I'd rather have you than children.' I laughed. 'Last year, we bumped into two of Peter's old school friends. They hadn't seen each other since they were fifteen. One of them asked whether Peter had children, and I said, "No! He's got me!"'

Celine laughed. 'Did they find that funny?'

'Sort of, but they weren't used to Dutch directness,' said Peter.

'It was just a joke.' I grinned. 'Our age difference is not some sort of a taboo that no one is allowed to mention.'

When Celine was about to leave the next morning, we stood and watched the sea. Beams of sunlight poked through holes in the clouds and sparkled on the surface of the ocean.

'You must have so many beautiful photos,' said Celine, as she took pictures of the cottage and the ocean.

'Oh, no, we don't have a camera,' I said. 'That requires batteries, memory cards, chargers and all kinds of equipment.'

'Also, when we look at an old picture,' said Peter, 'we miss the beauty we are living in right now!'

'I'm going to set this as my computer's desktop background.' Celine showed me a picture she had taken of the view from the cottage. 'So we'll have the same view!' She laughed, and stashed the camera in her blue parka.

We hugged goodbye, and she walked back to her car, carrying a leg of goat in each hand.

It rained for two solid months, and dried out only in November. In the springtime, the days grew longer and the sun warmer. One quiet evening, we sat outside on the verandah playing chess. While the last light was still visible in the west, the first stars had already begun to appear in the east. A slight breeze carried the sound of breaking waves up to us. Then, quite unexpectedly, we heard a strange tune: it sounded like howling dogs.

'What's that?' I asked, astonished.

'I think we are hearing seals on the rocks down below,' said Peter.

The next morning, we decided to venture 200 metres down the cliff to visit our neighbours. The wind was strong and gusty when we set off, but when we entered the dense subtropical rainforest it felt as if we had walked into a different world. The wind could not penetrate the vegetation and it was quiet and still. Enormous trees grew between boulders the size of houses. The smooth trunks of the nīkau palms, with their perfect rings, looked like pieces of art.

We zigzagged down a treacherously steep slope covered with slippery vines, until we were surrounded by kiekie, a woody climber with slender stems, that formed an impenetrable lattice. Sometimes we could slide underneath the kiekie, but at other times it was so thick that we could only walk on top of it. Our progress was extremely slow, but the thundering roar of the sea grew ever louder as we approached the coast.

At last, we found ourselves on top of a small cliff in a cold mist of salt and spray, looking out over the booming waves below us. The smell of salt and seaweed was on the wind. Rugged, spiky rocks stuck out of the sea, and when big waves crashed on to these black peaks a massive 15-metre-high fountain exploded upwards. The tops of the waves were blown sideways by the gusts of wind. It was a truly awesome sight.

After some nervous discussion, Peter lowered himself down the vertical rock face, holding on to a thin vine. When I saw that the plant held his weight, I hesitantly followed him. At the bottom of the cliff, we found ourselves in a thick mass of kiekie vines, with a tunnel into the vegetation. There was an almost nauseating smell of rotten fish. I crept into the tunnel ahead of Peter.

'Hey, this is a seal house!' I shouted to Peter, over the noise of the breaking waves, as I crawled over the packed-clay floor.

'We'd better hope we don't run into a bull seal!' he shouted from behind me.

I hadn't thought of that! In a panic, I tried to stand up and run, but I hit my head against the kiekie stalks above me. I had no choice but to continue creeping forward on my hands and knees through the labyrinth of stinky seal tunnels. I turned into a side tunnel, pretending to have gone the wrong way so that Peter would pass me. It was better to let him go first and deal with a bull seal, I thought, feeling cowardly.

'Find a stick to defend yourself with,' Peter yelled.

I spotted a strong piece of driftwood, and felt slightly better with it in my hand. Peter also had a stick, and he banged it on the ground to warn any nearby seals that we were there. I did the same. We sounded like big sea lions banging their giant tusks on stones. 'We're sea lions!' I shouted.

We escaped the labyrinth—happily in one piece. All the seals were fishing in the raging waves or sunbathing on the rocks. It was a sunny day, but the ocean was roaring in the wind as if we were in the middle of a violent storm. Enormous waves crashed ceaselessly on the rocks, the wind blew the tops off the breakers, and seagulls circled the sky with long cries and loud shrieks. It was almost frighteningly wild.

Thick foam was thrown high up in the air, and we sat in a salty mist that extended for as far as we could see.

The seashore consisted of massive boulders backed up by cliffs. Lush, vibrant vegetation grew above the rock walls. It was clear that nobody visited this part of the coast; this place was for the wild seals only. Big bull seals three times the size of the females were fishing in the ocean and occasionally coming back to the shore. Small juveniles were playing in pools between the big stones. Diving, turning and whirling, the seals moved so gracefully in the water; once they were on land, though, they lumbered awkwardly over the boulders. Amidst the wild waves and the gale-force wind, they looked perfectly calm and tranquil sunbathing and swimming.

We were looking at a million-year-old scene. What we saw now was the way this place had been for time immemorial. It was order within chaos, in which the gentle resided in a shell of resilience.

Peter climbed down from our rock-haven and collected some driftwood. The seals followed him curiously with their big brown dog-like eyes. He looked very small between the giant boulders. We cooked lunch over a fire, watched from every angle by seals. I spotted a seal skull, the white bones bright among the black stones, and skipped off my rock to fetch it, then ran back. While Peter was cooking lunch, I wiggled a big tooth out of the jaw. With my pocketknife I bored a hole in the tooth.

We spent two hours climbing through a maze of kiekie to avoid the seal house on our way back. When we climbed back into the calm forest, the sound of the waves slowly faded to absolute silence. I felt observed by every tree.

We arrived back at the cottage as the sun was setting. I found a piece of string, then attached the tooth to it and handed the necklace to Peter.

'Now you will carry the spirit of the seal.' I laughed. 'And you will know how to be tranquil, like the seals, in even the wildest places on earth.'

———

One morning in early summer, Daniel arrived and asked us to join him for a couple of nights working at the last Westland petrel colony in New Zealand. He was involved in a lot of conservation work, and one of his jobs was monitoring petrels, which are a type of albatross. There were only about 4000 pairs left, he told us, in an area of two by three kilometres.

We eagerly followed Daniel up a steep, slippery mountain. After many hours of bush-bashing, we finally arrived on top of a cliff surrounded by massive trees. This was clearly a 'bird city': between the trees, there were no plants, and the soil was barren and packed. We pitched our tent and waited.

That evening, a thousand big birds crashed into the treetops and literally tumbled to the earth, their falls softened by the trees' branches. Daniel explained that the petrels were designed to glide on to water, but could not easily land on a branch; their heavy bodies had to just crash into the canopy. This was the only place on earth where they touched land.

The birds' homecoming was accompanied by a deafening cackling, squeaking, screaming and howling—an unearthly and unbelievable cacophony. We looked around, wide-eyed, enchanted by the strange sounds. The magic went on for a long time, until eventually the birds all found the way into their burrows and the forest grew quiet again.

Daniel put on his gloves and sprang into action. He pushed his hand down into a tunnel and pulled out a bird. With a loud, raspy squeaking and screaming, the bird repeatedly bit Daniel's gloved hand. He inspected it, and told me to write down its band number in his notebook. To me, it seemed a contradiction to protect the birds by disturbing them in their burrows, but Daniel assured me that they were benefitting more than suffering from the human interference.

'Is ecological conservation all based on a feeling of guilt?' I asked.

'Yes.' He grinned. 'Humans have destroyed untold numbers of plant and animal species. We're undoubtedly the greatest pest on the planet. If animals and plants could, they would surely vote us out of existence.'

'I don't know much about conservation,' I said, 'but what I've seen in life is that any action derived from guilt usually just creates more confusion and distortion. It never solves conflict.'

Daniel was silent for a while. 'Yes, that might be true with people. But we have to do something on this planet, before it all goes to shit.'

Just before dawn, around six in the morning, we positioned ourselves behind a tree near the petrels' take-off spot—a steep cliff overlooking a forested valley and the ocean. It was incredible to see the chunky birds hobbling awkwardly towards the edge, spreading their wings, then taking off and gliding into the big sky with such grace and power. I could only sit there and admire the wonders of this incredible planet.

Each bird swung into an updraft, and beat its wings towards the great ocean. They would fly several hundred kilometres to islands far off the mainland to feed, then fly all round the whole coast of the South Island, before returning to their burrow.

Our summer on the West Coast happened to be the driest since records began. Between November and February, we saw no rain at all. Most creeks slowly stopped running; although it created problems for farmers, for us it was pleasantly dry.

We found another way to reach the coast without disturbing the seals. By walking a long way through the forest, we eventually arrived at the sea. We walked over sandy beaches, climbed over boulders and strolled across long stretches of smooth bedrock. I was just clambering over some gigantic washed-up logs when Peter pointed at some limestone cliffs to our left.

'There might be a cave there,' he called out over the noise of the breaking waves.

I looked up but couldn't see what he meant, but before I could answer he had already disappeared into the vegetation. It was so dense that I soon lost all trace of him. I called his name and struggled inland, until I came out on an impressive overhang.

'It's quite deep!' came Peter's voice from the darkness. When my eyes grew used to the low light, I could see that part of the big limestone cave was wet with a small trickle of water, but other parts were dry.

'Hey, we could live here!' I said enthusiastically. The idea of living in a cave has always been enthralling to me. 'We could bring in supplies by boat. Nobody would find us! We could eat mussels and goats, and sleep there.' I pointed to a dry corner. We checked the cave for signs of human habitation. 'Imagine if we find bones of some sort!' I said.

'In India I once found a skeleton in some underground caverns,' Peter said.

'Really?' It always amazed me how many stories Peter had that I hadn't heard yet.

'Yes, at first I thought they were monkey bones, but the legs looked too long. It had been there a long time and there was no skull or clothing. I measured my legs against a stick, and then placed it carefully alongside the bones. I saw that the leg bones were longer than mine. It had to be human.'

'Do you think the person had been murdered?'

'We'll never know, but after I found the skeleton I discovered some leopard shit nearby. Leopards are big animals—they can weigh up to ninety kilos. I knew there were leopards in that area, but I didn't know they were living in that cave.'

'Weren't you afraid?' I asked.

'Oh, of course. When I realised I was in a leopard's house, I was terrified! The fear almost paralysed me, but it ebbed away when I remembered that leopards would have been able to hear me easily. If they had wanted to kill me, they would have already done it.'

'What about the skeleton?'

'Well, I just sat there for a while, wondering what had happened to that person. I thought about the fact that this was my future too. One day, no matter what, I too will be just bones. I thought about what a strange life we humans have.' He looked at me for a moment. 'I stayed there for a long time, considering the fact of death. I understood that we're so focused on *becoming* that we miss *being*, and being is where we all are. When being ceases, we become bones and that's it: life's over. Kaput. Finished. No return.'

'Yes, it's strange to live for the future, because the future might never come,' I said.

'Yes, you will die too, one day,' said Peter. 'You might not think about it, because you're still young and very healthy. At my age, though, people get up in the morning with plans for the evening, but they fall dead by lunchtime. It feels different to be nearly sixty for that reason. I don't have time to waste doing things that I don't really want to do.'

'No, I don't either, really.'

We sat in silence and looked at the beautiful colours of the canopy outside the cave. Big ferns and long mossy strands hung over the entrance and swayed in the breeze.

'Did you take some bones from that skeleton, as a souvenir?' I eventually asked.

'No.' Peter laughed. 'It wouldn't be a good look, going through New Zealand customs with human bones hanging round my neck!'

The air in the cave started to feel very cold, and we returned to the coast with its warm wind and wild waves. Since it hadn't rained for a long time, we had to climb quite a way up a dry river to find fresh water to boil tea. When we finally came to a small trickle, we lit a fire for tea and toasted our bread. After lunch, Peter suggested we should have a look further up, and our efforts were rewarded when we came to a pool with dark water. Just round the corner, we could hear a roaring waterfall.

'Hey, let's swim to that waterfall!' I said, already getting undressed. I waded naked into the pool then swam slowly round to the waterfall. The noise was deafening, and the energy electrifying. The water in the pool seemed to be vibrating, and it was surrounded by high rock walls decorated with small ferns and flowers. It was an exceptionally pristine place.

I swam in a circle then slowly headed back round the corner to Peter. 'Hey, wuss!' I shouted. He was still standing on the edge of the pool. 'Come over here, you scaredy-cat!' I was laughing, holding on to a log in the pool. 'Have a look at this waterfall. It's amazing!'

'Water-bow-deals?' he yelled.

'What?'

'What about the eels?' he shouted, louder this time. 'See any ee—'

He hadn't even finished his sentence when I suddenly felt a sharp bite on my leg. I screamed and looked down to see a long black eel slithering round my legs. I climbed lightning fast on top of the log, while Peter collapsed with laughter on the pool bank.

'I thought that they—' He could hardly speak, he was laughing so much. 'I thought they'd be hungry!'

I crawled over the slippery logs, too afraid to touch water again.

'This pond is full of eels, scaredy-cat!' Peter said. 'I can see four here, and more are coming. So much for the brave Jane of the jungle, eh?' He was still laughing.

I grinned sheepishly when I finally managed to climb back to shore. The wound on my leg was bleeding, but at least the eel had let go— even with its backward-sloping teeth.

One beautiful autumn morning, when the air was warm and the sky blue, we took a little backpack with food and walked into the mountains. I showed Peter the secret places I had discovered on my hunting trips. When we saw hoof prints, I proudly told him how long ago the goats had been there by studying the shape and consistency of the upturned soil. We sat in my cave among the dry goat droppings and I broke some in half to show Peter the coarse grass inside, which indicated an older goat since the digestion of older animals is less effective.

When the sun was high in the sky, we found wood in the riverbed and Peter built a fire to cook lunch. 'There is so much land here. It is just unbelievable,' he said.

'Isn't it interesting that so many people want to *own* their land, to have something to their name?'

'Yes, most people in New Zealand are conditioned to believe that you should work towards owning your land and property. I did it myself.'

'I guess there's an idea that you'll feel very secure if you own property and land,' I said. 'Security must mean a lot to us human beings. But is it real? Can you find security by having something to your name? Did you feel very secure owning land?'

'No. It took me ten years to realise that I had built myself a very nice prison.'

'I'm feeling quite secure,' I said. 'Yet I don't own anything really, except my bow. But if I had to pay a mortgage every month, I'd be nervous about whether I could pay it or not. If I had a job, I'd be constantly worried that I might lose it. I don't think I would feel more secure in myself than I do now. It would have the opposite effect on me.'

'Yes, but, as Mouse pointed out, your security lies in me.'

'That's right.' I smiled. 'But what I'm trying to say is that if I owned land with a mortgage, I would be less secure than I am now.'

'Even when you own land freehold, you still have to pay rates to the council. And if you have milking goats, fruit trees and gardens, it ties you down. In a dry summer, you can't just walk off into the forest for weeks on end, without watering the garden.'

'Owning land suddenly sounds like quite a horrible restriction,' I said. 'I wonder if we really need to buy something?'

'No, maybe we don't.'

We finished our lunch, Peter suggested we explore the river, so we walked with our sandals in the water through a gorge. Spectacular cliffs, overhangs and waterfalls made us walk further and further. At one point, Peter guessed that the river would go round a corner, so we stepped out of the river and headed into the forest to take a shortcut of about a hundred metres across the land. But, to our surprise we did not find the river—it had flowed in a different direction from what we had thought.

'If we keep going left, we must hit the river again,' I said.

We walked and walked through the thick jungle. The ferns, rimu trees, nīkau palms and beech trees all became one big green blur. Everything looked the same. Soon we had no idea where we were.

'Which direction do you think we came from the river?' Peter asked.

'There,' I said resolutely, pointing to my left.

Peter stared at me for a moment. 'I thought it was there.' He pointed in the opposite direction. 'What the heck has happened? Where has that river gone?'

A black nanny goat and her kid appeared from behind a little mound. They looked at us with surprise, then casually continued on their way through the forest. I smiled and looked at Peter. 'They're not lost.'

'No, they can sleep anywhere and eat anything,' he said. 'It must be great to be so completely independent.'

It was hard to tell whether or not we were walking in big circles. The silent forest suddenly felt eerie. Even the birds seemed to have gone quiet. It was as if everything was waiting. I started to think about the possibility of spending the night in the forest. We had brought warm clothes, and we had matches and a little bit of bread left.

'How long have we been walking for?' asked Peter.

'Somewhere between half an hour and four hours,' I replied.

Peter turned round. 'That's weird, eh? There is no sense of time when you're lost.'

A kererū studied us quietly from a tree. The wood pigeon's eyes were bright red and it had a big white chest, which looked like a singlet, and beautiful blue-green colours on its back.

We walked in the silent forest, pushing our way through the under-growth, for what seemed an eternity. We came across big impressive trees with trunks completely covered in mosses, ferns and lichens. Living plants covered every square inch of this forest. In sunny patches the light was so bright that it made the green tree ferns look white, and in the shadow everything was very dark. We struggled through lush undergrowth and followed animal tracks up and down small hills. The longer we plodded onwards, the more disoriented we felt. Sometimes we thought we saw signs of the river, but it turned out always to be an illusion.

Then I spotted an opening in the trees to my left. 'The river!' I shouted, elated. Peter came running. 'But this is the left side of the river,' I said. 'How is that possible?'

We were so puzzled. We decided that we must have gone over a hill and arrived at another river. We sat down to rest because we felt safe, now that we could follow the river back to the coast. We were no longer lost. But we had only walked 20 metres downstream when we found our own footprints again, leading out of the river and into the forest. We exchanged an astonished look. 'What is this? An optical illusion?' I asked.

Without saying a word, Peter turned and followed the river up. After about fifty metres, it disappeared completely underground. Trees had grown over the boulders and there was absolutely no sign of a riverbed. The answer to the riddle of the lost river: we had walked right over the top of it.

One afternoon at the beginning of autumn, I was sitting on the verandah, sewing pieces of possum fur, when I heard a familiar voice. 'Pete, you here? Anybody home?'

I looked up and was overcome with joy to see Mouse appear. He put down his bags and hugged me jubilantly.

Peter arrived from the garden. 'How're you doing, Mouse?' They hugged too.

When we sat together at the picnic table on the verandah, and while we sipped at our tea, Mouse filled us in on the long process of his divorce and property division. He and Debbie had initially departed as friends, he said, but it had slowly turned nasty. By the end, they were communicating only through a lawyer. Now, though, everything was settled.

'Yep, I'm doing pretty damn well,' Mouse said. His main occupation, he told us proudly, was chasing women. 'You have no idea how handy a smartphone is.' He laughed, and tapped the device on the table. It was surprising to see him so enthusiastic about technology; he never used to do anything with computers. He looked at Peter. 'There's this app that'll link you up with the nearest chicks. You can have a root whenever you want!'

'With an app?' asked Peter.

'Yeah.' Mouse laughed. 'Look at this. I learned all this stuff. It's bloody incredible.' He was shaking his head in wonder, while scrolling through his phone. Mouse described all the interesting parties he'd been going to and the people he had met. He also told us that he had booked a trip to South-east Asia, starting in Thailand. Halfway through his story, he suddenly jumped up, grabbed a beam and started doing pull-ups.

Peter looked astonished, as if he was observing a dog suffering from an epileptic fit. 'What's he doing now?'

'I'm just doing,' Mouse grunted, 'some exercises.' He then lifted his legs into the air and, with a big swing, jumped down again.

'You are already the leanest guy in the country,' cried Peter. 'You haven't got an ounce of fat on you!'

'Keeping fit for the ladies, Pete! Very important!' Mouse laughed.

Of course we had an enjoyable time together with lots of laughter, but the Mouse we knew seemed to have disappeared, lost in the world of technology and all the wonders it had to offer. His passion for chasing pigs had been replaced with chasing women. Whenever one of us was trying to say something, Mouse would be staring at his smartphone. It was good to see him happy, but I felt a little sad. The gentleness that I had seen before in Mouse seemed to have evaporated.

After two days, he had to leave again. We walked him up the path to his pick-up truck.

'Strange to think that I'll be in Bangkok in two weeks,' he said with a grin.

'You'll be in a different world!' said Peter cheerfully. 'It'll be hot. Make sure you give yourself some time to adjust. I think you'll like the food.'

'Hey.' He shrugged. 'We'll keep in touch!'

We nodded.

'Get yourself a smartphone.' He looked at me. 'So I can text you.'

'No reception where we're living.' I smiled.

When he hugged me, he held me for a moment, then looked at Peter. 'If you guys are going further into the wilderness, I'm afraid I won't see much of you now.'

We all fell silent for a moment, then Peter said, 'Look after yourself, won't you?'

Mouse laughed and jumped into his truck. 'Of course! Don't you worry about me.' He wound down the window and leaned casually on his arm. When I stepped closer, his hand found mine.

'Bye, Ricky,' I said. 'Good luck.'

He smiled, but I couldn't tell what he was thinking.

His truck brushed an overhanging tree branch when he turned the corner, and it created a little shower of rain.

'Do you think we will see him again?' I asked.

'I don't know, sweetie.'

'It's like mourning the end of summer, with the first sign of autumn,' I said when we walked back to the cottage. 'The summer doesn't mind that it is changing. Only *we* resist autumn.'

On the autumn equinox, when the day is precisely as long as the night, the sun dropped below the New Zealand horizon and, around the same time, it came up in Stockholm. Right on the other side of the world, my older sister, Hanna, gave birth to a boy. They called him Rafael.

I sewed a soft possum blanket for him to lie on, and wrote a letter promising that one day I would show him the silence of the big mountains and the beauty of the clear rivers. Together we would watch the birds and listen to the songs of dawn. I would teach him how to sleep on the ground, hunt with a bow and roam the wilderness. In the evenings, we would light a big fire on the stones in the riverbed, and maybe the flames would one day become a fire in his heart.

At the end of the autumn, the first rain began again. The temperature dropped, the sky turned grey and the ground sodden. With it came that dreary feeling we had experienced last winter. We did not want to go through another wet winter on the coast. We did not want to be tied down by a garden, chickens, or even a house any longer. We wanted to move freely again.

Before coming to Daniel's cottage on the West Coast, we had entertained the idea of buying our own bush block, milking goats and fruit trees, but now we were glad we had not done this as we had both grown bored living in one place. We wanted to be independent and not rely on other people's land and baches. Something in us had stirred. We were ready for the nomadic life again: climbing mountains, roaming the valleys, hunting and gathering.

It was time to move on.

CHAPTER 8

MODERN NOMADS

'One and one is three, sweetie,' I said.

'Two, isn't it?'

'No, no.' I shook my head and laughed. 'If two people work harmoniously, there is a combined strength that is more than just two individuals.'

I felt excited. We were on a new adventure. It was winter, and we were driving towards snow-capped mountains. Peter was looking intently at the muddy track ahead of us, his hands on the worn steering wheel. Behind us were boxes of food, clothes and blankets, our possum furs and tent, and a big tarpaulin. We had exchanged our car for a 20-year-old Toyota Hilux, which was designed for driving in all seasons through water, mud, over stones, mountain tracks and through valleys. We were going to spend at least the next year driving from the top of the South Island all the way to the bottom.

Most of the rain in New Zealand falls on the west side; after a year on the West Coast we decided we would definitely stay east. We would follow old tracks into the mountains, cross rivers into isolated places and set up campsites in the wilderness. We were going to be modern nomads. If we had lived in 1900, we would have travelled with horses; now, we had a truck.

A fast-flowing river suddenly appeared in front of us. Peter brought the truck to a halt and we stared at it in silence. Large boulders created a surge, and the river looked like a whirlpool of white water. Peter nervously put his hand on the gearstick and tried to change gears. The old truck didn't respond quickly; it had already done over 350,000 kilometres.

'Over there, over there!' I said anxiously, pointing to a shallower spot.

The nose of the truck moved down towards the water, and all our gear in the back slowly slid forwards. I held myself in place by holding on to the handlebar near the glove box in front of me. We entered the river. In the middle we felt the full force of the current, and white-blue water churned over the bonnet. I held my breath. The truck moved staunchly through the torrents, then slowly climbed up the bank on the other side. I exhaled in relief.

'What did the mechanic say? Toyotas are bulletproof.' Peter laughed. We grinned in unison, and started to relax.

'Our journey is a bit like an expedition, isn't it?' I said.

'Yes,' Peter replied. We drove round a big boulder. 'Except we don't have a plan, schedule, sponsors, obligations or expensive gear.'

'Or somebody to rescue us,' I added uneasily.

We were not used to four-wheel-driving, and because we knew we were so dependent on our truck, it was thoroughly nerve-wracking. We were traversing the high country of South Marlborough, and most people came through here in summer and drove in convoys. They pulled each other out of ravines, rivers and mud with pulleys and winches. The only reason I felt confident was because I knew that, in an emergency, we could take our packs and walk out to get help.

The valley we were driving through was part of a cattle run, and the surrounding forested mountains were public land. The ranges to the east and west were so high that there was quite a lot of snow on the tops. Two brilliant rainbows—one just behind the other—were visible between the mountains. Despite the hazards and dangers, driving in our own truck through this deserted high country gave us a fantastic sense of freedom and independence.

We drove through the last station gate and travelled south into conservation land. The forest and the rugged cliffs disappeared, replaced by round mountains, with snow tussock in the valleys, the long yellow strands blowing uphill in the strong wind. The sky was deep grey, with dark clouds coming from the south. We nervously looked around for trees. We needed forest for shelter and firewood. We had never been here and we had no idea where we would make our camp.

Then we spotted some trees in a distant side valley. Even though there was barely any sign of a track, we drove right across the tussock, mud and rock, so eager we were to reach the protection of the forest.

We set up our camp among the stumpy mountain beech trees. I tied our big tarpaulin between the tree trunks to create a living room. There was quite an art to it: I had to take into account high winds, rainfall and snow, and it had to be slightly sloping so that it would direct water to one point. Peter dug a drain to guide storm water towards the creek. We had a cover for firewood and a separate flysheet over our tent. In this way, we had a roof for every 'room'.

I had made hooks from thick fencing wire and tied a rope between branches to hang up pots, cups and pans, just like in a kitchen. An elastic rope tied round our 'bathroom tree' was a handy spot to stick our hairbrush, shaver, toothbrushes and toothpaste. We had found an old-fashioned meat-safe, which we hooked on to a branch. It was a metal box with mesh on both sides to let the wind through, and it worked well, keeping flies at bay and meat fresh. When it was raining, we would sit underneath our tarp on buckets and play chess. Round our fireplace, we had collected big river stones to sit on. The whole set-up was indeed very tidy, organised and homely.

Our first morning, I woke up at dawn, and put on my possum jacket and hat. My breath was visible in the crisp air. When I reached the open clearing, the land was cold and still. There was no wind, and everything was waiting under a layer of white frost. I looked at the rock faces, which, aside from the occasional embracing plant, were bare. Vertical peaks on the tops revealed the bones of the mountains. Snow in meadows formed a trickle of water further down.

I breathed in the pure, clean air. The rising sun touched the tops of the western mountains, and the white snow turned red and orange. To see colour emerging in this silent world was magnificent. It was astonishing that we were living in such a beautiful place. The splendour was all-encompassing and I thought, *Why should I ever live in a house in town again, where I would be ruled by the clock, money and social obligations?* Then I was struck by a sudden clarity. *I won't. I will live free in nature.* It seemed the most obvious thing in the world for me to do. *There is a free life to be lived, and I will live it.*

This realisation was like a path ahead of me: all I needed to do was follow it. Even if I lost it, I would find it again, because I knew it existed.

We were living in magnificent beauty, but camping in winter at high altitude was very cold, especially when a south wind brought freezing temperatures from Antarctica. In our first year in the wilderness, we had slept in a tent, but the hut had always given us shelter on the worst days. Now, we only had a fire outside. We could sit in the truck to get out of the wind—if we moved all the buckets and boxes aside—but the truck was also cold, for we were too afraid to drain the battery by switching on the heater.

Our fur jackets, hats and gloves were invaluable. The possum blankets and mats we slept on proved to be very warm during the cold winter nights. We could not wash the furs, but we laid them out on bushes when the sun was shining. The best solution against the cold, though, was to keep eating and keep moving. If I failed to shoot an animal, we slowly grew colder and colder. Our well-being depended heavily on whether I could provide meat.

One afternoon, I went hunting up the valley. I climbed out of the forest and hiked into an alpine basin filled with golden tussocks. I was surrounded by impressive mountain peaks. I held my rifle in the curve of my arm and my eyes scanned the landscape. I meandered between the big, silent rocks. The shadows were drawing out and the land glowed red in the evening sun. Puffs of pink cloud slowly drifted past the mountaintops. With every breeze I smelled a different subtle scent.

Everything in nature had its own distinct colour. There were many different browns in the grass, rocks and shrubs, but only one was the soft brown colour of a hare. Suddenly I saw it. I froze. The hare's ears were high up in the air. It could hear every movement. It could hear me walking and breathing; it could hear wind bending round my body. Any sound now and it would run. In slow motion I crept towards a big boulder. I rested my rifle gently on the stone. My hands were shaking slightly. I did not want to miss. This was the first hare I had seen in two days.

Boom.

The gunshot echoed down the valley.

I sighed with relief when I saw the hare was dead. I ran to it and stroked its warm fur. It is strange that one can only touch a wild animal once it is dead. Its tummy was soft and snow-white. It had thick, furry padding underneath its feet to keep it warm in the frost. I picked up the hare, and smiled. Peter would be so happy to see meat for dinner.

I had left in the warmth of a sunny afternoon, but now the sun and all its colours had disappeared. The landscape had turned ashen, a kind of blue-grey. A cold southerly wind blew over the mountains. I had forgotten my possum gloves, and my hands were exposed to the icy breeze. I needed to do something because my hands were becoming painful and the return journey was long, so I carefully slit the hare open with my knife. The soft pelt easily detached from the warm body, and I was able to move my fingers inside the hare, as a sort of glove.

The hare's warmth was transferring to my body, its meat would soon become me, and its strength would grow into mine. *The living becomes the dead*, I thought, *and the dead becomes the living.* I felt like a wild hunter, connected with my nomadic European ancestors from ancient times. They had also roamed the mountains, and wandered through unknown valleys into open horizons to hunt for food in the coldness of winter.

It was dark when I entered the forest. In the past weeks, I had used my torch as little as possible and my eyes had learned to see in the half-darkness. Instinctively, I recognised the shapes of trees and stones and slippery boulders, which glistened in the moonlight. It was still in the forest, and the creek mumbled softly. An owl hooted in the distance. Every now and then I caught a comforting whiff of smoke from Peter's fire down below. When I arrived at camp, my hare was cold, but my hands were warm.

In the year ahead, I hunted for hares in the open grasslands. Conservationists detest hares, for they eat the fragile native alpine vegetation, but the more I hunted hares the more I admired them. Although low in numbers, they seemed to be able to live anywhere, even in the high alpine areas. They could survive where other animals could not. They lived mostly solitary lives, but never appeared to be lonely. Most of all, they knew how to run. When hopping casually, their ears would be held high; when they were on their guard, they would go faster with their ears halfway down. When a hare felt real danger, it would run like the wind. Its ears would lie flat on its back, its body would take the shape of an arrow and it would effortlessly fly at tremendous speed straight up a steep slope. It was a pleasure to watch a creature that could run so gracefully.

I often noticed that, high up in the sky, hawks would be watching me when I went hunting. They would circle up above, patiently waiting for their share. It didn't take them long to work out I was providing food for them.

Those winter months were cold, rough and uncomfortable, but something in me started to breathe again. Living on the edge allowed me feel alive. Something had touched the very core of my being. The cold mountains were cleansing, magnificent. The wind made me resilient, the icy water in the river made me strong, and the darkness made me endure. I had to surrender fully to the dynamic movement of the rhythms of nature.

One cold morning we woke to a profound silence. I had been sleeping wearing a hat, three jumpers and two pairs of merino leggings. When

I heard something sliding softly over our tarp, I crawled out of the tent and into a white forest. The branches bent and our tarp bulged under a thick layer of snow. It was exquisite. The bark of the beech trees suddenly looked very black compared to the white forest floor. Little flakes of snow had drifted into our 'kitchen'. All the pots and pans were covered, and even our toothbrushes had almost disappeared. A bird had hopped over our chessboard and left its prints.

I lit a fire, squatted beside the flames and admired the pristine wonder around me. When a little breeze came by, tiny snow crystals floated down. A beam of sunlight shone through the trees into the falling icy mist. It was magical.

I made a strong cup of tea with a lot of honey and milk powder for Peter, who looked at the white forest from his warm fur bed. The condensation from his hot cup of tea formed a dense cloud in the cold air.

We relished the peace of that undisturbed world. Our minds could relax and slow down, for we had not a worry in the world. We had just slept at least 13 hours—sleep comes easy when the mind is at peace—and a natural feeling of contentment came with having so much rest. We talked about our life, and the beauty around us, and discussed the necessity of having time for contemplation.

In the afternoon, I put on a pair of woollen socks and then my sandals, and we went for a walk through the snow-covered landscape. We discovered the presence of a wild pig in our neighbourhood: the prints were easy to spot in the snow. Countless tracks of rabbits and hares also showed up on the white carpet. We quietly followed the big hoof prints of a deer into a meadow. A load of snow slid off a branch, and the thudding sound made us look up: just 30 metres away, a stag was looking at the same branch. We could only see its head with large antlers between the bushes, and he stood there calmly. He didn't run. His big, pointy ears moved forwards and sideways, picking up the sounds around him. We watched him and he watched us with shared curiosity for a long time, before he slowly stepped back into the forest. His head moved gently from side to side, to avoid his antlers touching the branches of trees.

We spent the whole winter in several places in the same long valley. Only once did we meet another person—a hunter who had walked up our valley and stopped for a chat when he saw our camp. He was in his forties, had short hair, and was slightly overweight and tired-looking. I was very happy to meet somebody and I quickly made some tea and offered him some camp-oven bread. He was busy telling some stories when I noticed Peter observing me. When I glanced at him, he suddenly looked quite old and grey. When I looked up at the mountains, which had appeared so splendid in the morning, I saw that these too looked rather grim and dreary.

'Very strange,' said Peter, when our visitor had departed again. 'When I looked at you just then, you appeared so old and worn-out, but now you look normal again. Even the landscape looked kind of ugly!'

I was astonished, because I had felt precisely the same thing. 'It is as if we were looking at the world through that man's eyes.'

'Why would he see the world so negatively?' Peter looked puzzled.

'Well, I don't know. Maybe he suffers from depression?' I said. 'It certainly felt that way.'

Peter looked at me. 'It's bizarre that we both felt that. It can't be.'

'Well, our minds might not be so individual and closed as we think,' I suggested.

'I have no idea,' said Peter. 'I wonder how often this happens? It's interesting to feel another person's state of mind. Perhaps this is something that happens in the human world all the time, but we're just not aware of it.'

'Well, we haven't seen anyone for months now. Maybe that's why it's more obvious to us all of a sudden?'

We would experience this phenomenon again, and more often, but it would always come unexpectedly.

After four months in the high mountains, we travelled down the valley to where spring was already in full swing. Wild cherry trees with brilliant pink blossoms were spread over a whole hillside. We moved through a tunnel of astonishing flowering trees. With the arrival of spring came a sense of great energy.

From the cold, dry ranges we drove into the province of extensive glacial rivers, which had shaped the mountains over the last four million years. We found a beautiful, well-hidden spot in the forest overlooking one of those braided rivers. We pitched the tent on the soft grass in the middle of a sunny clearing amid mountain beech trees.

One morning we walked out of the forest to see the broad river. The turquoise water was flowing across the gravel and silt in a network of channels that changed with every flood. We were standing on a high bank and could see small white birds flying busily up and down. A column of spinning air, like a mini tornado, appeared out of nowhere and moved furiously over the sand, picking up dust as it went along. Then, just as suddenly as it had appeared, it died again.

If we had wanted to reach the other side of the river, we would have had to cross more than 10 channels. Some of the waterways were shallow, but others were too deep to cross, even in summer.

'See the water,' said Peter quietly. 'It never begins or ends. When a river meets the sea, water evaporates into the sky and becomes a cloud. Snow or rain falls in the mountains and comes back to the river.'

'Yes, it's easy to forget that water is constantly transforming itself,' I said, looking at the clouds.

'In a way, rivers are kinds of beings too,' he said. 'Lakes and pools are calm, the river is busy, the ocean endless, yet they are all of the same essence. Water is a symbol of the eternal. It turns upon itself with infinite grace, yielding and flowing in the lowest places and enduring beyond measure.'

'I should write that down,' I said, 'so I don't forget it.'

'Don't write it down.' He laughed. 'See it for yourself. Words are meaningless compared to direct experience.'

We lived quietly and peacefully in our campsite on the edge of the forest. We ate healthily, read books, played chess, talked and went for many walks in the forest. One day we rested in the sun on a bank of thick moss amid big trees, overlooking a small stream that had cut a little trench. Patches of sunlight moved over the little ferns and thick mosses.

'You know, sweetie,' I started, then fell quiet again, searching for the right words before continuing. 'Everything in this forest has a place. Every plant grows somewhere. All birds and animals have a sense of belonging. You also have a sense of place. You have strong foundations, but I feel that I don't have a place.'

Peter looked at me.

'I don't mean I need to settle somewhere. I mean that I don't have foundations in myself, the way you do,' I said, and looked at a little fantail that came by. It twittered excitedly as it hopped through the branches, its white tail flicking from left to right. It flew up and caught a small insect in mid-air, then returned to its branch.

'Sometimes I have an image of you in a chair with big armrests,' I went on. 'I feel like I don't have a seat for myself, so I have to squeeze you aside and we have to sit together in one chair.' My words suddenly felt vague and nonsensical. I regretted bringing it up. 'Does that make any sense?' I picked up a little twig and twisted it round.

'Yes, I do understand what you mean,' Peter said. 'I never thought of putting it in an image like that, but yes, sometimes I feel the need to create space for myself.'

'I don't know whether I'm imagining this—if it's even real—but I feel I don't have my own place, so to speak.'

We were silent for a while.

I found the whole conversation rather sobering. 'What is there to be done, once I notice this?' I asked.

'Nothing,' Peter replied. 'You can analyse your upbringing, past lives, future lives and all that. You can examine attachment, security and all those psychological aspects. But to see it clearly for yourself, as you do now, is much more important.'

So that's what I did: I kept looking. For a long time, nothing seemed to change, but I never forgot about it, and eventually, much later, I would see a change.

———

With our hardy truck we could drive into many isolated mountains and valleys, and make a home wherever we wanted. The one disadvantage of our truck, however, was leaving it behind: it gave us much freedom, but we were also tied to it. The vehicle was old and our belongings even older, but we didn't want to risk vandalism or theft.

So, when I discovered there was a good trail over the mountains, I shouldered my pack and set off alone into the dense and vibrant forest. On this warm day in October, the woods were gentle and idyllic. There was a spring perfume with the smell of damp earth. Everything was covered in moss—even the big stones and fallen logs. When I sat down to rest on the soft carpet, I saw one of New Zealand's smallest birds: a green rifleman was scaling up and down a nearby tree, fossicking for insects in the bark. It was so little, and it made a sound that resembled a cricket.

I followed a narrow trail over a pass and came out in an open valley with a beautiful river flowing over clean, round rocks. I heard all kinds of birds, and along the way I practised imitating their different tunes, melodies and hums. After a long day, I arrived at a big Department of Conservation hut. Confident that nobody would come, since I had not seen anybody else along the way, I took a bath in the river. There was a little breeze and plenty of sun, so I took the opportunity to wash all of my walking clothes in the river. I chopped wood, lit a fire in the firebox and was just sipping my tea when I heard voices, and two men came around the corner.

'How many in your group?' asked one of the men in a British accent. He was handsome, quite tall, and had a tanned face with hazel eyes and longish brown hair.

'Just me,' I replied. 'What about you?'

'Six. To be honest, we're a bit like the United Nations.' He sat down on the wooden verandah to undo his boots. 'I'm from the UK, Belgium is just behind us, and India and Japan are on their way too. Dave here is the only Kiwi, but his parents are originally from Cambodia. We're on a team-bonding exercise, and all these guys are PhD students in my research group.' He stood up and shook my hand. 'I'm Antony, but most people call me Fez.' He had a nice smile.

I felt cheerful when we were all sitting round the table, and I chatted all evening with the students. In the end only Fez and I were still awake.

'So, where do you live?' he asked, boiling water for tea on his gas-cooker.

'Here!' I answered with a grin. I gestured out of the window.

'*Here*?' He inclined his head and raised his eyebrows. 'What, all the way up here?'

'Yes, my partner and I are homeless. We live in a tent in the mountains.' I smiled.

He listened with interest to our way of life. When I told him about my hunting, he said he objected to killing animals. He had shot a pigeon when he was about 10 with his grandfather, and had decided that he would never kill any animals again.

'But do you eat meat?' I asked.

'I do. I used to be vegetarian, but I lapsed when an ex-girlfriend dumped me. Chicken tikka masala that night, and bacon sandwiches the next morning, and I've never gone back.' He shrugged.

'Everyone who eats meat should kill an animal themselves, to realise what it means to eat something that was once alive.' I smiled to soften my bold statement.

He laughed and replied that was an excellent ethical standpoint, and it would certainly turn a lot of people into vegetarians. He had a hundred questions about our way of life, and by the end of our conversation he concluded that our life was authentic, contemplative and adventurous. 'But,' he told me, 'unfortunately, there is a flaw. What are you going to do when you're old and your body can't cope with this lifestyle? What about doctors and healthcare? Can you live in a tent when you're in your seventies and eighties?' he asked. 'You won't have savings, a property or a pension to support yourself. People need assets when they're old, but you won't have any.'

'Well, maybe,' I agreed. 'But I refuse to spend the majority of my life worrying about my last days. My main asset, hopefully, will be the ability to be happy with very little.'

Antony told me he was 45 and his life had just been turned upside down. He had separated from his partner of more than a decade just a few months earlier, and his father had recently died from cancer.

'What will happen when *I* die?' he asked. 'A lawyer will read out my will and that'll be it, I guess. My life will have come to an end. Who'll notice or care that I've gone?'

He stared out of the window into the darkness for a moment. 'I flew through the UK education system. Straight As at school, the top First and then a PhD from Oxford, followed by post-docs in Paris and Cambridge. I was only twenty-seven when I was appointed a Fellow at Oxford. Lots of kudos for working there, of course. Intelligent, highly motivated students to teach, and lots of perks. But I got fed up with it. So I came to New Zealand, easily got a job in Christchurch. Some of my old colleagues thought I was crazy to leave Oxford . . .' He looked at me. 'I'd accomplished what society told me to achieve, but so what? What did I actually get out of it? Was I happy, or content? It's a cliché, but as time passes you start to wonder what it all means, what it's all for.'

We both looked at the candle between us. He poked the liquid wax with a match.

'Yeah,' I said. 'It's good to ask yourself whether you're doing what you really want to do, before it's too late.'

He sat back, lifted his hands in the air and asked me, 'Well, what shall I do?'

I was startled for a moment. How could this Oxford professor ask *me* what to do with his life? 'How do I know?' I laughed. 'What would you like to do?'

'Um, I like travelling—South America, Peru, trekking in Nepal.' He hesitated. 'I don't know. My ex was always anti-children, and because of her I never really thought about them, but now we've separated maybe kids are what I need? I'm a bit of a Dawkins-ist: maybe passing on your genes is the real point of living? Of course, I'd have to meet the right person first . . . which is easier said than done.'

'Maybe all you need is a younger wife,' I said to cheer him up. 'My partner is thirty years older than me.'

'Thirty.' He nodded.

'No, no—thirty years older. He is sixty!'

'Bloody hell! You're kidding?' He leaned forward, put his hands on the table and laughed heartily. His amusement was contagious. 'How did you meet?'

'In India.' I was laughing too. 'I guess India allowed us to forget about social rules and reject conformity.'

We talked for a long time about travel, having children and the effect of nature on the mind, before finally going to bed. The next morning before he and his group left to hike back to their cars, Fez invited me and Peter to his house in Christchurch.

I went on alone into the high mountains. For many hours, the conversation with Fez replayed in my mind, especially his words: 'The lawyer will read out my will, and that'll be it.' *One day*, I thought, *all this natural beauty will not be here for me any more.*

I waded through a big river, where a flock of geese were resting. When I quietly walked past, they started honking. Some of them stood up nervously, but they didn't fly away. Their call echoed in the trees, a beautiful and mysterious sound.

I followed a small track through a thick, untouched forest and came out at a pristine blue pond. It was a stunning place. Several small waterfalls dropped over high cliffs into the lake. A white bird floated quietly in the middle, and sometimes it dived down and stayed underwater for a long time. It was very peaceful to walk alone in the deep, still forest, with light falling softly through the leaves. Apart from an occasional quivering in the thickets, it was so quiet that my own footsteps seemed loud. The constant chatter of my thoughts never really stopped, but sometimes there was a moment of silence. I sat down on the banks of the lake and looked around. I saw that there was complete order: everything was at peace, because every plant, tree, bird and animal had its place.

I continued my hike, spending a few nights in old huts, and on my last evening I decided to camp. I arrived at a grassy meadow very high up in the mountains. Since Peter was in our tent, I had only a small flysheet. I rolled my mat out on the grass, then spent an hour making my shelter possum-proof. *Of course, I'm not afraid of possums*, I told myself. *I just don't want any surprises in the night.*

I lit a fire, cooked and ate. Just when I was about to fall asleep, the wind picked up and it started to rain heavily. With every gust, my tarp was pulled away from the logs. I cursed; if I hadn't been so worried about possums, I would have put up the tarp with the wind in mind instead. Now it was too late. The wind blasted the cold rain through the door and wet my gear. I looked out at the menacing dark clouds. The tarp flapped constantly in my face. I piled my gear into the middle of my shelter, then found a piece of half-rotten log in the grass at my side that could function as a tent pole. As long as I held the one-metre log upright, I would stay dry.

Then I heard thunder rolling down the mountains and saw flashing lights to the north. The distant rumble quickly became loud claps that echoed between the rocky summits. I fearfully started counting between the lightning and thunder, to calculate the distance between the storm and me. It was moving in my direction. This show of nature was frighteningly powerful. I lay down, curled round the tent-pole log. The crashing thunder was deafening. There was enormous energy in the air, and it caused a strange sensation in my head, as if a big hand was trying to lift me up into the air.

I felt the ground vibrating, and I was painfully aware that I was in an open meadow beneath the one tree: one stroke of bad luck, and the lightning would hit me. I wondered whether there was a deity or universal force that could save my life. I tried, but could not believe in a creator or an over-arching spirituality that dictated my survival. To me, death seemed random: for the animals that I hunted, for people who contracted diseases, for people in war or traffic accidents, for every small, individual being like me. I stared into the darkness, waiting for the next flash.

After many hours, the storm eventually blew over. I had survived; I felt greatly relieved. I had never been happier to see the dawn creeping across the sky. As soon as it was light enough, I started packing. I stuffed all my damp gear into my backpack and hurried down the steep forested mountain.

After an hour it began to rain again and I heard more rumbling in the distance: another lightning storm was coming. Above me, the tops of the big trees were tossing violently to and fro. As I hurried down the muddy track, it seemed the thunder was getting closer and closer until it was right above my head. My instinct was to run even faster towards our camp. The rain came down in torrents, turning the steep track into a muddy slide. I slipped over. My trousers and the bottom of my pack were now covered in brown clay.

'Slow down! Slow down!' I told myself. I thought of the calm seals on the West Coast, who casually accepted all weather conditions and never worried about a thing. I could not afford to have an accident, because there was no backup for me. I had completed several first-aid courses, and I had a kit with strong painkillers in case I had to drag myself off the mountain, but I didn't have an emergency-locator beacon, no button to press when I wanted a helicopter, no cell phone to call, no mountain radio to ask for help. It forced me to be completely responsible for my own actions. It forced me to slow down, to not take any risks. My only rescue would be Peter: if I didn't return today or tomorrow, he would eventually come and find me.

I forced myself to move at a snail's pace down the slide. I grabbed trees and branches to slow myself down. The thunder and lightning were all around me, but the forest felt like my protector.

When I finally arrived back at camp the storm had passed and Peter was very happy to see me alive. He had been as terrified as I had in the storm. All my stories came tumbling out at once. He was clean and dry, and I was soaking wet. I thought of Fez and his students, who would be back in their offices by now. Their clothes would have already been in a washing machine and dryer. For Peter and me, it was not good to get our gear wet and dirty, because we had no opportunity to clean it. Wet clothes on wet days are one thing I have never got used to.

After several weeks in our beautiful forest spot, we packed up and drove into barren tussock country. A lot of the land we were travelling through had previously been farmland but was now conservation land. In between vast areas of tussock and small bushes, there were sometimes small patches of forest that had survived the blazing fires and grazing stock. Those were the places we looked for.

It wasn't always easy to find a quiet place to live. Although the east side of the country had plenty of public four-wheel-drive roads, access was sometimes denied, with locked gates, fences and signs. When this happened, we had no other option but to keep trying and to keep looking. We met quite a few locals who were angry about losing their rights to this so-called public land, and I could well understand their frustration.

We drove over a narrow, muddy four-wheel-drive track towards a patch of forest that Peter had spotted on the map. Several times we had to drive into slippery gullies to ford a creek and creep back up the other side. I stared wide-eyed at the road ahead, keeping a look-out for potential disasters. Floods had washed away the road, and the truck had to crawl slowly over big boulders. With every scraping sound, I held my breath. With every rock hitting the bottom of the truck, I jumped.

We were forced to stop when we came to a swamp situated between us and the trees on a spur. We carried all our gear across the knee-deep bog and made a camp between the trees. We were not the only creatures that longed to live here: the forest was a little sanctuary full of birds, lizards, insects and hares. Some day in the future, these few trees would give rise to many seedlings, and slowly this would all grow back into a big forest.

From our camp we had a magnificent view over a grassy meadow with a beautiful pond that was home to paradise ducks. Their feathers were pretty colours: green and blue patches, and even some orange and chestnut among the black and white. I often walked past the pond to look for hares on the other side, but every time the paradise ducks saw me coming they would raise the alarm. 'Ahu, ahu, ahu!' they would repeat until I had walked past, then they would call out, 'Ohw, ohw, ohw!' which meant that I was not so dangerous after all. Over the weeks I began calling 'Ohw!' myself, so that they would stop telling the hares that an intruder had entered the area. We learned to understand each other.

Slowly Peter and I felt we had become part of the valley, instead of being just observers. One sunny day in November we went for a walk up our valley. We followed a stony creek with flowering speargrass growing on either side. The grass's yellow heads—big cone-shaped structures with small flowers hidden in the middle—towered above the ferocious spear-like leaves. My eye was drawn to one plant in particular: a formidable two-metre-high speargrass. Its six heads swayed gently in the wind and when I looked at it I could, oddly enough, also feel it. It seemed as if the plant's spikiness had penetrated my whole being; it felt as if I was standing in front of a dangerous animal. This feeling filled my stomach and my heart. I had sensed plants before, in our vegetable garden the previous year, but this was a much more powerful experience and quite overwhelming. I looked at it for a long time, then eventually Peter and I continued up the valley. We lit a fire for lunch and sunbathed on some warm rocks. On the way back, we walked past the speargrass plant again. It still looked impressive, but the feeling had gone.

I sat down next to the plant. 'What did I see before?' I wondered out loud. 'And why is it not there now?' I looked at Peter.

'I often feel strong connections with plants and trees,' he said. 'That awareness does exist all the time. It's natural. You don't have to meditate to see this, but for some reason most of the time we just don't notice it. Maybe we are too occupied with our thoughts, or maybe we're just not aware enough. I really don't know.'

'We must miss an awful lot of this world.' I thought of the little bird we had seen whistling a tune that we couldn't hear, all that time ago at Base Hut.

'Yes, but you can't manufacture it, can you?' said Peter. 'That's why you can't come back to this plant and force the connection. Those things happen spontaneously, or not at all.'

We lived for a month in this little sanctuary next to the pond. We enjoyed a beautiful spring and not a drop of rain fell. Living outside in a dry place is infinitely easier than living in a damp, wet environment. To be able to sit on the ground brought a great sense of relaxation.

About 50 metres away from us, two magpies were sitting on their eggs. They were very watchful neighbours. Every time we walked out of our camp, they called out authoritatively before gliding out of their tree and diving directly at our heads in attack. They never actually hit us, but every time I thought they might. The birds, with their immaculate black-and-white feather coats, could produce many different calls. Their warning call sounded rather harsh, but their songs were lovely. There was not a more wonderful, enticing sound in the world than the cajoling melodies of the magpie. It sounded like stones in a clay pot filled with water: 'Cockle oodle ardle doodle.' We lived with the magpies and the ducks, the butterflies, rabbits and hares. Everything lived quite peacefully—except, that is, on Saturday mornings.

Gunshots heralded the weekends. Repeated salvos echoed through the desert-like mountains, as if we had been somehow transported to a war zone. We were quite far away, but I felt very vulnerable underneath our plastic tarp. I could hear from the intervals that it was unlikely anyone was hunting: it sounded more like the rampant discharging of high-powered guns. We had seen bullet holes in many of the road signs along the four-wheel-drive road down the valley.

To us, this place was a little sanctuary where we lived quietly; to whoever was firing the guns, it was an uninhabited wasteland. We wondered about the mindset of some of these people who roamed the hinterlands when we once discovered eight dead cattle up another valley. We had smelled the bloated bodies before we saw them. Two of them had been caught up in an old fence before the big bullets had found them, and I could almost see the terror in their eyes. What were these cattle doing here? Why would anyone shoot a 2000-dollar animal and leave it to rot in the grass? What kind of person would want to fire at the hills, road signs and cattle?

Happily, on Sunday afternoons the place grew quiet again. We stayed near our camp during the weekends and explored the wider area during the week. We once climbed a big mountaintop. As soon as we emerged out of the gully, we were met with a strong westerly wind that swept mercilessly over bare rocks where only red lichen managed to grow. On the summit we gazed at a turquoise lake below us. The amazing opaque colour of the glacial water was absolutely breathtaking. A braided river with a hundred courses glittered in the afternoon sun, and in the far distance we could see farmland with its straight roads and square paddocks. We sat between the clouds and enjoyed the view, as we had done many times before.

Suddenly we both felt the presence of another dimension. We were struck with awe. On that high mountain, we were witnessing something immeasurable. It was as if we were sensing the unspeakable energy that underpins all of reality. In comparison to this immensity, thousands of years of human history and sophisticated achievements seemed quite insignificant. In this light, even the existence of mankind seemed irrelevant. This sense lasted only a short time—half an hour at the most. We saw it once and never again. We tried talking about it, but we couldn't find the right words. Later, I wondered whether this was what Lao-tzu called the great Dao.

When our food diminished, we started to prepare for a trip to restock our supplies in Christchurch. While Peter studied the maps for four-wheel-drive roads and patches of forest, I walked two hours over a pass to a lake surrounded by boulders and tussock. It was a hot day and the air was very still. At first I thought that a post had been erected in the lake, and only when I looked closely did I see that it was actually a fisherman. I sat down on the stones for perhaps an hour and watched in silence. Eventually the fisherman waded out and started packing his car. I approached him and explained that I had walked over the pass because I needed to send a text message. I asked if I could borrow his phone. He smiled, surprised, and handed over his device. I stared at the screen for a while, before handing it back to him: I had no idea how to type a message.

'You belong to a rare species, nowadays.' He chuckled and tapped the words I recited. There was no reception to send it now, he said, but he promised to do so as soon as he was back in range. He opened his chilly-bin and showed me a grey speckled fish. He was adamant I should have it.

Peter and I ate the fisherman's tasty trout for dinner. The next morning, we drove out of the mountains, past a small forest of flowering broom. We had been living in a very brown environment, and to see so much yellow had a very positive effect. The colour and its sweet smell made my heart leap with joy.

We drove into what felt like a very fancy part of Christchurch, and I was suddenly aware of the mud and dust that covered our old truck, and of our faded clothes that smelled of wood smoke. We drove past big villas and beautiful flower gardens, until we reached the address that Fez had given me. There was a folded note taped to the big mahogany door at the back of the brick villa: *Welcome, Miriam and Peter! The key is in the letterbox. Please make yourselves at home.*

We grinned excitedly as we entered the house. There were several bedrooms upstairs, and two living rooms downstairs. The house seemed enormous for just one person.

When Fez came home that evening, he was delighted to see us. We sat at the table and talked about the passing of time and the effects of working in an institution. Being in this mansion was such a contrast to our life in the mountains, but I loved it; it made me look at things with different eyes. While we talked, I realised how, in nature, everything is living: the trees, birds, animals, and even fire and the weather are lively. Everything exists in relation to everything else. A house, on the other hand, with its totally indoors environment, is quite dead by comparison.

Fez took us to the university staff club one night. I found it stimulating to talk to people from all over the world about a wide range of topics, and I enjoyed seeing Peter converse with lecturers and students. I had never seen this side of him before, but it was evident that he felt very much at home. It was hard for me to imagine that he had once had a life in a city like this: lecturing during the day and marking assignments at night.

After five days in the city, the wild was calling to us again, so we drove south towards a valley in the Southern Alps. We turned off the asphalt road and bumped along for 40 kilometres on a dirt road pitted with potholes. The valley was covered with small bushes and yellow flowers, and its sides were heavily forested with colossal mountain beech trees. In order to reach these trees, we had to drive through rockslides and creeks. Eventually, we found a magnificent place amid the small ferns to pitch our tent. Our camp beneath the tall beeches was so beautiful that we wanted to live there for a long time.

We soon realised that we had neighbours: two blackbirds were feeding four young chicks in a nest just above our living area. We watched fondly as the chicks grew bigger and stronger.

One day a falcon came by and perched on the branch next to the nest. The bird was so close that we could admire it in all its glory: its legs were clad in orange feathers, and round its beak and eyes was bright yellow. It pulled out a chick from the nest with its razor-sharp notched beak, then flew away without remorse. Each day after that, it returned to steal another chick. On the fourth morning it put a claw on the last chick's neck. While the baby bird squeaked, the falcon looked at us for a surprisingly long time before casually pecking out one of the chick's eyes. Then it lifted the chick out of the nest, spread its pointy brown wings and sailed down the valley—maybe towards its own family of hungry chicks.

If I looked into the heart of nature's rhythms, I could see that sacrifice was part of its cycle. All around me, I was aware of a sweeping power that had the ability to destroy living creatures so casually, but with the same movement could also create profoundly. I saw that same energy in the vast landscape around us.

An ice-age glacier had moved through the valley where we were living and had left a wide riverbed, in which a beautiful turquoise river now flowed. In dry periods, it was possible to wade across the river, but in times of flood the cold water would cover at least half a kilometre. From our camp, we could see an impressive mountain range on the other side, with great peaks towering high into the sky. Even in December, the tops were regularly covered in snow. One afternoon in midsummer, Peter pointed at the snow-capped ranges and predicted the existence of a mountain lake.

So, the next morning, we set off very early. Crossing the river required great attention, and we walked up and down to look for the best place to do so. After some discussion, we waded through the strong current, using our long walking sticks as pivots. We scrambled up the bank into the forest, which slowly made space for alpine vegetation. In between the rocks and lichen grew little white snowberries, which we ate like sweets on the way. The mountain was incredibly steep, and soon we were puffing and panting. The higher we climbed, the further away the summit seemed to be.

Then the stream became a waterfall and we were faced with a big wall of rock. We thought we must be just underneath the lake, so we started climbing the cliff, but the rocks weren't solid; they seemed to break apart dangerously easily. I moved towards the small shrubs that clung bravely to the wall with strong roots, and used these plants as climbing ropes. Once we were above the treacherous bluff, we found ourselves in a gigantic boulder field. By now it was midday and the sun was burning hot. The rocks shimmered with heat, and we rested in the shadow of a big one, looking out over the majestic Southern Alps. Each pinnacle had its own name and shape—some tops were sharp, some round, some had gathered a cloak of clouds, and others stood naked in the blue sky. Every time I saw these magnificent ranges towering into the sky, I was overcome with joy and astounded by the beauty. I felt immensely grateful that I was here to see it.

When we stood up, we saw a chamois 20 metres behind us. I was mesmerised: I had never seen one so close before. It had a goat-like body, with straight little horns that curved backwards at the top. Its face was whitish, apart from a black dash on its cheeks that went from its nose to its pointy ears. It was magnificently elegant, and it watched us with shy curiosity.

While looking at its eyes, I understood that beauty does not come through *becoming*, but only with *being*. The chamois was not working towards a better version of itself; it just lived. I, on the other hand, was always trying to become nicer, better, stronger, smarter and prettier, which caused me to lose my authentic self. I understood that the process of becoming disfigured my being. This chamois showed me, in that moment, that *being* is the most beautiful form of existence.

After a long time climbing, we finally reached the summit, and at the foot of a wall of snow, in the heart of a basin, we at last found a pristine blue lake. We sat down in wonder beside the crystal-clear, tranquil water. The lake was absolutely still—it looked as if it had been undisturbed for millions of years. It was as if we were looking at the origin of all water, the first creation of life on our blue planet. We were silent in the presence of this ancient lake that felt so holy.

Even though it was the middle of summer, the weather in the mountains sometimes resembled winter. At regular intervals, freezing-cold winds brought snow and hail. It was so cold that the bumblebees often sat immobilised on their flowers, and we would use the opportunity to stroke their furry backs. On these cold days we sat round the fire in all our winter gear until the wind changed direction and brought a sweltering-hot summer day again. We came to expect any season at any time.

One good sunny day we decided to walk to a big waterfall a long way up the valley. We followed a trail through the forest and came across a huge landslide. We sat down and lit a fire with the abundance of firewood. While Peter was toasting his bread on a stick, I told him that I had felt a huge build-up of energy in the last few days. So much so, I said, that I felt like jumping up and down like a Masai warrior from Kenya. Peter laughed and gestured to show that I should certainly take no notice of him and feel free to jump about if I felt like it.

We continued our way up the valley. Slowly we walked out of the forest and into a giant basin, where the steep mountains were virtually cliffs, and little streams and waterfalls cascaded down the rock walls. Eventually we came to a point where a river had carved a smooth channel through the massive rock. The power and beauty was astounding. Peter climbed the rocks, while I stood still.

I was looking at the turquoise colours in the silky water. I was not doing anything special, but suddenly it felt as if a lightning bolt entered my head, as if the right part of my brain suddenly opened, and with it came an extraordinary clarity. I sat down in wonder, and saw that the whole of reality was in fact moving like a kaleidoscope. I saw that everything, including my own mind, was constantly transforming; I was not really fixed in one place. I saw that this changing reality was an eternal movement in a timeless world.

Eventually I climbed up to where Peter sat. He looked at me and understood at once that something had happened, for he had experienced similar things himself in the past. We sat down, and we were so in sync that with only a few words he intuitively understood what I was trying to say. While looking at the world, my mind seemed so clear. It was as if I had been driving a car with the handbrake on and suddenly it had been released.

We spoke about humanity, and good and evil. We discussed how children are taught right from wrong, and how these words affect our way of seeing the world. While talking to Peter, I saw myself thinking according to these culturally conditioned values. I could see how I interpreted, judged and analysed my own thoughts, thereby restricting my own mind. I realised that these social rules were made in the past, and had nothing to do with the ever-changing present.

We climbed to the roaring waterfall round the corner. A white river was thundering down to earth, and an eternal, drifting spray covered the fall like a jacket. The wind shaped the mist into different patterns. The spectacular 100-metre cascade had carved a shaft through the solid cliff, before it rushed over smooth slides down the mountain. The power of the waterfall engulfed me. I felt part of its pulsating movements, which glided through the hard rocks to find the lowest levels of the land and reach the sea.

After that remarkable day I didn't suddenly walk around with a smile all the time. I didn't feel an eternal bliss. Quite the contrary, in fact: it felt as if someone had removed my rose-tinted glasses. The world had become crystal clear, and I was forced to look at everything—the good, the bad, the beautiful and the ugly—in a direct and unconditioned way. It was immensely sobering, but also profoundly connecting.

In the following weeks, we went for long walks. We came across flowers that I had seen a hundred times, but it felt as if I saw them for the first time. I spotted a big plant with yellow flowers and when I touched its soft green leaves I felt, intuitively, that these could have a medicinal property for the lungs. When I saw another plant, which Peter recognised as ragwort, I felt that it should not be eaten, but could perhaps have a use for skin treatments. We walked from plant to plant, and each one told us something of interest. I realised that in the past people would have had a sense for the medicinal values of plants, and that this insight was now rendered obsolete by modern science and technology.

Not only was I fascinated by the world of plants; birds and insects also captivated me. When we saw a giant dragonfly on the ground, I lay down next to it. It looked like an alien, with its long black-and-yellow tail. Its enormous eyes on its swivelling head looked at me, and I wondered what it saw.

When we returned to the forest, I was in awe of the big, tall plants that we call trees. They suddenly felt like friendly giants. I sat on the roots of an old tree and felt my own heartbeat resonating with its pulse. I was connected. The whole world was magical, and everything in it had such a beautiful design. My mind was empty; the world was complete, full. There was nothing to miss or desire.

The nights were equally as intriguing as the days. When I dreamed, I knew I was in a dream and I could look around without waking up. It was interesting to observe how real the dream world seemed. I touched people's faces to test if I could feel their skin. I could jump high or fly at will. I listened to orchestras and was at the same time astounded that my brain could make up and play all the instruments. If I didn't like the course of my dream, I was able to change it.

This state of mind—this extraordinary sensitivity and connected-ness—only lasted for a few weeks. After a month, I felt mostly 'normal' again, although some aspects of my understanding had changed forever. My dreams, especially, are still very enjoyable.

We spent more than two months in this quiet paradise in South Canterbury, but at the beginning of February we had to move on again, as we had run out of food. We drove down the valley into a town, did our shopping and continued our journey south on a sandy four-wheel-drive track into a golden desert. The tussock-covered hills of Central Otago rolled smoothly before us like a gentle sea. Under the big sky, there was an immense sense of space. The only features in the landscape were natural rock sculptures that rose high above the grass. They were smoothed by the wind, battered by sandstorms, baked in the scorching sun, and covered in snow in the freezing winters.

This desolate wilderness seemed devoid of people, but in the 1860s gold miners with picks and shovels had worked here. In between the round mountains were the ruins of the old stone cottages in which these miners had survived tremendously cold winters. We found one of these stone ruins in a small valley. There was little left of the tiny dwelling besides three half-broken walls, which we restored with flat stones. We then stretched a tarp over the top as a roof.

I experienced exactly the same enjoyment I had once felt as a child, when I used to make huts in the garden. Peter pulled out the weeds that had invaded the hut and cleaned up the interior. I dragged a big stone inside—this was our table. We couldn't stand up in our cosy little hovel, but we could sit down on the dry sand and drink tea at the stone table. We were sheltered from the strong wind and protected from any rain by the tarp. I felt very happy to know that we could make a home out of ruins.

In the evenings we admired the brilliant sunsets: orange, red and even green covered the heavens, and every second the colours changed. The sky never stopped moving. At night we watched a dome of stars. The Milky Way was revealed in its fullness, and the whole earth and universe seemed infinitely pure.

During the day we searched the hills for wild thyme and berries. More than a hundred years ago miners had planted gooseberries as well as red and black currants. Their cottages had long gone, but their fruit plants had quietly survived. We picked buckets of fruit, and ate until our stomachs burst. Then we stewed the berries and tried to eat more. There was not a more satisfying thing in the world than picking our own fruit. We were immensely grateful to those hardy old gold miners.

From Otago we drove into Southland. Peter had found an isolated valley on the map, and we followed a vague track into the forest that led into the mountains. When a mud pool emerged in front of us, Peter drove to the side—and promptly got the Toyota stuck on a hump. The bottom of the truck was caught on the clay mound and its wheels spun in the air like turtles' legs. I jumped out and furiously started digging, while Peter ran around looking for flat stones and branches to give the wheels something solid to grip on to.

Once we freed our truck, we followed the track into a boulder-strewn riverbed. We crossed the river countless times, and every time I got out to direct Peter away from the deep pools and treacherous rocks. The gravel at the edges of the river looked solid, but was often as perilous as quicksand. When we saw a suitable place to pitch the tent, I was very glad to stop.

One day we climbed out of the forest towards the mountaintops. When we reached the last tree, we built a fire and cooked lunch while there was still firewood. We walked up a steep, rocky spur covered in moss and beautiful alpine flowers and herbs, and came out on the summit. The view was astonishing. We had seen smooth, round mountains in Otago; now we were suddenly looking at a horizon of rugged peaks with steep crags. The pinnacles were so sharp that they were like pieces of broken glass. This was a lesser-known part of the South Island, and we were in one of the wildest places we had ever seen.

When we saw a hawk gliding over the forest far below us, I suddenly remembered the billy. I had left it at the tree line, and I worried that somebody might find it.

'There is nobody here to steal it!' said Peter, when I expressed my thoughts. 'The only person who stole that billy was you, anyway.'

A few months earlier, we had found the cute little billy in an abandoned cottage. It had been dirty and rusty and I had spent a long time cleaning it up. Now I regarded it as mine, but Peter was right: I had taken it. It was not mine. When I realised this, my worries dissolved instantly. If it didn't belong to me, I didn't need to worry about it.

Fewer possessions meant less anxiety.

'What is actually mine?' I said. I looked at my clothes. I had not made these clothes; I had not even bought them, because most had been given to me. I had bought some of my gear in second-hand shops with money that had been given to me for singing. As we talked about the notion of possessions, I realised I could not justify any of my so-called 'belongings'.

'The only thing that really belongs to me is my body,' I said. 'That's what I should worry about: keeping my body healthy.'

On one of our walks we met a deer hunter who was carrying a stag's head. He was a trophy hunter, about 40, with a short-cropped beard and blue eyes, and he was wearing a camouflage jacket. He was quite friendly and we stopped and chatted to him for a while. When he made some small movements to indicate he was about to move on, Peter asked where the rest of the stag was.

'Over there.' He waved vaguely down the valley. He had big, strong, calloused hands. 'But the flies have been on it for yonks, mate.' He looked at his watch. 'I shot it about four hours ago.' Once he understood that we were serious about finding the stag, though, he launched into a complicated explanation of how to get to it.

We returned to our camp and took two empty backpacks. Peter had memorised the route the hunter had described very precisely, and he led us into a valley, along a river, up the side of a mountain and through thickets and forest, all the way to the animal.

We heard the flies before we saw the carcass: there were thousands buzzing around. The hunter had taken only the head and left the rest of the beast intact, including its skin. Methodically, we cut and piled 30 or more kilos of meat into our packs.

On our way out of fly city, we spotted the brain, which the hunter had cut out of the skull, lying in the grass. The flies were not interested in this curly mess. Peter picked up the brain and inspected it with interest. 'We can eat this!' He flicked some blades of grass off.

'What?' I felt slightly nauseous. 'Are you sure?'

'Oh, yes.' He laughed. 'My mother used to cook sheep's brain. Wait till I fry it up.'

'No way,' I said. 'I wouldn't want to die of that laughing disease.'

'Don't worry, I think that's only when you eat human brains.'

The route back to camp was much more difficult with our heavy packs. When we finally arrived back at our campsite, we stored the heart, liver and kidneys in our meat safe and stashed the rest of the venison in buckets, which we placed in the cold river with rocks on the lids.

Peter lit a fire and heated up the pan. He sliced the brain and rolled it in flour. He ate the fried brain with relish. 'Here, have a bite!'

I declined and began cleaning the stained bags instead. When Peter insisted, I very hesitantly took a small bit of the whitish substance. To my surprise, it was delicious and the texture was like marshmallows. Deer brain was the tastiest thing I'd ever tasted in my life! I laughed enthusiastically and reached for more.

'Don't laugh too much now.' Peter's eyes twinkled.

In April, we drove slowly north again, heading for Mavora Lakes. We harvested a lot of wild food in the autumn—for me, there is no greater enjoyment than eating healthy, fresh fruit, nuts and herbs. We arrived at North Mavora lake with a truck full of supplies, boxes of apples and buckets of walnuts. It was a time of abundance. We felt very rich.

The lake had forest at one end and tussock at the other. We followed a narrow four-wheel-drive track into the forest. There was no space to drive around the potholes and mud pools, so we were forced to plunge straight through every obstacle. Peter just grinned; by now he had become a confident four-wheel-driver.

We built our camp in a beautiful spot between some old beech trees, with a view out over the shimmering lake and the mountains beyond. We could see several spurs coming down to the valley floor. In the early morning, birds would call over the lake, and their hoots and honks sounded mysterious, even magical. Sometimes the air was so still that the mountains were reflected on the water's surface like a mirror. A breeze often came up in the afternoon and created a thousand horizontal lines on the water. When the ripples became waves, the lake sounded like a small ocean.

We drank the lake water, as it was very clean and pure. Every time I fetched a bucket of drinking water, I felt delighted. In Holland I wouldn't ever drink from a river, let alone from a lake. I felt very blessed to be living in a country with clean water.

One day we walked to the head of the lake. 'Over there is Shirkers Bush.' Peter pointed to a small forest on a spur. 'A hundred years ago, some men who didn't want to fight in the First World War hid in that piece of forest. They followed Archibald Baxter's example—he was a conscientious objector and pacifist who stood up to the military machine. He said that he would never in his sane mind surrender to the evil power that had fixed its violent roots like cancer on the world. They shipped him to the trenches in France, put him deliberately in a firing zone to get him shot, and tied him to a pole in the snow.'

'Really?' I gasped. I wondered if I would be able to stick to my principles if forced to endure physical and mental torture to that extent.

'It nearly drove Baxter insane, but they didn't kill him. I reckon he was a hero, because he dared to speak out against war.'

We climbed up a spur, through the rocky mountains. Hardy speargrass and alpine flowers grew in the green meadows. It always amazed me what could grow in these harsh environments.

'You know what this is?' Peter pointed to a bush no higher than a metre that grew like a thick carpet over the stones. He reached down and picked a small red berry. 'This is a tōtara tree. If you dig this out and plant it down in the valley, it'll grow into a big tree!'

I looked at the tōtara bush, which was disguised as an alpine shrub, and sat down next to Peter to pick my share of berries. While we were busy picking and eating, I looked up. Above us on the rocks walked a beautiful tahr. We had never seen one of these Himalayan mountain goats so close. He had long horns, dark fur and was strong and healthy. He was incredibly dignified with his long mane. He stood still for a moment and looked at us, before he continued climbing a vertical crag.

As autumn slowly descended beside the lake, toadstools began to emerge beneath the trees. In the heavy early-morning dew, the threads of magnificent spiderwebs became visible between the branches. The nights were growing colder again.

One evening I walked silently with my rifle through the big beech trees in search of a rabbit. I was hoping to find one nibbling the soft grass at the edge of the forest, but the clearing was empty. There was a faint pink colour in the sky and, as is often the case at twilight, the silence was profound. It was as if heaven had pulled away from the earth and created a space in which everything was still, serene and complete.

I could see more clearly in the evening than the day. My eyes seemed to be made for twilight. When my eyes opened, my skin did too. Everything opened up, and I could smell the earth's secret scents. On the faint breeze, I could hear the whispering tussock, the murmuring flowers and the sighing trees. I could feel all there was and, while the birds sent long calls from tree to tree, I moved silently into a clearing.

Then I saw that I was not alone. About 20 metres away walked another hunter, at the same speed as me and with the same air of importance. A wild cat. The big black tomcat was strong, proud and determined. I marvelled at its wildness. This was a tiger compared to a domesticated house cat. I thought about how humankind had gradually grown tame; once upon a time, humans had been as wild and proud as this tomcat, and deep in my heart I felt that one day, in a faraway future, humans would be wild again. We had been living in nature for four years, and I had begun to see that everything must return, sooner or later, to its natural order. The forest had been burned in vast areas of the country, and one day it would grow back again. It might take millions of years, but nature has time. Like the forest, one day we humans will reconnect with the earth on which we were born, and return to what I believe to be our natural order.

Several lone hikers came past the edge of the lake on their way along a 3000-kilometre walkway called Te Araroa—New Zealand's trail. This trail goes all the way from the top of the North Island to the bottom of the South Island, and the hikers we met had been walking for almost five months. Although they looked tired, there was something quite uncommon in their eyes—a kind of inner peace and confidence. They had a resilience and strength that they had acquired through enduring hardship and walking in beauty.

One morning we met Jean-Charles. Like the other young hikers we'd met, he was tanned, thin and strong. His clothes were ragged and faded, and his lower lip appeared to have cracked and healed over again several times. We lured him to our camp—a bit like we would a weka—by offering him bread and butter. He had twisted his ankle the day before, and we suggested he should rest with us for a couple of nights. We discovered just how hungry he was when he wolfed down three plates of possum stew and brown rice. He ate as if he was on the verge of starvation.

He told us that he had walked every step of the trail and was determined to finish his mission. 'I'm looking forward to reaching Bluff and I'm dreading it at the same time,' he said. 'In two weeks, I'll be on a plane back to Paris, where life's so trivial—matters are so tedious, and people so superficial. After walking for nearly five months through nature, the whole human world seems meaningless.' He had a very concerned look in his blue eyes.

He told us all about the trail, his preparation, organisation and planning. He spoke with enthusiasm about the most beautiful places and the most difficult parts.

'What do you think about when you're walking by yourself?' I asked.

'Well, for the last few days I've been thinking whether there is ever a moment in life that you know who you are.' He looked at Peter.

'Well, I don't know,' said Peter.

'You should know. You are sixty!' Jean-Charles liked to speak frankly.

'Say life is a river,' I said. 'If I threw myself into the current, into the unknown, I'd be subject to all sorts of random events and it would automatically change me. I'd never be the same person for very long. So, I think—and I might be wrong here—that the moment I know who I am and settle into a routine, I will be stuck on the bank instead of flowing with life.'

'I agree,' said Peter. 'But maybe there is an expression of an authentic being in each one of us—something that isn't constantly being moved or changed, but belongs to you.'

The morning that Jean-Charles left, Peter and I went for a walk. We followed a small trail over the roots of the big trees next to the lake. We sat down on the soft moss and looked out over the water. A group of birds on the lake was making a sound very similar to a squeaky wheel. Their call resonated over the still surface of the water.

I patted the moss next to me. 'Wouldn't it be nice to walk onwards and just camp wherever we found a nice spot in the forest?'

'Yes indeed. I was just thinking that.' Peter looked at me with a faint smile. His blue eyes were twinkling with a new idea. 'Don't you think we should walk Te Araroa too?'

'Leave the truck behind?' I said. 'Live with nothing, only our packs?'

'Hmm.' Peter nodded slowly. 'Walking into the unknown.'

'That's the best idea I've ever heard.' I laughed and hugged him.

—— CHAPTER 9 ——

CIVILISATION

This wasn't the first time we'd thought of going on a long walking journey. The first time I met Peter, when we played chess together in that little restaurant in South India, he had told me all about his travels in the Himalayas. Later, when he suggested undertaking a 600-kilometre journey through the Himalayas together, I agreed without a second thought—all my life, I had dreamed of doing such things.

We had set off in late spring with minimal gear. We walked through forests, across high snow-covered ranges, through barren deserts. We slept under the stars or in caves, or stayed in remote villages and ate meals with the locals. Crossing the mountain passes often took four or five days, and we carried flatbread, roasted-barley flour, dried fruit and muesli. We crossed eight mountain ranges on our way to Ladakh, and three of the passes were over 5000 metres high. The nomadic people we met while travelling in those majestic mountains were an inspiration to me. If they could live in the beauty of that rugged wilderness by becoming hardier and tougher, I had realised, then so could I.

Now here we were preparing to lead precisely such a nomadic way of life again, this time on Te Araroa. We would walk with very few possessions. We would hunt and gather, see the country and discover its beauty. I felt a fierce excitement to see all there was, and to explore all dimensions of reality.

We arrived in Wellington in our truck when winter had descended upon the land. Celine had recently moved to the capital, and we stayed with her at her new house on the south coast. She was very happy to have company—and for somebody to cook her dinner when she got home from work at the hospital at eight or nine in the evening.

We arrived at Celine's on a Sunday afternoon. We had a cup of tea together, and afterwards I went and had a shower. I had not felt a hot shower since we had stayed with Fez in Christchurch seven months earlier. The sensation of the warm water on my skin was amazing. I changed into some fresh clothes, and looked out of the window at the foul weather outside. It started to rain heavily, but, for a change, I didn't need to worry about all the items that could get wet or blow away. I grinned at the luxury of it all—being in a house was so comfortable and cosy. Going outside in this stormy weather suddenly looked very unappealing; going outside to live in a tent in the winter seemed almost nonsensical.

When it had got dark outside at six, instead of going to bed (as we would have done if we were in the wilderness), we just switched on the lights and started cooking an egg curry. Since I wasn't able to hunt while we were in the city we had reverted automatically to vegetarianism. We ate together at the big table. I was amazed by how comfortable the wooden chair was; as though it was made exactly for my body. My back precisely fitted the backrest, and my feet touched the ground just perfectly. I placed my elbows on the wooden tabletop and grinned at the marvellous ingenuity of the person who had invented the chair.

'Do you know how brilliant a chair is?' I asked Celine. 'And how handy a table is? After squatting for a year to cut bread and meat on the ground, I think tables and chairs are the best inventions ever!'

Celine looked at her table, surprised. 'What else did you miss?'

'The news,' said Peter. 'What's been happening in the outside world?'

We spent some time discussing recent world events, then Peter asked Celine, 'So, what are the medical concerns today—still a pandemic, is it?'

'Pandemic?' Celine looked surprised.

I laughed, as I remembered our first conversation quite well.

'Oh, no,' said Celine. 'Don't worry about pandemic. I'd say obesity is the latest worry. People are losing the ability to take charge of what they eat and how to prepare their food. Another problem is mental health. People are working horribly long hours, which causes depression and burnout.'

After the dishes Celine suggested we watch a movie. 'What would you like to see?' She looked at me. If she had asked me to list all the cities in China, I would have had a similar mind-blank. I couldn't think of anything. 'Um, you can choose,' I said.

'Life in the city is quite lonely without a partner or children,' she said, as she scrolled through the movies on the screen. 'I often watch romcoms. The characters simulate friends I don't have the time to make. Pathetic, isn't it?' She laughed. 'Watching these cushy, undemanding movies gives me the illusion of belonging. I feel I'm not so different from everyone else.'

'Really?' I said incredulously.

'Yes. Plus, sometimes I just need to zone out and stop thinking about work and cancer.' She looked up. 'Every week I tell people they have cancer. When I save lives, my job is wonderful and rewarding. But sometimes there's nothing I can do for a patient, and that's really tragic.' She glanced at the coffee table, silent for a moment. 'Now,' she said, 'let's watch this one. I think you'll like it.'

Celine's house was on the shore and overlooked the wild waves, which occasionally washed over the footpath.

On sunny days, Peter and I went for long walks along the ocean's edge and gathered wild silver beet, parsley and fennel for dinner on the way. The salt and wind had made the silver beet leaves thick and tasty. There was a colony of seals on the rocks a few kilometres away. It was such a wild, weather-beaten place that it was hard to believe there was a city just round the corner.

One day, in a sheltered spot among the dunes from which we could see the mountains of the South Island, we discussed Te Araroa. Most of the hikers who had passed through Mavora Lakes had planned their journeys quite precisely, and some of them had organised food parcels containing special dehydrated supplies. Although it would make our walk easier, we thought that arranging food parcels might ruin the spirit of the journey; we wanted to be able to change our route whenever we needed, and we didn't want to be hindered by a pre-planned itinerary. Not organising our food, however, would mean that I would have to hitchhike to town for new supplies whenever the opportunity arose—and this would sometimes mean I'd have to walk for many hours to reach a road to hitchhike from. But I still thought that was a better option than predetermining our route.

To keep their packs as light as possible, most of the hikers had been living on things like two-minute noodles and dehydrated potatoes. This seemed part of the reason that their bodies were so run down by the end of the journey. Our aim was to arrive at the southernmost tip of the country as fit and healthy as possible. To accomplish that, we would need wholesome food. So, like the Himalayan shepherds, we would carry wholemeal flour to make flatbread or chapattis. I would take a gun and hunt along the way. Since we wouldn't be able to carry a whole goat with us, we would rest for the time it took to eat any animal I shot. Peter would also need this time to recover. He maintained he was fit enough to walk 3000 kilometres, but not at the same pace as the young hikers we had seen speeding by. Most walked the trail in somewhere between three and five months, but, since we had all the time in the world, we decided to take twice as long. We would walk the North Island in the summer, then rest for the winter. The following spring, we would walk the South Island. Our aim was more than just doing a long trek; we wanted a walking life, like that of the nomads we had met in the Himalayas.

I woke up on Saturday morning when I heard Celine getting up to go to work. I went to her computer in the living room and opened my email. When Celine came into the kitchen to make breakfast, she told me her work schedule and other chores for the morning.

'Don't you miss having a job?' she asked, opening the fridge.

'Well, I'll go back to teaching if I need to,' I said, 'but I don't think I'd like the monotonous routine. My life would be chopped into days of the week. My future would be planned and organised.' I laughed. 'I'd probably die of stress or boredom.'

'What I like about a job is the responsibility. Don't you miss that aspect?' She fed celery, cabbage and avocados into a blender. It made a very loud noise.

'Well, in the past I had some responsibilities that made me feel important for a while, but you know what happened? The moment that I walked through the door of responsibility I found myself in the room of obligation.'

'Well, that's a pity you see it that way.' She drank her smoothie. 'I'm sure you would be a good teacher. You could be a great inspiration for students.'

I laughed. 'Maybe, but I'd much rather sing in the streets to make money.'

She nodded and smiled, rinsed her empty glass and looked at the clock. 'I've got to go now. My patients are waiting. You have a nice day!'

When Celine had left, I walked to a market in the city centre with my guitar, which we had picked up on the way to Wellington. I planned to do some busking. I watched the men and women on the street. Most of the people I saw around me had a job. It suddenly struck me as bizarre that I had enough money to do everything I wanted to, without working. For the past years, I had lived off the interest earned on the savings from my teaching job, and while we were on the West Coast I had made money busking. We had also been living off the land by hunting and gathering. My money didn't seem to run out—as long as I didn't buy things I didn't need.

Then I spotted some men sitting round tables with chessboards. There was a sign out saying that they were recruiting new members for their chess club. I nervously walked over to one of the empty chairs. A man of about 60 was sitting on the other side of the table. I indicated that I would like a game.

'Do you know how to play?' he asked.

I'm not sure that he would have asked me that question if I was a man, but I nodded shyly. Little did the man know that I had been playing every day for the past eight years with Peter. For most people, chess is a boring game, but it was our main source of entertainment. We had played countless games together.

As I took my seat, I instantly felt a rush of adrenaline. The start of the game was easy enough, and we both moved quickly. When the game became complicated, my opponent started chatting with his neighbour while I studied the board intently. I forked his queen and his rook. He was losing. By the time he finally started paying attention, though, it was too late. He resigned and insisted on another game. The second time around he beat me, but I felt proud anyway—it turned out that the man was some kind of local champion. He tried to get me to join the chess club. They needed more women, he said. If I had lived in the city, I assured him, I would have joined.

I picked up my guitar and went and found a spot to busk. 'We walk in the mountains, I hunt in the valleys. We sleep on the ground in a place that we have found. The call of the geese echoes in the trees. We receive our energy straight from the earth . . . straight from the earth.' I sang many songs with much enjoyment. I found different places in the city to busk, and made enough money to top up my savings.

That first hot shower I had when we arrived in Wellington was wonderful, but it surprised me how quickly the extraordinary fact of endless hot water began to feel normal again. That seemed to be true for all comfort. Everything—the soft bed, clean sheets, clothes that smelled of flowers—very quickly became disappointingly ordinary. After a week in Celine's house, I started to miss the breeze and, above all, the fire. It felt as if I had lost the company of a good friend. The convenience of the heat pump did not match the sparkling beauty and warmth of a fire. Living indoors once again, I was slowly losing touch with the real world. The weather was irrelevant, we passed the longest night without noticing it and I lost track of the moon's phases.

My period, which had over the years synchronised with the full moon, slowly became more irregular again. Even though I showered daily, I never felt as clean as I did in the wilderness. It was as if the cold, pure rivers washed both sides of my skin.

While Celine was at work, I typed long emails and we watched news and documentaries. Before I knew it, another day had gone. Time seemed to vanish quickly when I was behind a computer; the machine ate the hours away. I noticed its predictability created a sense of comfort, which in turn created a resistance to stepping into the unknown. I could see how the comforts of a modern life—with computers and hot showers and everything else—could make it difficult to surrender again to randomness and the spontaneous flow of reality.

We had brought a lot of food with us, and we stored it in Celine's cupboards. I could eat as much as I wanted. There was no need to use it sparingly—if we had run out of butter, we would just walk down the road and buy more. This felt luxurious. But, since we weren't getting the same long sleeps we'd had in the wilderness, I had less energy and wanted to eat more. I soon felt bloated and worried about gaining weight. However, the more I told myself not to eat, the more I ate. Instead of letting my body tell me when I was full, I started calculating how much I had already eaten that day and whether that meant I should—or shouldn't—eat more. While I was baking bread in the kitchen one Sunday morning, I spoke with Celine about the world of appearances.

'I know it's terribly frivolous,' said Celine, leaning on the bench with a mug of herbal tea in her hands, 'but in France, my friends—who are mostly doctors, engineers or lawyers—and I used to talk a lot about weight and comment on other's people's bodies.'

'I'm very happy to be away from all that.' I poured some flour into a big bowl. 'I'm glad I live without a mirror. In nature it doesn't matter what you look like, really.'

'No, that's right.' Celine smiled. 'But appearance is an important part of society. Comparing myself with others is so deeply ingrained in me,' she admitted. 'I always think I should lose some weight.'

I looked at Celine, surprised. She was already very slim.

'Or I see you, for example,' she continued, 'and I think immediately I should also have strong, toned biceps like you.'

'What for?' I asked incredulously. 'You don't need to haul a heavy backpack over the mountains. You work in a hospital.'

She nodded a little sadly. 'My parents have always encouraged my brothers and me to reach for the best. The disadvantage is that I feel that nothing is ever good enough. I am constantly assessing myself against others, if you see what I mean?' She paused. 'It's a kind of permanent yearning, but it also gives me the energy to keep aiming for an ever-moving goalpost.'

I told her about the day I had seen the chamois and realised that real beauty lies in *being* not *becoming*. It had made perfect sense in the wilderness, but I now saw that in civilisation everything was about comparison.

I started mixing the yeast and water with the flour, then began to knead the dough.

Celine nodded. 'Oh! I have something for your bread.' She opened several drawers before she found a tiny bottle containing a liquid that made everything taste smoky. 'It's very expensive to buy.' She laughed. 'If you use some in your dough, it might taste like the bread has been cooked in a fire.'

When we left Celine's, we went to stay with our friend Bennie. His father was German and his mother a New Zealander. He was my age, but looked younger. He was quite tall, and had green eyes, very pale skin and blond hair. He lived alone and rented a tiny cottage perched on a hill overlooking the city. We slept in a tent in his garden. Compared to the mountains in the South Island, we found the winter in Wellington very mild.

We liked Bennie's frankness, perceptiveness and sense of humour. He had an ability to attract people of all ages and from all walks of life. Groups of friends would come round and hang out in his small backyard with glasses of wine and cigarettes, talking about everything from 3D printing to nanotechnology, from following Elon Musk to Mars to whether or not quantum computers would result in radical social change. Nobody—Bennie included—ever showed any sign of being tired, even at two in the morning. We would crawl into our tent when the last people finally left, then wake up a few hours later when the first birds began their morning cacophony in the kawakawa tree next to our tent.

Just after seven one morning, Bennie came out of the bathroom brushing his teeth with one hand and combing his blond hair back with the other. He disappeared into his bedroom then reappeared five minutes later. He nodded at me. 'Ready to roll?'

'Ready to roll.' I grinned.

I wanted to walk him to his office, to see where he worked as an IT specialist. We strode down the road into a park. Big eucalyptus trees loomed over the path. Their smooth, colourful trunks looked as if an artist had painted them. In the branches were four magpies, all cawing at once. I thought of our valley in the dry mountains with our magpie neighbours.

'We're a bit on the late side. We might have to walk a little faster,' said Bennie when we entered the busy streets of the city centre. Seven-thirty in the morning appeared to be rush hour for all the people going to work. The noise of roaring motorbikes and buses vibrated through my body. Fumes entered my lungs. The hissing airbrakes of every passing bus felt like a punch in the stomach. It was as if I was walking about naked, without protection from the growling engines, pollution and crowds. This surprised me, because once upon a time I had lived in Amsterdam, which was a lot busier, noisier and more polluted than Wellington.

'I recognise perhaps fifty faces on an average morning,' said Bennie, marching down the footpath. 'These people walk here every weekday. Same place, same time. It's fixed, a gridlocked pattern.'

We stopped at a red light. About 70 people stood waiting with us. The system wasn't very efficient, for at one point all the cars were waiting too. Then a young man came flying down the hill on a skateboard. I couldn't see how he was possibly going to be able to stop in time—and he didn't. He flew right through all the red lights while everyone else was waiting! My mouth fell open.

'He's incredible!' But my comment was lost when the great mass of people started moving again at the nervous *Pew! Tick-tick-tick* sound that came at the same time as the green walking man lit up. Everybody hurried across the road.

'See everybody rushing?' Bennie said. 'We all think we're getting somewhere, that we're making progress, but we're in fact just struggling to keep our spot on the treadmill. People have become like sheep. Sheeple.'

I noticed that everybody was alone. Nobody, besides Bennie and me, spoke or walked in pairs. All eyes were concentrated on some point in the distance.

'Now,' Bennie glanced briefly at his phone, 'we have ninety seconds spare for shopping.' He led me out of the main stream of people and into a supermarket, then meandered through the aisles. Our only traffic jam here was the queue at the checkouts.

'Every day I wonder what I'll choose for lunch,' Bennie said, while we got slowly closer to the self-checkout machines. 'The idea of having a choice is very satisfying, yet every day I buy the same thing.'

'Why is that?' I asked, surprised.

'I can't be bothered spending time thinking what to buy! And, actually, this fruit smoothie's pretty good.' He shook the plastic bottle in his hand. 'All these people buy just enough food for today's lunch. Tomorrow, they'll be here again at exactly the same time, to buy exactly the same things.' Bennie smiled. 'Like me.'

'Why don't they make sandwiches at home and save themselves some money and time?' I asked.

Bennie swiped his card through the EFTPOS machine. 'No, no, no. We don't feel like thinking about tomorrow's lunch. There's so much else to organise in the evenings, so many chores and responsibilities.' We walked out of the supermarket. 'Remember last night? I had to wash my work clothes, organise a meeting for work, text some friends about a party on the weekend . . . I was busy from the moment I got home, right? Sorry, we lost time in the supermarket queue. We'll have to run. I have to be through the gates before eight.'

I jogged after him, and was glad I'd worn shorts and sandals.

'Run, lemmings! Run!' Bennie called out, as he raced along the footpath in his black suit.

'But why is everybody doing this, day in, day out?' I asked.

'We've got to pay the mortgage or the rent,' he said over his shoulder. 'For a house we only see at night.' He trotted down a long flight of steps, lightly touching the silver railing with his left hand. His body seemed to stay still while his feet moved at an incredible speed. He held up his smartphone. 'And to buy more and more and more convenient stuff. All those laptops and phones—they're so convenient!'

At last he came to a standstill in front of a big important-looking building. He straightened his suit while he waited for me to catch up. 'It's called comfortable slavery.' He moved his right arm towards a sensor and the glass doors opened. I followed him into a foyer with thick carpet and high ceilings.

'Thank you for your company, ma'am!' Bennie said to me in a British accent.

'My pleasure, sir. Have a nice day.' We shook hands to complete our performance, then he disappeared through the electric gates into the office. The big electronic clock above the entrance read 7:59:10. He had made it just in time.

I exhaled in relief and sat down on a sofa to recover. When I walked out, the clock read 8:02:17. Other cultures have deities on the walls; here, we had The Clock.

I walked outside and looked up. Bennie worked on the third floor. I couldn't see inside, as the building's windows were like mirrors. Reflected in them, I saw three seagulls circling in the blue sky beneath a white cloud that looked a little bit like a dog with a very long tail.

'Let's go for a walk,' said Peter one sunny Wednesday morning. We followed a marked trail in the forest that cuts right through Wellington city. The trail went up a hill, and the streets and houses lay below us. While we walked through the town belt, I realised that life here in the city called for extra meaning besides just living. If I was to live in a town again, I would need a hobby, an interest or an occupation too. Yet in the wilderness I never felt I needed any projects other than our daily chores, like baking bread, lighting fires and washing clothes in the river. These activities were all fulfilling and enjoyable, and living in beauty was meaningful enough.

After an hour walking, we stopped to rest under some giant pine trees. The ground was dry and soft, littered with fine brown pine needles. Several birds were singing high up in the trees. The light shone through the branches and created beautiful golden-brown patches in between the trees. We looked out over the city and the harbour below. The city centre is quite small—only a few blocks with high-rise buildings. I pointed out to Peter where Bennie worked. It was characteristically windy, for we could see the waves on the water in the harbour as vague white dashes. With its view over the big mountains in the distance, Wellington must be one of the most beautiful capitals in the world.

We continued along the trail until we were able to admire the other side of the city. We rested several times in quiet places. It was so still we could barely hear any traffic, and only heard the occasional aeroplane. Then we heard a very peculiar sound.

'That's a lion roaring!' said Peter.

I laughed. 'Of course not, silly.'

'There must be a zoo nearby,' he said. 'Let's go and have a look.'

We bush-bashed through the forest until we did indeed come out at the back of a zoo. On the other side of the fence lay a sleeping cheetah. When we came close, the cheetah woke up, and looked very annoyed. It reluctantly stood up, stretched its powerful body and loped off to the other side of the enclosure. The fitness contained in its muscles was astounding.

'See how strong the cheetah is? After our three-thousand-kilometre journey, we will look like that.' I smiled.

'Hey, I don't even know whether I'll be able to make the first kilometres!' Peter laughed. 'I might be dead by the time we reach the end of Ninety Mile Beach!'

I put his arms over my shoulders and kissed him. 'No, you won't.'

We walked onwards and came out at a children's playground. The slide was quite high, and I impulsively climbed the steps. It had been more than 20 years since I had played on a playground. I went down the slide at high speed. I climbed a tower and went down the flying fox. Each object gave a different sensation. It was really quite enjoyable.

There was a boy of about nine there with his younger sister. We took turns on the swings and I showed them some simple tricks on the trampoline. When we were climbing to the top of a rope-tower, the girl suddenly called out 'Look!' and began to laugh.

Her brother and I turned round. At first I couldn't understand why she was laughing so much, then I noticed she was pointing at a big dribble of spit that had stuck to her chin. Her joyous face, her carefree laughter and her joke all reminded me so much of Sofie, my sister, when we were young. The boy and I grinned at each other. After a little while, the children went home and I returned to Peter.

'Adults take themselves way too seriously,' I said as I picked up my Swanndri jacket. 'I should actually laugh a bit more about my own foolish quirks.'

Peter stood up. 'Such as playing like a kid in a playground?'

'That's not that foolish. I mean all things I regard as failures or embarrassing or shameful. I should just laugh about them.'

'Yes, but it takes a bit of confidence to laugh at your own mistakes,' he said. 'Even as a kid I was shy. I had very little confidence, and I wanted to defend that little bit of self-esteem I had.'

One night, I decided to go with Bennie to a pub in the city centre. I had bought pants and a silk blouse for a few dollars from a second-hand shop. My new outfit was a world apart from my patched-up Swanndri, ripped merino tops and faded shorts.

When we arrived at the pub, a band was getting ready to play later in the evening. Leaning over the bar, Bennie asked me, 'So, what would you like to drink?'

I had not drunk much alcohol for the last 10 years, but I wanted to experience the effects of it now, since it is an ordinary part of Friday nights for many people in the city.

'Vodka,' I said. It was the only thing I could think of besides beer and wine, which I didn't like the taste of much.

We took our drinks outside, where big heaters stood on poles. I wondered how much it cost to turn winter into summer like this.

'Cheers!' Bennie said. 'This is the working man's reward for a life of comfortable slavery. Work all week, make money, then spend it immediately on expensive poison with friends who have nothing to say to each other, because everybody had a boring week.' His laughter was contagious. We raised our glasses and took a sip. I felt the strange sensation of the alcohol burning my throat and down into my stomach. I looked at the people around us. Everybody had come in pairs or groups.

'Shall we talk to somebody?' I said.

'No, no,' said Bennie. 'Too early. Wait until everyone loosens up a bit.' He leaned on one elbow and swirled his glass. 'I told my brother that you guys live in the mountains in a tent,' he said suddenly.

'Oh, did you?' I grinned, and also swirled the vodka in my glass.

'Yes. His first reaction was, "So they're homeless? What's their problem? They probably have mental issues."'

'Did he really say that?' I was dumbfounded. 'Mental issues?' I asked, suddenly realising his brother probably wouldn't be the only one who thought this.

'Oh, yeah.' Bennie shrugged. 'He believes that happiness is secured through money. He would never understand your lifestyle.'

'I guess that is very democratic thinking,' I said. 'What the majority choses must be the right thing!'

Bennie pondered this for a moment. 'Well, you've chosen a totally different way of life compared to most people. My brother runs his own IT company with over twenty employees. The majority of people would probably agree with his way.'

As we drank our vodka, our surroundings seemed to gradually become friendlier. The people looked happier and more attractive. The clouds reflected the city lights with an interesting yellowish colour. Even the high-rise buildings around us, which had looked so ugly to me when I arrived, looked quite artistic.

We walked over to the bar to get another drink. While I was waiting, a young man appeared next to me. 'Wow, you have really long fingers,' I said. 'Do you play the piano?' I pointed at his hands. He laughed and replied that he played the bass guitar then held up his hands to compare them with mine. We walked back outside together, and talked until the band started up inside. Even from outside, the sudden noise was deafening to me. I was so shocked by the blast that I blocked my ears and wrinkled my nose. My new friend thought it was the music I didn't like, rather than the volume, and he said angrily, 'What are you doing here if you don't like the music? You just want to stand here in your pretty little blouse and be a cute little princess, do you?' He even wiggled his hips in a derogatory way. My mouth dropped open, and I laughed wholeheartedly. It was the funniest thing I had heard for a long time. The young man appeared to be quite astonished by my reaction.

At midnight, Bennie and I left the happy people in the noisy bar behind and walked along the city streets. The night-time atmosphere was completely different to what it had been like during the day. We passed drunken folk on the footpath, and long queues outside nightclubs and bars presided over by bouncers in black leather jackets. In between the noise of cars and shouting people, I was amazed to see homeless people with their few bags of belongings sleeping on benches beneath the streetlights.

Bennie asked whether I had ever been to a sex shop. I could not say I had, so we walked into a shop which was illuminated as brightly as a supermarket. I looked around with interest. There were some videos and a few magazines, but the bulk of the products were tools to inflict pain of one sort or another. The salesperson behind the counter was the strangest individual I had ever seen. He had a man's face, complete with a two-day beard, while his body was that of a woman, including breasts. He had dressed himself as a woman, too, with a colourful skirt over his big stomach. I was so curious I wanted to study him more, but restrained myself.

'Excuse me,' I said instead, 'what is this for?' I pointed to a metal ball that looked similar to hammer-throwing equipment used in athletics.

'Ball-stretching,' he said irritably.

Still uncertain of the function of the device, I asked for clarification. He must have thought I was mocking him, because he became quite angry and said curtly, 'To stretch the testicles!'

I was a little shocked by his gruff tone—I had only been curious about the product. I signalled to Bennie that we should leave and I was relieved when were back out on the street again.

'It's strange that a sex shop should be full of torture equipment, don't you think?' I said to Bennie as we crossed the street.

'Well, I reckon people have so little connection with their bodies that they need to feel pain to be reminded of their physical existence,' he replied.

'Really? That's sad, isn't it?'

'Yeah. Life in this society is one great assault on the senses. We're constantly overloading ourselves. We eat too much, because we can't feel whether our stomach is full or not. We don't taste anything, so we need more MSG and salt and sugar. The music we listen to—like the band just now—causes hearing damage. Did you know that one in four people have hearing loss? And I'm one of them. I've already lost thirty per cent of my hearing.'

We walked for a while longer, and I silently reflected on modern life. It struck me that humans are becoming increasingly desensitised and therefore slowly losing the ability to see the beauty of the world.

Soon we approached a big road. A vehicle slowed down, and to my astonishment a group of teenagers leaned out of the windows and started throwing eggs, before driving off again quickly. Luckily I saw it coming, so I ducked, but the security guard who was working for the nightclub behind us received most of the eggs. We asked if he was OK. He told us that he was often the victim of drive-by egg-throwing. 'People think we are police because we wear this blue uniform,' he said. 'Eggs are nothing,' he added. 'Sometimes we get knives thrown at us.'

Bennie hooked his arm into mine, and we turned into a small, deserted alleyway. We marched up a hill and it was very quiet. The air was fresh, but I wasn't cold. It was strangely exciting to walk past rows of houses inside which people were sleeping. When we got home, I wasn't even tired—probably thanks to the vodka. Bennie and I tiptoed past the tent where Peter had already been sleeping for five hours, and continued to chat inside in the kitchen until daylight.

In the spring, Peter and I got married. I basically had to drag him along to the registry office, as he was opposed to marriage. He believed that wedlock would turn into a ball and chain that would ruin our relationship. As for me, I did not believe a marriage certificate would make that much of a difference, since we had already been together for eight years. However, I wished to become a New Zealand citizen and be able to keep my Dutch nationality, and getting married was the only way I could do this. Despite his resistance, Peter managed to smile quite cheerfully when our friend took a picture that day. After that, I had to complete the process of obtaining citizenship, and these bureaucratic events delayed the start of our journey for several months. At last, though, we were ready to head to the Far North to begin Te Araroa.

Peter had an old friend from university called Nick—Nick Maverick, I called him. I had known him for quite a while now, and regarded him as a good friend. He drove us in his very small car 1100 kilometres northwards to Cape Reinga. It took two days.

Nick was a few years older than Peter, and had blue eyes and thick white hair that had grown wild and long. He used to be a mountaineer when he was younger, but in recent years he had suffered from an autoimmune condition called inclusion body myositis, which is an inflammatory muscle disease characterised by slowly progressive muscle weakness. Every year he lost more strength, and he had trouble walking. If the condition worsened, he could eventually end up in a wheelchair.

As I sat in the back of his small car, hemmed in by our packs, I looked at Nick's blue eyes in the rear-view mirror. Watching the road ahead intently, he told us in a casual manner about the things he had seen in the most remote corners of the world. As a university lecturer, he had journeyed with students to visit and learn from indigenous cultures all over the world. The future of many of these cultures was under threat. What he had seen was destruction: of people, of their way of living, of their sacred sites and of the earth. It had all left him with a sense of immense sadness.

'We're in a bizarre position,' Nick said. 'In the West, we've ended up with a civilisation that is focused on progress and development, but is in fact an appalling make-believe on a gigantic scale. It encourages— almost insists upon—distraction at any cost. In the public sphere we see violence, venality and greed. There is dishonesty, propaganda and obsession with the trivial . . . The list goes on and on. The system in which we live is a forced consensus of a self-created monster.'

The landscape we saw as we drove north was mostly farmland. Sometimes Peter pointed to forest in the distance and said that we would be hiking through those ranges in a few months' time. It was inconceivable that we would walk the whole length of this island. We drove over the high-altitude Desert Road, and past magnificent volcanoes. We got stuck in traffic jams in Auckland, and once we entered Northland we began to see more forest. It was like a different world. I opened the car window. The summer air in Northland was warm and heavy, the temperatures high. I looked out at the rolling hills and the patches of forest with big, strong trees. Small creeks wound their way through the hills.

While we drove, Nick talked about what he referred to as 'the mavericks': the courageous people who had freed themselves from social conditioning and dared to make a stand. In his mind, they were the last hope for changing the social and economic structures that he felt were crushing everybody into nothingness and despair.

'I feel bereft at the whole monstrous, appalling system. How can humans be so ignorant and stupid? How do these selfish and hedonistic beliefs evolve? How do they take root? How do these self-serving maniacs get the ruling power? It's madness of the highest order, eh?' He laughed softly. 'Best thing to do, I reckon, is build local resilience, have as little to do with the destructive system as possible, and let things take their course—downwards.'

His face in the rear-view mirror was constantly changing expression. His blue eyes turned from passionate fury and anger to wonder and surprise. Sadness and sorrow was swept away again by love. All the expressions of humankind were to be found in Nick Maverick's eyes.

We drove into Kaitaia, the northernmost town we would go through. We saw very few white or pākehā faces, and many Māori. People were talking with each other on the streets and, in the heat of summer, nobody wore many clothes and most walked around barefoot or in jandals. I had the feeling we had somehow driven to a Pacific island like Fiji or Samoa. I instantly felt more relaxed.

Our Te Araroa journey officially started at Cape Reinga, but we drove a few kilometres east to a beach called Spirits Bay. Peter had been there years ago and suggested that we should start our journey there because it was so beautiful.

As soon as we arrived, Nick opened the car door to let the sea breeze in. He shaded his eyes from the sun. Several white seagulls were flying overhead, calling wildly to each other.

'Isn't this incredible?' he said. Beautiful old pōhutukawa trees with red flowers grew on the rocks in the distance. The wind carried the sound of breaking waves from over the white dunes in front of us.

'In a sense, society is a horror,' said Nick. 'Individuals can do such wonderful, creative things, act with kindness, generosity and sacrifice. But, at a larger level, evil and destructive systems have taken root everywhere. But we can't allow that to sink our hearts. We can't. We have to find harmony within. All that is left to do is to reconnect with the heart of the wilderness, the spirit of nature. Like you guys, I've had several mystical experiences in the past. Once you see the mystery, it never leaves you, eh? I want to keep feeling that fundamental generosity and creativity of life.'

Peter and I sat in the grass next to the car, while Nick remained in the driver's seat. I sliced some bread, which I had baked a few days earlier, and handed him a sandwich.

'I wish I could come with you guys,' said Nick. He shifted his legs out on to the white sand, then slowly worked himself out of the car. When he eventually stood up, he leaned on the open car door and looked ahead. 'I want to walk along beaches, over mountains, wander between ancient kauri trees, be on a journey,' he said. 'If I could get the use of my legs back, I'd be unspeakably happy. I'd dance with joy.'

I nodded. I lifted my eyebrows to try to keep the tears out of my eyes, but my eyes became misty anyway. I looked down at my feet, moved a hand through my hair. My heart ached for Nick. I wanted to say 'I'll carry you!' but the words did not come out, and I knew I could not carry him, no matter how much I wanted to. He looked down at his thin legs, which were withering away from the disease.

'You don't realise what it is to be able to run until it's too late.' He laughed softly. 'I mean it, eh. The only thing I regret is taking my legs for granted all those years.' He leaned forward, looking where to put his feet. I moved closer to help him. He laughed softly and leaned on my shoulder. 'You have a good journey, my dear.'

CHAPTER 10

TE ARAROA:
THE NORTH ISLAND

We tied our sandals to the side of our packs and walked barefoot through the water. Every now and then a big wave made me run into the soft sand.

'Don't worry, sweetie! Everything will dry in an instant.' Peter laughed, swinging his walking sticks enthusiastically through the air. His jubilant mood was contagious. We walked side by side into freedom, and felt great excitement about this new adventure.

The sun shone cheerfully and a little breeze lightened the warm air. The waves dragged pebbles backwards, creating a beautiful sound. Seabirds spiralled above into the blue sky. As far as the eye could see, the sand on the beach was untouched. Nobody had walked here. For a moment it felt as if we were the first people to explore an uninhabited island. It felt so natural to be nomadic, to follow the ancient footsteps, dance to the rhythm of the mysterious earth, and to see the world as new.

Along the shoreline grew ancient, gnarly pōhutukawa trees. Their long arms reached for the ocean, and countless red flowers covered the trees like a special blanket. The blaze of red against the green hills and the sandy beach was absolutely magnificent. The heat and the flowering trees had moved me into a world of wonder. The pack on my back contained everything I owned in the world. I could carry it anywhere. I loved the idea of sauntering into the unknown, without returning to the same place. We would go on and on, unfolding our journey with every step.

The first hour of walking along Spirits Bay towards Cape Reinga was exhilarating—but after about five kilometres we suddenly started to feel very tired. We were pushed into the deep, soft sand by the incoming tide, and every minute the weight on my shoulders seemed to grow heavier. My head was throbbing in the midday heat and the sweat on my back was soaking into my clean T-shirt. Under the scorching-hot sun, we dragged ourselves through the blinding white sand. Our burdens made us hunch over so badly that, from a distance, we could have been mistaken for four-footed animals.

'This is way too heavy,' I groaned. It was only the first day. How were we going to fare with all the beach walking awaiting us over the upcoming months? Hoping to find firmer ground, we climbed over the dunes to a dirt track, but the sand on the track was just as deep as on the beach. Our suffering continued.

Just when we had sat down to take a rest, we heard an engine. A ute loaded with people drove up to us. Heartened, we smiled as they approached.

'Jump on the back, bro!' said the driver cheerily. With happy faces, we climbed on to the back of the ute and sat between the five kids already there.

'Where're you fellas from?' asked the oldest boy. He looked to be about 13.

'Well, we live nowhere and everywhere,' I said.

'We're going to walk three thousand kilometres to Invercargill,' said Peter cheerily. I could feel his pride and, like me, he looked as though he had instantly forgotten our recent hours in the sand.

'Where will you sleep?' The boy looked at us curiously.

'Wherever we find water and a flat space to pitch our tent.' I pointed at our yellow tent bag.

'You're like gypsies,' said a girl who looked to be 12. 'I want to be a gypsy, too!' She looked at her brother, who nodded approvingly.

'You should,' I said. 'It's too boring to live in one place all your life!'

They laughed. These children seemed so happy and content.

When the ute could go no further, everyone jumped out. The family was going to fish in a nearby lagoon. We thanked them all profusely, then continued our journey through the soft sand. It was just as tiring as before, but at least we could now see the cliffs that marked the end of the beach. When we finally reached a sparkling little creek, I was relieved to take my pack off and sit down in the shade.

We rested there, without walking any further, for a week—we had planned it that way. I had packed extra food, so that we could give ourselves this time to recover and let our bodies adjust to the idea of walking 3000 kilometres.

We pitched our tent beneath a magnificent solitary pōhutukawa. The crimson stamens drifted down like red snow in a gentle wind. We sat with our backs against big stones and looked out at the ocean. After years of living in the cold mountains, being warm was remarkably relaxing. It helped us quickly forget the suffering of our first day, and we didn't even think much about the journey ahead.

We explored the coast and found hidden beaches with steep cliffs. We gathered mussels and seaweed, and dug edible raupō roots from the swamp, then boiled them together with wild spinach.

While we gazed out over the rolling waves, we reflected on the past months. I realised that I had found urban life quite tiring. I had become sleep-deprived with all the socialising and time behind the computer, combined with the electric light that kept me awake at night. I felt as if life in the city had taken away some of my vitality and clarity. But, during our first week on the beach, I started to ease back into the rhythm of nature again. Slowly, I felt less bored and restless, and more at peace.

After a week, Peter had recovered from that first day and we began our journey to Cape Reinga with renewed optimism. I knew that, at his age, he would struggle more than me with a heavy pack, and his recovery time would also be significantly longer. Our solution was to slow me down by making my pack heavier, so that we would walk at the same pace. Food included, my pack weighed 25 kilograms, and Peter's just 15. Some people would comment on our different-sized packs, but I was very proud of Peter for even attempting to walk Te Araroa.

We hiked through the hills towards the lighthouse at the cape, where two oceans meet: the Tasman Sea and the Pacific Ocean. For Māori, Cape Reinga is a spiritually significant place—according to mythology, it is where the spirits of the dead begin their journey north to the land of their ancestors. For Peter and me, it was the start of our long journey south.

'Te Araroa trail.' Peter tapped the little black-and-white sign with his walking stick. 'Ready?'

We had been looking forward to this day for many months, and I felt proud to be standing here. We looked at the vast oceans below and took a deep breath. Then we turned round to face south. This was going to be our direction for a couple of years.

'Ready!' I said. I felt very excited.

We were on the west coast and walked over high sand dunes. This part of the country was such a narrow strip of land that we could sometimes see the eastern coast from the top of big dunes. After two days, we arrived at Ninety Mile Beach, where our surroundings were flat and expansive. Ahead of us was a great, featureless, misty void over which we would walk for the next week. The ever-present wind and moving waves created artistic patterns in the sand, which were constantly shifting. We walked barefoot over the hard sand, our moving shadows reflected in a thin film of water.

At certain times of the day, we saw air-conditioned buses speeding past. Young people wearing headphones waved enthusiastically from behind the tinted windows. As I lifted my wooden sticks in the air in greeting, I couldn't understand what could possibly be enjoyable about driving in a bus over the beach. The bus passengers undoubtedly thought exactly the same about us.

Once, we thought we saw a person in the distance, but when we got closer we saw it was a lone black-backed gull—like the ones we had seen sweeping over the Southern Alps. It rested on one leg and looked out to sea. Those solitary gulls stood so proud and noble that we called them King Edward birds. When a King Edward saw us, it would regard us with mild curiosity but would never move. There were seagulls and business-birds gathered in big groups that expressed their annoyance raucously whenever they spotted us. After some noisy screeching, one gull would take off and the rest would soon follow. They would fly a kilometre south before gliding down on to the beach again. We would meet them over and over, until they flew graciously north again into the immeasurably blue sky.

The sea breeze kept the temperature down, our shoulders grew used to carrying our packs, and with each day, walking became a little easier. During the day we were always searching for fresh water. At night, we often found shelter in the pine forest behind the dunes.

One afternoon, we followed a big stream inland. After struggling through high reeds and small bushes, we found a flat spot underneath a copse of planted trees. Glad to have discovered such a convenient site, I immediately pitched the tent. I was just laying out the bedding when a wildly barking Jack Russell came running towards us. I was a little afraid of strange dogs and I warily grabbed my walking stick to defend myself.

Then, to my astonishment, a brown donkey with a long nose and big grey ears also appeared. It looked puzzled when it spotted us. It started to bray loudly, and another black dog emerged, followed by a man clad only in a pair of shorts. In his hand he held a bag containing small white tuatua shellfish.

'Kia ora,' he said.

The man looked to be in his late forties and was strong and fit. He didn't smile as he glanced at the tent. I followed his gaze, and at once regretted pitching it. Peter stepped forward to save the situation. 'Sorry, mate.' He smiled. 'We didn't know we were on private land. We just walked up the creek looking for a shady place to camp.'

There was a moment of silence during which the man looked at us intently. Then he said, 'You're all right. No problem.' His words were slow and careful. 'Haere mai, welcome.' He shook our hands. 'I'm Anaru. You should come see my house. I'll make you a brew, bro.'

Peter and I followed Anaru and his donkey and two dogs through a small forest. I was walking last, so nobody saw the little Jack Russell attack me. It sneaked up on me with cunning swiftness and bit my heel repeatedly. I considered yelling out for help, but Peter was chatting so amicably with our new friend that I didn't want to make a pathetic first impression. Instead, I rotated nervously as I walked in order to keep an eye on the darting little dog. Only when we reached a white house in the middle of a grass clearing did the terrier retire to its designated mat—as though nothing untoward had happened whatsoever.

The wind was warm and the sun had yellowed the grass. With the surrounding smooth-barked eucalyptus trees, cicadas and lush, beautifully scented flowers, I was reminded very much of parts of Australia. Once we were seated on a blue bench with a cup of mānuka tea, Anaru began his storytelling. We learned about his whānau—his uncles and aunties, nieces and nephews—and his tribe and culture. He showed us a book with pictures of the area marked as 'places of significance'. Where I could see only ordinary grass hills, for Anaru's people these places were sites of historical significance or where one god had betrayed, fought with or given birth to another. He told us he was training to become a guardian of this piece of land by the sea—a kaitiaki. By taking care of a particular place over many generations, he said, kaitiaki had accumulated a knowledge that included a spiritual link between all the plants, animals and seasons. The spring growth of certain plants, for instance, told him something about hunting or planting and harvesting. I found it so interesting to see how he braided his role as kaitiaki with his religious beliefs and scientific understanding into a colourful world view.

While Peter was resting the next day, Anaru and I took a boogie board and went walking through the dunes. He wore yellow sunglasses and a hat over his shaved head. His feet were broad and calloused from walking around without shoes for many years.

I was fascinated to hear about the time he had discovered a washed-up whale on the beach. He explained what he had done with the teeth and ambergris, which were very valuable items. 'I gave a lot away to my marae, but the biggest teeth I gifted to another tribe. This token of peace solved an old dispute between that tribe and our people.'

I learned a lot from Anaru about New Zealand. I knew that there had been conflict between early European settlers and Māori tribes, but I had thought that these things were in the past. Anaru taught me that this was still very much a current issue. There is no denying that early European settlers took land from Māori tribes that they had no right to, and that the debt for this theft is still far from settled.

When we climbed up a big dune, the sand was very warm under my feet. The sky was a deep blue and the landscape looked like a desert. Everywhere I looked were huge dunes covered with wavy patterns created by the wind. I wondered what it would be like to live here. Maybe Peter and I could come back one day, and camp in this warm dry place for a while?

We reached the top of a dune and Anaru sat down. 'What about your people?' he asked me. 'Tell me about your people.'

My people? I thought. I had never really given this much consideration. 'Holland is a small country, where three big rivers meet the sea,' I said as I sat down next to him. 'The river silt is very fertile and accommodates a big population. We might have had sacred natural places in times before Christianity, but now cities and towns have been built over the top, I guess.'

'So, what is sacred in your country?' He scooped up a handful of sand and let it slip through his fingers.

'Some buildings, like old towers and churches, are protected, and some nature reserves are fenced off. I'm not sure, but for the Dutch, maybe the family is sacred. Family provides security and a safety net.'

'It's the same with whānau here.' Anaru nodded. 'What about your siblings. What do they do?'

I had never met a person who took so much interest in my people.

I told him how Hanna lived in Sweden and Sofie had moved to France.

'How come all of your family has moved out of Holland?' he asked.

'My people are not so place-orientated. The Dutch like to travel, and they emigrate easily.'

'Yeah, I know one of your people: Abel Tasman. Don't think he liked the Ngāti Tumatakokiri warriors down south when he ran into them at Murderers Bay.' Anaru laughed and stood up. 'OK, ready? Who's going first?'

'You,' I said quickly. 'Show me how it's done.'

He took two steps then dived on top of his boogie board and glided with extraordinary speed 60 metres down a very steep dune, holding his feet up behind him. Right at the end he lifted the tip of his board and skimmed over a pond for several metres, before sinking into the clear water.

After several days with Anaru, we returned to that other world: the beach.

We walked to the rhythm of the rolling waves. On our left were endless dunes; on our right the infinite ocean. Our surroundings didn't change for days on end, yet we were amid the most ancient movement of the earth: the eternal flow of the tides, coming and going with the rhythm of the moon. The wind seemed to drive the salty mist on ahead of us. We could never reach it, yet we were always in it. Nothing ever stopped the sea or the waves, the wind or clouds or beach. None of it had stopped since the beginning of time. It kept moving, and it kept us moving.

One afternoon Peter spotted a little trickle of water coming out of the gravel and shells, just before it reached the sea. We traced it back into the dunes and found a little pond surrounded by some trees, beneath which we created a little space for our tent. When the sun set over the sea, the sky flaunted vivid orange and red clouds.

I was just walking through the gentle ribbed patterns in the soft sand to take a bath in the pond when I heard a sound. I looked up and saw three wild horses also walking towards the pool. It was magnificent to see big, strong-muscled creatures. I exchanged a look of surprise and wonder with Peter, who stood in front of the tent. When the wild horses saw us, they fled like wary deer. Their long manes and tails flew up in the air as they galloped at full speed inland. It was a remarkable sight. Horses are naturally very elegant, but these wild ones were indescribably magnificent. These free horses almost felt like a gift from Ninety Mile Beach.

A week later we reached the end of the beach. We had eaten most of our food so, once we were back on the road, I hitchhiked to the nearest town for supplies. Although there was not much traffic, I had no trouble getting a lift. In the years to come, I would hitchhike hundreds of times. Sometimes rich people with expensive cars would stop. Other times homeless people with old cars would give me a ride. Every now and then, I rode on the back of a ute in the fresh wind, and on a few occasions I was folded up between furniture in the boot. All of the people who gave me a lift were extraordinarily kind and helpful. I had no reason not to trust people's good intentions, but I also had a knife in my pocket and an ability to defend myself in case I needed to. Luckily I never found myself in any threatening situations.

I returned with enough food to last us two weeks, and we loaded it into our packs. We followed the Te Araroa trail into the forest. I had grown used to walking on the flat beach, so to suddenly climb with a 25-kilogram pack up a steep, slippery trail was a form of physical torture.

I trudged upwards for a short distance, then stopped, bug-eyed, while my heart pumped alarmingly. There was no wind to cool me down, and I was sweating profusely and panting noisily. My legs protested with every step up the near-vertical slope. When I finally made it to the top, I swung my heavy burden on to the ground. The movement and weight of my pack nearly pulled me down after it. Completely out of breath, I leaned with my hands on my pack and glanced through my arms to see where Peter was.

'Peter?' I called out.

There was no sign of him. I stood up, turned round and looked down. I waited a while. When I heard no sound, I slowly walked down. I kept going, until I saw him sitting at the bottom of the slope. His pack looked as if it had been hurled into the bushes.

'Your mule-wife has come back to save you!' I called, smiling.

'You don't have to take it,' he said, slowly getting to his feet.

'Of course I don't.' I laughed as I shouldered his pack. 'But I don't want Te Araroa turning into Te Horror-roa for you.'

The mountains over which the trail sent us were not a bit like the South Island, where a track would gradually reach a pass, followed by a long descent into a broad river valley. The big hills in Northland were steep up and steep down, which was incredibly demanding. Te Araroa was at times an ordeal for Peter, and I wanted to do anything I could to make his burden lighter, his journey more enjoyable. This journey, like our life together, was one of cooperation and symbiosis.

One hot afternoon we were climbing a muddy track up a very steep hill. Because of our heavy packs, we had to rest often and our progress was slow. We had soon drunk all our water. Every time we stopped for a rest, Peter taught me the names of trees. Some of them had tasty edible berries that lessened our thirst. Over the years I had learned the names of most of the plants and birds in the South Island, but this part of Northland was home to many species I had never seen.

When we finally reached the highest peak, we could see a great deal of Northland. Below us, we viewed the entire stretch of Ninety Mile Beach. In the east were all the bays and inlets touching the Pacific Ocean. Towards the south was a lot of farmland, forest and more sharp hills—all of which we would traverse.

'It's very different to drive through the country and look out of the window, compared to walking it all, isn't it?'

'Yes, incomparably different.' Peter smiled. 'In a car you can watch the scenery, but you can't feel the land.'

I was a little surprised when the day began to fade and we still hadn't come across any water. I began squatting down to lick drops of water off moss-covered logs. The situation had become somewhat worrying. Just when we were about to look for a spot to spend a thirsty night, Peter found a small muddy pool. We stared for a silent moment at the murky brown water.

'We'll boil it,' said Peter. He took his pack off and with a cup carefully scooped the top centimetre of brownish water into a bottle.

In the twilight we made one cup of tea before going to bed. Even though the night was very warm, I put on all my clothes to stop my sleeping bag from getting covered in mud. As I lay there, exhausted, I could taste the sweat on my lips. I was suffering greatly—not just from the thirst or the long, tiresome days walking, but also from the punishment of having to sleep with dirt, sweat and mud caked on to my body. I had grown used to the abundance of rivers in the South Island, and had always washed myself clean before sleeping. This was for me the hardest thing to deal with on our walking journey in waterless places: crawling into my sleeping bag dirty.

We walked most of the following day feeling very thirsty. Only in the late afternoon did we come upon a good creek. We stopped, pitched the tent in a beautiful little place and drank as much water as we could.

I was in a state of shock when I woke up the morning after. Being dehydrated had prevented my body from recovering at night, and I had never woken up with such discomfort.

'My body!' I whimpered. 'I can't move. My legs feel like lead.'

Peter grinned. 'Now you know how I feel most mornings!'

I looked at him wide-eyed. 'How can you endure walking all day?'

'Sometimes I have to take a painkiller, otherwise I can't sleep. My hips, back, legs and feet ache after every walking day. Unfortunately for me, there's no way round it. To do these hard journeys with an older body, I have to endure pain. To choose comfort would be so easy, but I'd never get fit and I'd never do a journey like this.' He lifted his knees.

'If you could jump into my skin, you'd be shocked.' He laughed. 'You have no idea what it is like. But when you are sixty-one just consider walking three thousand kilometres and remember me.'

I looked at his face. The corner of his eyes had gone down slightly over the years. I thought it made him look more gentle. His hair had gone quite grey now, and his beard had some white in it. He looked younger than his age, but whether he looked 51 or 61 didn't really matter to me. His health was significantly better now than when I had met him in India, and his body was certainly much stronger than it had been nine years earlier. I always said we were growing older at exactly the same rate: day by day.

The next morning, my legs felt normal again and I set out with my rifle. The gun and the bullets weighed three and a half kilos, which was heavy compared to our other items, so I tried to go hunting as often as I could to make carrying it worthwhile.

One of the most common wild creatures in Northland is the turkey. Originally from North America, these grass-eating birds are considered a fast-breeding pest and hunters are encouraged to shoot them. I had never actually seen wild turkeys before, and it took me a while to understand their behaviour.

When I heard the distinct gobbling sound, I quickly crouched down. The large birds looked quite strange, with their wattles and small red heads. Their plumage was mainly black with some white and grey speckles. I crawled towards them, but a run of 15 turkeys has many alert eyes; when one of them saw me, they all began running, one after the other, over a grassy hill and into the dense, low bushes. I stood up in full view, and walked casually in the other direction, pretending I had no interest in them. When I saw from the corner of my eye that they thought they were safe and had returned to grazing, I crept back and hid behind a shapely tree in the middle of the clearing.

Then I fired.

The sudden noise startled the turkeys. They gobbled nervously and fluttered about a bit. When the run saw that one among them had fallen to the ground, the rest all bent over the lifeless body to see what had happened to it. As I approached them, they scattered—very reluctantly.

I hesitantly lifted the dead bird by its leg. I had grown so accustomed to touching animal fur that the scaly feet of a turkey were a bit creepy. It felt like a skin of a crocodile and looked like an enormous chicken leg.

Back at our campsite, I made a tripod with three of our walking sticks, a piece of string and a hook, so that the billy could hang over the fire, rather than sitting on top of the flames. Peter cooked the turkey meat with powdered coconut cream and watercress that he had found in the creek. It tasted delicious.

We had been on our journey for several weeks now. We'd had no injuries or problems with our feet, which were clad only in sandals. Slowly, we adjusted to the weight of our packs and to the physical hardship, and we started to appreciate our nomadic wandering life.

Living in this way meant that everything was uncertain. We didn't know what tomorrow would bring, where we would sleep, whether we would find good drinking water, if there would be animals to hunt. Life on the edge was invigorating. Moving every day demanded attention to the present. Yesterday quickly became totally irrelevant; tomorrow was impossible to predict, so we were left with the present. Slowly, our long walk was cleansing our minds of the past and the future. Even though we walked with a physical burden, the walk relieved us from the mental burden of time. This gave a glorious sense of freedom.

One day, we decided to take a detour from Te Araroa, which went over a steep ridge, and walk up a river instead. We had to cross the water often, and sometimes we had to clamber over big rocks to avoid deep pools. We were amid fantastic lush forest full of bird life. The trees on the side of the river were all covered in small ferns and leaned towards the light, creating a beautiful arch over the water. The bank was sometimes rocky and steep, and covered in a carpet of moss.

We hadn't seen anybody for many days, and we were very surprised when we saw two men on horses coming round a bend in the river. They, like us, were using the river as a highway. When we saw their dogs, we understood that these men were pig hunters. I admired the way they rode their horses without saddles. One man looked to be around 50, with a bulky frame and a friendly round face. The younger man was rather shy and let the older man speak. They wore oilskin jackets and long trousers with gumboots. Round their waists they had belts with hunting knives. They knew the area very well and told us where we could find goats and pigs.

'So you fellas are gonna walk all the way to Invercargill?' the older man asked. He spoke in the same slow manner as Anaru. When I nodded, he shook his head. 'You people are crazy!' he said with a smile, and stroked the long mane of his horse.

I grinned. I had thought exactly the same thing when we had first met Jean-Charles at Mavora Lakes.

'Yeah,' said Peter. 'Sometimes we feel like that too! But walking through the entire country is a unique thing to do. We'll see a lot of different things.'

'Yes, it's amazing that the trail is here,' I said. 'We are doing it because we can, really.'

We said goodbye to the pig hunters, and eventually left the river and moved into a forest filled with kauri trees. Kauri are among the world's most impressive trees—they can grow up to 50 metres tall and live for over 2000 years. These were the biggest and oldest trees I had ever seen. Walking between these kauri created a similar inner reverence as walking into an old cathedral: I felt I was in a sacred place. The trees grew at a respectful distance from each other, and I could almost feel how their roots were connected, as if all the kauri together were one.

To be in the presence of these giants also made me realise that, once upon a time, most of the island would have been covered in enormous trees. When I expressed my sadness for what had been lost during the sawmilling years, Peter said, 'Sanctuaries are so important now. The forest only needs one good seed tree in order to come back. For us it is sad because we won't see the giant forests return, but in a thousand years they'll have regenerated. The milling of native trees has ceased in this country. Given enough time, the forests will come back.'

We sat down at the foot of a large kauri. It was so huge that all the surrounding trees looked small and spindly in comparison. Its straight grey trunk had a girth of more than 11 metres. The first branch was at least 15 metres up. Many little ferns grew on its limbs, living their entire life in the crown of this majestic tree. It was a truly awesome sight.

Whenever we needed drinking water, I walked down to the creek to fill up our bottles. On one water trip, to my astonishment I saw a possum near the creek. When it spotted me, it quickly climbed a nīkau palm. I raced back to Peter, and hastily pulled everything out of my pack to find my gun.

'What happened?' asked Peter.

'There's a possum!' I whispered, then I looked up. I smelled peanuts. Peter was eating peanuts! He was breaking our self-imposed travel code and eating them in secret. Everything was *supposed* to be shared equally. I rolled my eyes at his hand in which the peanuts were hidden, then ran on silent feet with my gun back to the possum. I waited motionless beneath the nīkau. The sun went behind a cloud and all the light patches in the forest disappeared for some minutes. I waited a long time until I saw a piece of fluffy black possum tail. Guessing where the rest of the body was, I fired.

It was unusual to see nocturnal possums during the daytime, so I checked the liver and kidneys to see if it had been sick, but it looked fine. When I returned to Peter with the skinned possum in my hand, I could not have met with a happier face. Now that we had meat, we could rest for a couple of days.

While we searched for a spot to camp, we found a kawakawa shrub. This shrub's leaves have medicinal values, and it made a very healthy and tasty tea. Eventually we found a stream with a small space beside it. This was a good place to rest. Our fire sent up a little pillar of smoke, which found its way through the canopy. While Peter cooked the possum, I looked at the stream. The water tumbled down, making a beautiful tune. I saw movement in the water, and caught sight of a small eel. Peter fed it little pieces of the possum that we wouldn't eat. In the forest, there was no waste. Every part of everything was used. Everything was part of nature.

That evening we ate cooked possum with rice. It was a very healthy meal and it tasted marvellous. After walking all day and burning up so much energy, there was no greater pleasure than to eat meat.

In the middle of the night we woke up when we heard an animal very close to the tent. It sounded like a small child clumping up the track. I listened intently, before Peter whispered, 'Kiwi!'

My eyes lit up. The famous kiwi! We lay quietly, enjoying the presence of the big flightless bird, which was now touching the tent. A minute later it began its enchanting, piping call. Twenty-five times it called out its high-pitched sound. All three of us listened for a reply from its mate in the forest, but there was none. A few minutes later, the kiwi began calling again. The kauri forest remained eerily silent in response.

After three days resting, we packed our bags and set off again. On our way through the forest, we saw baited traps, designed to kill possums, halfway up some trees. Even though I understood all the reasons for pest-control, especially in kiwi territory like this, I still got a big shock when I saw a possum hanging by one paw from a trap. Something had gone horribly wrong here. Instead of its head, the possum had put its paw in the trap and could neither escape nor relieve its suffering. It would have been many days before it had died of thirst. This was a cruel death for a helpless creature. Sometimes in the wilderness I saw things I wished I hadn't.

We walked through the hills for several days until the world of the forest came to an abrupt halt at a fence. Suddenly we found ourselves on a road amid farmland. The glaring light on the white gravel was blinding, without shielding trees the fierce wind was gusty, and without shade the sun was swelteringly hot.

Large parts of the North Island have been deforested, and the trail crossed a lot of farmland, but the road was easy to walk on, and I enjoyed the comfort of a flat surface for a change, where my pack felt light again and where we could cover 20 or 30 kilometres a day. It was often on the side of those quiet farm tracks that we found watercress, wild herbs, mint and lemon-balm to make tea. We also saw wild fruit trees. Peter had a good eye for fruit and often spotted the trees from a long distance. We would increase our pace to get there faster. I would throw my pack in the grass and climb the tree without delay. I would eat greedily as much as I could, handing fruit to Peter, and fill my pockets to eat more on the way. In this manner, we picked many peaches, plums, passion fruit and figs. To eat food—and especially precious fruit—without having to carry it was sheer luxury.

We walked over steep mountains and small hills and eventually arrived on the east coast. This part of the country was drier and more cultivated. While walking over the gentle hills, we had stunning views out to the clear blue Pacific Ocean and many offshore islands in the distance.

On one particularly hot day we had run out of water. When we saw a house, I walked up the long paved driveway with my empty bottles. I rang the doorbell and looked through the window. The place was luxurious, and the furniture expensive. It was so orderly that it looked as if nobody had lived there for a long time. This was obviously a wealthy person's holiday home.

I looked up. A red eye was watching me. A small camera followed my movements. I smiled generously. 'Water!' I said and dangled my plastic bottles in the air. I casually strolled round the house to look for an outside tap. The extensive flower garden gave off a beautifully sweet perfume. In exchange for a handful of ripe cherry tomatoes, I watered the small vegetable garden that was right next to the tap. With my full bottles and a mouth stuffed with tomatoes, I walked past several more electronic eyes and mouthed, 'Thank you!'

If the people who owned the house had been home, I imagine we would have had a cup of tea together underneath the umbrella. While I walked back to Peter, I thought of the poor and isolated communities we had passed in the forest, where the people lived so differently to this house, but had invited us to share tea, stories and music. Wherever we went, we seemed to encounter friendly people.

Over the years we had learned to recognise the faintest trace of deer and goat trails, so to follow an existing path with maps and track notes was relatively simple. We had been living outside for so long that we had no need of camping grounds or hostels. Occasionally, kind people offered us a bed in their house, but we felt most at home in the forest.

We just needed trees for shelter and firewood, and drinking water.

Intuitively, Peter always found the most beautiful sites. As soon as we had found a good place, I would level the ground and pitch the tent. In the meantime, Peter would gather firewood, then he would cook dinner while I unpacked all our gear. By the time we had eaten, we would both be exhausted. Feeling on the verge of collapse, it was quite difficult to remain friendly to one another. Sometimes I had to put in the utmost effort to remain cheerful. On those occasions, I always thought of my father, who once said to me, 'It's very simple to smile when life is easy, but difficult times will show your true character.'

We followed the azure coast past stunning bays and beaches, some of them accessible only by foot. The fine sand was easy to walk on at low tide. We used seawater to cook our food, and at the end of the day we often found little spaces to pitch the tent. We discovered beautiful secret coves and lagoons, and camped under the long arms of big pōhutukawa trees.

We were very lucky with the weather. Since the day we first set off, there had not been a drop of rain. The journey went well—until we met with The Sign. We glared in silence at the huge placard that heralded AUCKLAND CITY. Even though we were more than a hundred kilometres from the outskirts of the city, we had apparently already walked into its council's regulations. Among 10 other restrictions, the sign said it was strictly forbidden to freedom-camp on public land or light fires.

We were standing in barren, windswept dunes. We now needed trees not only as a shelter from the wind, but also to hide our orange tent. When we saw a stand of pines in the distance, we marched optimistically towards it. About a hundred metres from the trees we were suddenly accosted by a terrible stench.

A new set of signs informed us that it was illegal to enter the refuse station in front of us without permission. We had no reason to climb the gates, but we followed the surrounding fence towards the trees. We struggled through nettles, vines and prickly bushes to find a safe haven between the pines. The trees were festooned with plastic bags that flapped continuously in the wind.

While cooking our dinner on our emergency gas, a warm westerly breeze carried whiffs from the rubbish tip. Years ago, I would have felt very uncomfortable sleeping with the stink of garbage in the air. I would have felt too dignified or full of self-respect to do such things that I thought were only fit for beggars. Now, I laughingly remarked to Peter that my attitude had completely changed. We had been walking for almost two months by this point, and we were starting to feel very fit. With our physical strength, we were also starting to feel mentally stronger.

'It's good to be able to sleep anywhere,' said Peter. 'It gives me confidence that I can adjust to any situation.'

I felt a kind of inner strength too—not from having reached any status within society, but from having no standards of what was supposedly 'good enough'. Actually, anything was good enough: even a rubbish tip! If I placed myself in the position of the lowest of the low, and didn't demand anything, I could be happy with anything that came my way.

We continued down the east coast until we walked into so many restrictions that we just took a bus right through Auckland. We picked up our route just south of the city, and meandered through lush dairy farms. One night we hid our little tent among green willows and tall poplars on the banks of a wide slow river. With some dry twigs we lit a smokeless fire to cook our food. There were several blackbirds in the trees and a couple of starlings singing their melodious evening songs. The sky was adorned with gentle cloud patterns, and when the sun set, wind-feathers glowed a beautiful indigo. There were large black-and-white Friesian cows in a nearby paddock, and it felt as if I was back in the Netherlands. There was a farmhouse in the distance, and we could hear cars driving on the road. Except for the volcanoes, this part of the country looked so similar to where I had grown up. I felt comfortable in our little hiding place amid the green trees.

The trail then directed us through Hamilton and over a very big, forested volcano: Mount Pirongia. From its top we had a brilliant view over the green land, which was dotted all over with smaller and bigger cones.

One day we left Te Araroa behind, and Peter led us into quite an unknown and wild part of the North Island. For many days, we hiked over the hills through an old tawa forest towards the west. Even though we were following a path, it felt as if hardly anybody ever came here. The place seemed very secretive and left alone. We came out in a canyon and found a small cave in a tall white cliff. Its limestone walls were fluted by rainwater and overhanging in places. Little white flowers grew in the cracks. We rested for several days in this enchanting place. In the quiet hours of the morning and evening it came alive with the songs of many bellbirds. We drank water from a clear river that flowed through the gorge. The exquisiteness of this land, in the warmth of the late summer, never failed to astonish me.

One afternoon while we were looking at the reflection of the creek shimmering against the ceiling of the little cave, Peter said to me, 'Solitude is important at times, but it is really very nice to share this beauty and journey with somebody.' His voice was tender.

I looked at his shining eyes. 'Yes,' I replied.

'I'm very glad to be with you.' He held me tightly. He was not often this vocal about his affection, and it was very touching. We stood for a long time in an embrace, while the creek babbled softly and the sun made beautiful patterns through the forest. It was true: love, friendship and cooperation was a gift.

We had seen many goats in this forest. Their presence always made me feel joyful, because it gave a third dimension to the land: the dimension of survival. Goats were not difficult to hunt and their numbers always seemed plentiful. If I ever found myself in a survival situation, I would have my best chances in goat country.

I had seen a family of goats walking on the edge of the forest. By predicting their route, I had ambushed a small one. We were overjoyed to have meat, for we had been voraciously hungry. We were so ravenous that we even fried the fat from around the kidneys in the pan. We devoured that goat in the same manner as our friend Jean-Charles had wolfed down his possum stew.

The energy we burned by walking over the mountains with our heavy packs was so enormous that we were often hungry despite the wholesome food we were carrying and the meat I shot along the way. We walked at a slow pace and had many rest days, but we still burned more energy than we could take in, and over the weeks and months we lost weight. We were becoming long walkers.

While Peter waited in the forest, I hitchhiked to the nearest town, Te Kuiti, to restock. I found myself on a quiet little road that hardly anybody drove along. I waited for about half an hour before an old Land Rover appeared in the distance and slowed down well before the turnoff.

'What're you doin' here?' An old man leaned out of the open window. He had brown eyes with a blue rim.

'Hitchhiking,' I said cheerfully.

'There's nobody out here!'

'You are!' I laughed.

'Where're you from?' His voice sounded stern, but his eyes glistened merrily.

'Holland,' I chirped. 'My partner and I are walking the length of the country and—'

'Holland! Have you heard of the camp ovens that they call Dutch ovens?' he asked.

'I sure have.'

He turned his head sideways. 'Tell me how they work.'

I laughed affectionately. Only an old man would take the time to listen to a long story on the side of the road, as if the day was empty, with nothing else to do. I like old people. They have a different quality to young people—perhaps because they grew up without technology in a world that still had spare time.

When I finished explaining how we baked our bread in a camp oven, he looked at me with renewed respect. He opened his door, then one leg swung like a slow pendulum out of the vehicle. With help of the handle above the window, he climbed stiffly out of his Land Rover. 'Joe is the name,' he said and shook my hand. He was dressed in an old-fashioned tweed jacket, with a white shirt underneath. His grey trousers had folds ironed into them.

I was just about to stash my pack in the back, when he said, 'Hold on. Hold on, young lady.' He slowly made space for my pack in the boot, which was filled with old stuff.

We drove along the quiet country road at 50 kilometres an hour. I appreciated the gentle pace; I had grown used to walking speed, and anything over 10 kilometres an hour was fast to me.

'You been picking some field mushrooms?' Joe asked.

'Yes, heaps of them. They're good eating,' I replied.

'So, you're walking a trail south, you say? Where are you camping now?'

'We're at the start of Pureora Forest. Tomorrow we're heading up the mountain.'

'Be careful in the forest, won't you? Every year people get shot by deer hunters. Personally, I wouldn't go near the place in the roar. But, if you absolutely must—' he looked my way— 'then make sure you talk. Keep talking, so that the hunters can hear you.'

I nodded and looked out at the farmland that we were passing. At my feet was an old milk-powder tin with staples, a pair of pliers, a wire strainer and a hammer in it.

'You still do a bit of fencing, do you?' I pointed at the tin.

'Not any more. I used to have a five-hundred-acre sheep farm.' He told me about his sheep and the price of wool and the life of a farmer, until he said, 'I've done a bit of tramping and that, but never more than a fortnight. What's it like to walk for so long?'

'We've taken many rest days, but we've been walking for more than three months now. It's an adventure,' I said. 'There're moments of pain and exhaustion, brilliance and wonder, fear and excitement, but it's never boring.'

He patiently waited for me to continue.

'I've learned about endurance, I guess. Walking with a heavy pack up a mountain is never easy. We've got to put up with physical pain, sweat, dirt, hunger and thirst. If we can't find water, we have to continue walking until we do, or sleep without it. If my clothes stink, I have to wait for a good creek and a sunny day to wash them. If I fail to hunt something, we go hungry until I shoot an animal. If there's no one on the road when I'm hitchhiking, I have to wait.'

He laughed. 'It's great to have an adventure when you're young and still fit and strong.'

I just smiled at that.

It took us over an hour to drive to town, and in that time I learned all about his farm and family, his hopes and fears. For that short time, we were the best of friends. I recognised that friendship is a precious coincidence.

The following morning, Peter and I entered the forest. The previous week it had been warm—like summer—but today it felt as if we had walked into winter. I was glad I had bought some extra merino jumpers at the Salvation Army shop in Te Kuiti. The damp air was so cold, though, that even while climbing a spur with all our woollen clothes on we barely kept warm. The moment we stopped to fry some peanuts in ghee over a fire, we started shivering again.

We followed Joe's instructions and kept talking to try to avoid being shot at. It was strange how difficult it was to think of something to say when our lives depended on it.

'This must be what animals feel like all the time,' said Peter, anxiously looking through the trees for any sign of hunters.

I kept singing songs and calling out the most boring anecdotes, but after two days we had nothing new to say and grew quiet.

We walked between the old trees in the silent forest. Tall podocarps like the ones around us had once covered big parts of the island. In the 1940s, Pureora Forest was one of the country's last native forests to be opened up for logging, but in response to protests in the late seventies the government eventually shut down all native logging in the forest and it is now a protected area. We didn't see many birds, and there were no rivers or babbling creeks. The forest was completely still. Mist hung in the tops of the trees, keeping the outside world out. The mountain guarded its tall trees, and any sound suddenly felt like sacrilege. Between the ancient trees grew little sky-blue mushrooms— thousands of them. Their perfect shape and colour turned the forest into a magical place.

Then the first snow of the year drifted down through the motionless branches, slowly covering the forest floor. We moved through the soft, white forest, feeling invisible until we came to a gap in the trees with a breathtaking view of the enormous crater lake at Taupō. It was an awesome sight.

'We are right now walking on the edge of a super volcano,' said Peter, pulling a water bottle out of my pack. 'All these ranges were formed by the ash that came out of the Taupō volcano about eighteen hundred years ago.'

'Wow,' I exclaimed. 'Could it erupt now?'

'Any time. If it goes off, half of the island could be burned to the ground or covered in ash. It's good to remember that, no matter what we do to make our civilisation secure, this volcano here has the last word.' He took a few mouthfuls of water, before passing the bottle to me.

I looked at the calm lake. It was hard to imagine such violence.

'It seems as if we're looking at the past,' Peter continued. 'It looks as if the crater is dead, but there is an indescribable energy just beneath the surface. It is like a living animal down there that can't wait to jump out again.' He leaned on his walking sticks. 'Everything on earth is dynamic,' he said. 'The world is like a living organism.'

On the fourth day we heard a roaring stag. We knew that if we could hear it then any hunters could too, so we immediately started talking loudly again. A little later we crossed paths with a high-visibility hunting dog. It had been dressed in a bright orange jacket to prevent it being shot accidentally. Its owner soon turned up, also dressed in orange camouflage gear. Everybody here, it seemed—humans and animals alike—feared being shot.

Once we were off the mountain and out of the forest, we could relax again. As we strode through the rolling farmland, we talked about our upcoming journey down the Whanganui River in a canoe. I had been looking forward to this for a long time. Peter told me animatedly about a rafting trip he had done on the Whanganui River with his students 15 years earlier.

In the beginning, he said, the river flowed through grassy hills with willows. When this farmland turned into the national park, we would paddle through the middle of a magnificent rainforest with many tree ferns and countless wild goats. Gradually, the banks of the river would grow steeper and we would float in a leisurely way through a gigantic canyon with walls clad in soft green moss. After the gorge, we would glide so silently on the water that wild deer and pigs on the riverbanks wouldn't even notice us. Towards the end, we would find ourselves amid the brilliant autumn colours of poplars, maples and liquidambars. At nights, we would be able to pitch our tent near the water's edge. We wouldn't have to carry anything on our backs, since it would all be packed in our canoe, so we would be able to enjoy great quantities of good food, such as eggs, potatoes, vegetables and even apples and bananas. Peter added that, thanks to the canoe, the pain and agony of walking would vanish. It would cost us a small fortune to do this trip, but hey—it was a once-in-a-lifetime opportunity. A kind of a holiday, as Peter said. With every vivid description of the river, I grew more excited and impatient to step into the boat.

When we arrived in the town of Taumarunui, however, we found it difficult to find a company that would hire a canoe to us; most told us that the water was too cold at this time of year. After much asking around, we at last found an outlet that was willing to let us rent a canoe for 10 days.

The man arrived in the early morning with our canoe on a trailer. It surprised me how quickly he went through the instructions, and his laconic attitude led me to think that the canoeing was not going to be very difficult. The Canadian canoe was loaded with blue plastic barrels for us to store our gear and food in. We put the canoe in the water, then stepped into it. I took the front seat, Peter the back.

'Have a good journey!' Smiling, the man gently pushed us off. We immediately glided away down the river.

'Thank you!' I called out, lifting my paddle in the air to indicate my enthusiasm and enjoyment. The big, quiet river was very peaceful, and it was a wonderful sensation to be afloat.

'Isn't this brilliant?' I turned round to meet Peter's happy smile.

At last we could rest our tired legs, while we drifted gently down the river. There was a cold wind, but I was quite warm in my three layers of wool.

We passed underneath gentle willow branches that almost touched the shimmering water. The sun made curly shadows on the water's surface. I looked over the edge of the canoe into the river and saw the tops of underwater plants waving in the current.

'Keep looking ahead,' said Peter.

I raised my eyes. The upcoming bend in the river suddenly looked very rough. Some large rocks had transformed the quiet flow into a noisy, wild monster.

'Which route do we take?' Peter yelled over the sound of the fast-approaching roaring rapid.

I hesitantly stood up to try to get a better look, but when I nearly lost my balance I quickly sat down again. 'Keep left! Turn right at the boulder!' I shouted back.

The moment we entered the thundering rapid we lost control of the canoe. Leaning dangerously to one side, we charged at high speed towards the rock. I started furiously paddling right, to go with the main current, while Peter kept to the original plan. As a result, we hit the rock at full speed. When we were very nearly tipped into the cold river, I let out a terrified scream. For a confusing second, we stayed stuck on top of the rock, then the end of the canoe swung us round. The current jerked us free, and we wobbled on down the river—facing the wrong way.

I paddled forwards, Peter backwards, and consequently we didn't manage to go anywhere at all. Eventually, we drifted into a shallow eddy. When I jumped out to pull the canoe up on to the bank, I noticed how freezing the river water was.

I had never seen Peter so angry.

He told me to stick to the plan and cooperate. I stared dully at the bank, while he grew more heated. 'I'm already freezing,' he said angrily. 'If we fall into the river, we risk getting hypothermia! If we get tipped out and lose the boat, we won't even have any dry clothes to put on because they'll still be in the barrels!'

This was a very bad start.

This was just the first rapid. Our little guide booklet showed us that there were precisely 202 more to come.

I solemnly promised to keep to the plan and follow instructions from now on.

Unfortunately, things only deteriorated. An icy sou'wester blew up the river, forcing us to paddle hard to move downstream. With every stroke, cold water leaked into my sleeves. From where I was seated, I could only see half a metre of the canoe and—apparently, for me—it was difficult to guess the position of the rest of the boat.

Often, when I thought I was heading in the desired direction, the rear end of the canoe would swing the opposite way. When I was quite certain that I should paddle on the left side, Peter was convinced we should paddle on the right side. In combination with a strong current, we had many close calls.

With every rapid, I grew increasingly anxious, and my anxiety didn't aid my ability to navigate the rapids one bit. For reasons unclear even to myself, I managed every time to do exactly the opposite of what I should have been doing.

'Thousands of people do this every year! Whole school classes! How is it possible that you are not able to do this?' Peter said in a tone that expressed his frustration, despair and fear of falling into the icy cold water.

I grew so wretched and miserable over the days that I wished I had never set foot in that boat. With misty eyes, I looked longingly at the riverbanks. *If only I could get back on solid ground*, I thought.

Several times, our canoe was nearly tipped over by treacherous willow branches looming dangerously over the rapids. On many occasions, the fierce current almost rammed us into submerged logs, and after every rapid we were sucked in by eddies that threatened to tip us over. We made it through very few rapids without nervous shouting matches. We had reached the limits of our cooperative abilities. There was no enjoyment left in it for me. This canoe trip had become nothing more than a chain of horrible, stressful and dangerous incidents. When the river finally met the sea after 10 long days, I crawled on hands and knees out of the boat and on to the land.

'Oh, I am so glad to get out of that boat!' I nearly cried with relief.

'What? Why?' asked Peter in a surprised voice. 'Nothing bad has happened to us!'

I didn't learn how to steer a canoe through rapids, but I did learn something about anger that altered my thinking forever. I had seen Peter's anger and observed my own reaction to it, and it had occurred to me that this raw emotion was often a result of fear. The fear of losing something we thought was precious—our status, our dignity, respect or, in the more elementary cases, our life.

The weather never really improved after our trip on the Whanganui River. The autumn had conquered the land and the days were now noticeably shorter. We had to hurry in the morning to break camp, because by the time we had had breakfast the day was half gone. The forest was wet, it was increasingly difficult to find dry firewood, and the nights were becoming quite cold in the tent.

The biggest mountains of the North Island were still waiting for us: the infamous Tararua Ranges. These ranges were subject to the worst weather from all directions. We had been told that rain and snow invaded the tops even in midsummer, and I grew very nervous because it was already the middle of May. The southern winter was near.

Rather than going up the ridge track, we followed a river into the high, forested mountains. There was no trail, but Peter had seen on his map that there was a hut near the river's source. At first, walking in shallow water was easy and very enjoyable, but slowly the small stones became slippery boulders. Eventually, we were forced to clamber over huge rocks wedged in by cliffs on both sides. Just before dark we arrived at the hut.

The next morning it started raining, and we decided to rest for a day. The more it rained, the more concerned I grew. The river had risen quickly and the way back was now closed. We were forced to go over the tops. A 1300-metre peak lay ahead of us, and I had visions of finding ourselves in the fog, maybe even in thunder and lightning, and losing the track, with no idea where to go, walking off the wrong spur into an impenetrable gully, getting lost and dying.

We sat in front of the firebox in the hut, each of us engrossed in our responsibilities: I was anxiously counting our food, while Peter was silently studying the maps.

We toiled for two days through the forest towards the tops of the mountain ridge. Every 100 metres, the air grew colder. Then it began to rain. Soft drizzle covered the ancient beech trees, and the fog hanging between them gave a very mystical feeling. These trees had lived here for centuries, yet they were barely two metres tall. The lichen seemed to be illuminated in a dozen shades of bright green. Soft moss was draped over every living and dead thing. The dripping forest was surprisingly quiet, and our voices sounded strangely sinister in the silent mountain air.

We followed the spine of the mountain, and the track went up and down and up and down. When we stopped for a moment to eat some sultanas, I had to tear the zip-lock bag open with my teeth, because my frozen fingers wouldn't work. After the first mouthful, we were both shivering so severely that we quickly got going again. Our packs were slowly getting waterlogged and very heavy.

Just when it began to pour, we came to a tiny orange tin shed. It had only one bunk and a narrow bench nailed to the wall, but I was very grateful for the shelter. I took my wet shorts off and exchanged them for woollen leggings with a pair of trousers over the top—warm layers that had been kept dry in the special dry-bag in my pack. We made tea and a meal using our emergency gas.

Wearing three woollen jumpers, I hardly fitted into my sleeping bag on the top bunk. Lying on my back, my nose was 10 centimetres from the ceiling. Even with all my clothes on I still felt cold that night. Somebody had left behind one old woollen glove. It looked and smelled as if it had been deserted 30 years ago, but it kept my left hand warm.

In the morning it was still pouring. We wriggled into the previous day's wet gear and set off into the rain. The first 10 minutes were horrible, but after that I grew used to the soaking clothes I was wearing.

We had to follow a slippery forest path down. I was holding on to trees to stop myself from sliding in the mud. It was toilsome, dangerous work, and I knew that one moment of carelessness might send me sliding down. After a while, I grew aware of a roaring noise in the distance. We were very high up in the mountains, but we could clearly hear the flooded rivers in the valleys far below.

The path climbed out of the forest, on to the barren spine of the mountains. I lost all sense of direction in the mist and fog. I simply followed Peter. He had studied the map so closely that he knew the route by heart. I could only see his tanned slender legs in front of me. His sandals left clear footprints in the yellow-brown soil. Our whole world was a thick blanket of mist. Civilisation and other humans felt very far away.

I noticed Peter stumbling as he climbed over the rocks. I could see he was tired. Worried, I tried to think of what else I could transfer from his pack to mine.

'I'm totally out of energy,' Peter said, when I reached him near the top of another peak. I clicked the two-kilogram tent off his pack. I put my pack into the soggy tussock grass and tied the tent on top of my pack.

'You've already got too much weight, sweetie,' he said wearily.

He pulled the map out of his pocket. It had been folded so often that there was now a big white cross over it that had wiped out some details. His long hair hung sadly down. Big drops fell on the flimsy piece of paper. Eventually he slowly turned round and continued towards the mountaintop.

We were very glad to finally see the hut. It was built high above the bush line. If the weather had been clear, we would have had a fantastic view, but we were in a world of mist and clouds. There was a firebox, but no wood. A whole pile of cardboard boxes had been left on a shelf in the ceiling by people who must have flown in on helicopters and brought their gear in the boxes.

'We'll light a fire with the cardboard.' Peter smiled.

I was surprised at how long the cardboard could burn for. While we played chess in our sleeping bags, the fire dried our gear.

'We've got to make the most of the good weather,' Peter stated the next morning.

'Good weather?' I saw nothing but a sheet of rain out of the window.

'This is a northerly wind,' he said, looking at his compass. 'This is warm, considering we're at about thirteen hundred metres. If the wind turns east or south, we'll become ice-blocks the moment we're back on that ridge.'

I remembered the stories I had heard about Mount Everest, where climbers passed the frozen bodies of the dead on the side of the track. I started packing.

We stepped out of the hut and straight into a curtain of rain. It took 15 minutes to climb back on to the mountain ridge.

The storm came from the other side, and we were nearly tossed into the air and blown backwards at the same time. The wind roared. The harsh raindrops battered my face and bare legs like small stones. This was not a place for humans. 'Let's go back!' I yelled in panic.

'We have to go on!' Peter's words were almost drowned out by the screaming wind and rain.

The water in my eyes prevented me from seeing anything. Battling a howling storm was the last thing in the world I wanted to do. I wanted to return to the hut, burn cardboard boxes and play chess.

Peter pointed with his stick in the direction of the trail. I wanted to tell him to go back to the hut. 'Wait!' I shouted, but when I started walking towards him, he took that as agreement and turned into the storm. The noise of the rain on my hood was so deafening that I held my walking sticks in one hand, and used the other to shield my right ear.

We climbed further into the daunting weather. It was now just step by step. I was soon exhausted. I was carrying most of Peter's gear, and my waterlogged pack was incredibly heavy. The dense cloud had transformed the tops into a sinister world of gloom. The ridge was sometimes so narrow that it gave me the impression that there was an infinite crevasse on both sides.

We had to climb over a big rock, and Peter let me go first. I pushed my walking sticks under my armpits so I could use my hands. One stick started sliding into the abyss. Luckily, Peter was right behind me and grabbed my stick in time. I looked at the trustworthy sticks that had saved me countless times from falling. They were varnished by years of being held in my oily hands. My shiny golden-brown poles had given me balance and confidence, and I could not afford to lose them.

Slowly, we climbed into the dark clouds, while the rain continued falling like stones on my hood. Watching Peter's feet was very comforting: I was not alone, and he knew the way. He was constantly meeting the void. I was overcome with a great admiration for my courageous man. For all he knew, he was alone in the misty world. He could only see five metres of the narrow pathway ahead, wedged in by tussock and stones. He must have been exhausted and afraid, but he kept our journey unfolding.

Here we were, in a storm on top of a mountain. All our belongings were on our backs. There was no house waiting for us in the valley, with a kitchen full of food or wardrobes full of clothes. This moment was our life. There was nothing else. We would walk to the next hut, dry our gear, wash our clothes, walk on, pitch our tent and hope it would stop raining. Then we would walk again.

On and on we would go.

After an arduously long ascent, we suddenly met with a signpost that marked the summit. Peter turned round. The merciless rain pelted his face. He smiled and stretched out his hand. I grinned. We shook hands while the storm howled all around us.

I kissed the back of his wet hand.

Peter pointed with this stick down the mountain.

'Down!' I yelled and we both laughed.

We were the very last people to leave the Tararuas that year. Behind us, the road collapsed and was not rebuilt until a nearly year later. Wellington had been flooded and people had died. Once again, we seemed to find ourselves in the midst of the worst storms in the country. After six months of walking, we finally arrived in Wellington, where it was already winter. We rested.

CHAPTER 11

TE ARAROA:
THE SOUTH ISLAND

It was September. We thought that spring was near, but dark clouds loomed over the sea as we walked on to the ferry in Wellington. While we cruised towards the South Island, I anxiously looked out of the window at the approaching rainstorm. I didn't feel like walking into horrible weather.

The trail officially started in the northernmost part of the Marlborough Sounds, but when we heard that the whole area was flooded we decided to take a bus to Pelorus Bridge, the beginning of the forest. On the way, we saw flooded farmland in the torrential rain.

'Good morning, ladies and gentlemen. In ten minutes, we'll make a quick stop to drop off two passengers,' said the cheerful bus driver over the speakers. 'I hope you've brought your togs, because we're in a weather bomb!'

When other passengers turned round, I saw a look of pity on their faces.

'Right,' said Peter, and put on his raincoat.

'Where are you walking to?' asked a man in front of me.

'Invercargill.' It felt like a punishment, rather than something to be proud of.

'Oh, well, good luck,' he replied. He sounded as dispirited as I felt.

When we stepped into the rain, I felt miserable. My pack was heavy and uncomfortable. My hood fell over my eyes so that I could only see the dirt road underneath my feet. We didn't say much for the first hour.

As the road slowly morphed into a walking track, the rain eased. A little breeze dried out our clothes as we approached the forested mountains. Patches of mist in the gullies were lifting in the warm spring sunshine. We eventually came to a clear turquoise river that had carved a slide through solid rock. I stood still and watched the beauty in awe. Here we were, in the middle of a pristine forest, and I suddenly saw that everything in nature was innocent and complete. Every stick and stone on the riverbank was pure and unblemished. I took a deep breath. 'It's good to be back in the South Island.' I looked at Peter's shining blue eyes, so similar to the river at my feet.

I had not missed the South Island while walking in the North, but now that I was back I appreciated the wild southern beauty even more. There are just over a million people in the South Island, and most of them live on the coast. The rugged Southern Alps are admired, even worshipped, and mostly left alone.

We had to adjust to the hardship of walking all over again, but this time it took only a few days to return to the rhythm of a nomadic life. The weather cleared, the clouds lifted and, when the sun came through, it was suddenly very warm.

Several days later, we were following a track that ran steeply up a mountain. On our right was a stream that had carved out a deep gully. In the late afternoon, we climbed down into this forested ravine to look for a ledge to spend the night on. We pitched our tent in soft leaf litter near a spectacular little waterfall. All around us were gigantic boulders on which very old trees grew. It was wonderful and secretive—as if it came out of a fairy tale.

I washed our clothes in the river and, while they dried in the last of the sunshine, I sat beside our fire. The smoke wound its way up through the trees. Peter, standing on large tree roots, was gazing down the waterfall. In his hand were two branches for the fire. His red merino shirt stood out in the light of the sunset. His strong shoulders were broad, his hair curly and healthy, and his face tanned. He was beautiful.

When night fell, we were—as always—grateful to lie down. We had only pitched the inner tent because there was no sign of rain. Through the gauze we looked at the shapes of the trees, which were peacefully swaying in the warm breeze. I could see part of the Milky Way through a gap in the branches. The sound of the swift creek was soothing, and we lay there quietly for a long time.

'Miriam, are you sleeping?'

'Yes.'

Peter laughed softly. 'This is what we're walking for, eh? To find places like this.'

I slowly turned to face him. He was lying on his back, looking up at the night sky. I lifted myself on to one elbow and kissed him softly on the forehead. 'Yes,' I whispered. 'To live in beauty.'

The following morning, we reached the edge of the forest and climbed into alpine country. As we got higher, the air became colder and we had to put on several woollen jumpers. When the ridge merged again with the forest, we came across a little creek and a flat spot where we pitched our tent. Not a minute later, it began to hail. I couldn't see the hailstones falling; I could only see them bouncing when they hit the ground. The little dancing pellets were a magnificent sight.

Slowly, the thick green moss on the forest floor turned white. While I tied our walking sticks into a tripod, Peter gathered firewood and stashed it underneath the trees to keep it as dry as possible. Then the hail turned into snow. Thick flakes floated silently down through the mossy branches, concealing everything under a 10-centimetre blanket. We huddled round our fire to keep warm. Big plumes of breath rose into the sky when we talked. We went to bed with all our clothes on, including a hat and scarf, and we were still freezing.

In the morning, the wind changed again. The air was fresh and the sky blue. I set off into the snow with my rifle and followed the creek up between stunted beech trees. The mountain was very steep, and when I rested for a moment against an old tree a bird down in the gully sounded the alarm. I waited in silence, and a little later heard a rustle in the thick ferns. I lifted my rifle, but I knew from the hurried swoosh that it was not a goat. My eyes flashed anxiously over the snowy ferns, until I spied the black back of a boar. It was moving swiftly up the mountainside. It stubbornly pushed through the bushes and shrubs with its big, strong neck. The pig wasn't aware of me standing there until it got quite close. Then it froze abruptly, its short tail and one leg still in the air. It stood completely motionless. For a moment, there was not a sound in the entire forest.

With its hairy body and long white tusks, the boar was magnificent and strong. In my state of awe, it didn't occur to me to try to shoot such an animal. Then a little breeze betrayed my scent and signalled danger to the boar. It snorted loudly and scarpered into the bush at an incredible speed.

As I continued up a long ridge, I realised that every type of animal has a totally different character. I wondered what animals make of humans. They must see us as very unpredictable creatures—sometimes friendly and kind; at other times violent and ruthless.

I came out in alpine country, where the tussock was covered in a layer of snow. As I climbed towards a ridge, I placed my feet carefully between the slippery stones. My gaze followed the line of the mountain and I spotted a dark speck near a big rock. A minute later the dot had moved, and I knew that it must be an animal. Over the years, my eyesight had improved. Without binoculars, and thanks to endless hours peering into the distance, I had learned to recognise shapes and movements across big spaces.

This terrain was so open that I feared the animal had seen me too, so I cautiously crept to the shady side of the ridge, where the snow had piled up thickly between the rocks. The air was so warm that my bare feet in my sandals didn't feel the cold snow at all. After climbing for a long time, I reached a big pillar that I could hide behind to spy. To my surprise, there were a dozen wild goats grazing the alpine herbs. I slithered on my stomach over the snowy stones until I was able to fire at a small brown goat. At the sound of my gunshot, the rest of the goats disappeared into the forest. I looked at the sky. Two hawks had been following my movements and were circling overhead.

When I removed the insides of the goat I had shot, I noticed that, even though the animal was dead, its intestines were still working. I watched in fascination and realised that, underneath my own skin, my internal organs were moving like that. Intestines are like an organism within an organism. I left some of the carcass for the hawks and walked back with our share of meat.

I felt incredibly happy. To roam through the wild, desolate mountains, where extreme weather reigned, and be able to hunt for my own food gave me such a feeling of independence and freedom. Our nomadic life was extremely demanding physically, and the wild meat gave us the energy we needed.

The next morning we rolled up our tent and followed the trail towards the top of the mountain. It was warm and there was no wind. We sat down and lit a small fire with the dead branches of alpine shrubs. There were no creeks up on the ridges, but there was still snow in the shade, so I scooped some into the billy and we were able to make tea and flatbread. While we ate our lunch, we gazed at the fantastic panorama around us. In the crisp air the view was crystal clear. Towards the west, we could see Nelson.

'That was once my whole world,' said Peter, who grew up on a sheep farm on the edge of the town. 'Can you believe it? It felt so big as a kid. From here it looks tiny.'

Across the sea we could see Abel Tasman National Park, where we had lived for a year in the little rat-cottage beneath the mountains. To the east, we could see the province of Marlborough, where almost six years earlier our wilderness adventure had started. I remembered myself with my bow and arrow, cautiously exploring the wild riverbeds, always a bit afraid of getting lost.

It was interesting to sit and look at all these places where we had spent so much time. In each bay, valley and mountain a story now nestled. When I looked at each of these corners of the wilderness, I was looking at a part of my own life.

We walked for days along the incredibly steep spine of the Richmond Range. In these rugged mountains, progress was slow. Sometimes we would only cover 10 or, at best, 15 kilometres a day. After two weeks, we had walked down our first range of mountains and were looking up at the second. Since it was the tail end of winter here in the high country, the pass was still covered in thick snow. We were not equipped to mount the snowy saddle, so we decided to walk the long way round.

For many days we walked along a deserted four-wheel-drive track amid snow-capped mountains. Eventually, we came out in a broad valley with beautiful side rivers and longstanding forest. Geese gathered in the riverbed, and paradise ducks flew noisily overhead. It was a wild and remote place, but once upon a time the valley floor had been part of a sheep station. One day while walking through the long green grass, we came to the archaic abandoned homestead. It had the same ambience as Elisabeth's place had had. Some of the fruit trees around the house were still alive. There were shepherds' cottages and big old barns where all the horses had been stabled. When I looked through the kitchen window, I saw a coal range and wondered what life had been like for the family who had once lived here.

We rested in the shade of an old willow tree. Its leaves were bright green with spring growth. We lit a small fire in the sand and boiled some water to make tea from lemon balm, which grew abundantly around the house. I watched the water boiling in the billy. Big bubbles were pushing the small ones out of the way. It was quite beautiful.

'Do you know that peak?' Peter pointed at a snow-capped mountain in the distance.

I shook my head. 'No, never seen it.'

'Yes, you have!' He laughed. 'You know that mountain very well. On the other side is Bob's Hut.'

'Oh, yes. Of course!'

'Remember sitting in Downie's Hut for three weeks?'

'Yes, it almost feels as if we were there yesterday! Remember how happy we were with the blue sky after all that rain?' I looked at all the mountains around me. 'In those early days, the forest and mountains sometimes felt ominous and frighteningly wild to me. I haven't felt that way for a long time now.'

'I think that if you don't have a house and live out in the wilderness the mountains become your home, and those forbidding aspects are not so fearsome any more.'

'And the thing reverses,' I joked. 'The deadly silence in a house becomes creepy and ominous!'

'Yes, but you've also naturally matured over the last ten years,' Peter said. 'You're not afraid to be alone any more. Instead of finding security in me or in our relationship, you've found security in yourself, I think. Remember years ago you created security in what you called the cocoon?'

'Hmm . . .' I nodded.

'Well, I reckon the cocoon has dissolved. The butterfly has flown out.' He slowly reclined in the green grass. His head rested on a big branch as if it was a soft pillow.

After a long lunch break, we entered the mountain beech forest and it began to rain. While searching for a big tree to shelter under, we saw a herd of wild horses. They stood solemnly between the trees, simply enduring the rain and the wind. They calmly watched us walk past from a safe distance. They appeared impervious to the weather; nothing seemed to matter to them. Except for the occasional flick of the tail, they were perfectly still. Resilience and endurance were their main attributes; the valley and the forest were their home.

After many weeks following Te Araroa, we eventually came out near a highway through Lewis Pass, where I could hitchhike to a town with a supermarket. I left our camp very early in the morning, but when I reached the road there was not a vehicle in sight. I waited for a long time in the cold wind before I heard an engine. A shiny blue car raced round the bend at enormous speed. It hurried past, then came to a shrieking halt some hundred metres down the road. I ran to it.

'Thank you for stopping!' I yelled over the blasting rock music.

The woman behind the wheel smiled, turned the volume down and asked me how I had ended up here in the middle of nowhere. I told her about our way of life while she brought her car back up to speed—100 kilometres an hour. For the first half-hour, I was terrified. I saw potential accidents waiting at every corner and with every approaching car.

'Just you and your partner? Twenty-four hours a day?' she exclaimed. 'You spend more time together than couples who've been married for fifty years! You say you've been together for ten years?' She tucked her straight blonde hair behind her ears, picked up her smartphone from between her knees and looked at the screen for a split second. 'How do you do it?' She smiled, showing white teeth. She looked to be about 40, and had a friendly face, beautiful skin and nice perfume.

'I don't know, really.' I glanced at the mini dreamcatcher that dangled from the rear-vision mirror. 'Choose a life you like and a person you like, I suppose.'

She laughed. 'That's a good one!' She touched my arm briefly, in a way that made me feel as if we had been friends for years. 'I married the father of my kids. Little did I know he would turn into such an arsehole!'

I laughed at the carefree manner with which she spoke about such serious things.

'We stayed together for seven years,' she continued. 'The youngest one was four when we finally split up. I'm seeing someone else now. He's nothing like Roger was.' She looked at her fingers on the steering wheel, and I followed her gaze. Her long nails were painted purple. 'So what do you reckon is the key to a good relationship then?' she asked.

The key? I thought. Relationships are very complex. I wasn't sure there was a simple answer. 'I greatly dislike conflict,' I said eventually. 'But, if Peter expresses criticism, I always try to listen and not to defend myself. If he's been unreasonable, I'll bring it up again a few days later, but often it's hardly relevant any more by then.'

'Is that right? I'll give it a try.' She looked at me an instant, before returning her gaze to the road. 'So, you live in the bush?'

'Yeah, that's why your whole car smells of wood smoke!' I laughed.

She assured me she didn't mind the wood smoke, then asked, 'But what the hell do you do when you have your period?'

'I've got a Mooncup. It's a silicon-based thing that looks a bit like a wine glass. You wash it out in the river when you need to, then just put it back in. It's very light and handy.'

'In the river?' She laughed and shook her head. 'Fucking hell, girl. You won't catch me living in the sticks. Do you have your stuff stored somewhere in a container, then?'

'What stuff?' I asked, grinning.

'Your furniture and that.'

'Actually, I don't own much at all, really.'

She looked at me for a moment. 'You only have what's in your pack?'

I nodded.

'Wow. That must be quite a relief, in a way, I guess. At least you don't have to worry about bills and getting all the stuff you own fixed!'

She dropped me in Amberley, a town surrounded by farmland. The difference in temperature was enormous. October in the mountains was mostly cold and windy, but here in the lowlands it already felt like midsummer. There were beautiful flowers everywhere. On my way to the shops, I reflected on her last comment. I appreciated not owning much. Life was simpler without a lot of belongings that require care and maintenance. It seemed to me that possessions have a crafty way of possessing the owner.

After shuffling for some time along the supermarket aisles, I stood still and watched the everyday busy-ness around me. Music was playing, and the scanners at the checkouts were bleeping noisily. I felt confused for a while, until I realised that I was looking around with a hunter's mind. I was trying to take everything in—all the products and people—rather than just focusing on the task at hand. Then I remembered my shopping list.

I used to be quite selective when it came to food, and would only buy very healthy items. But, after walking for eight months on Te

Araroa, the quality of the food became less important. A one-dollar loaf of bread tasted just as good to us as a five-dollar loaf. That night, we would eat a dozen eggs with our cheap bread, a tin of corn and baked beans, and everything would taste delicious.

A hundred and fifty years ago, the only route between Christchurch and the West Coast was a narrow pack-trail through the mountains. It had been made with picks and shovels and was designed for horses. When they first marked the track, they had blazed the trees with an axe. The scars were still visible on some of the old beeches.

In those early days, walking this trail would have been a necessary part of life. Over the years, the relationship with the forest had changed. Now people came for their enjoyment, and saw the environment as scenery.

The pack-trail's perfect gradient was very pleasant to walk on. Near the path were several natural hot springs, where we soaked our tired muscles. Summer was coming, and the first small berries appeared. After bathing, we spent hours picking and eating wild fruit.

The old pack-trail led us over Harpers Pass, and as soon as we were on the other side we smelled the fragrance of lush, jungle-like vegetation and moist air. We were entering the west side of the range. The mountaintops were lost in the clouds. The cliffs looked grim and uninviting, yet the green valley floor was very pleasant. In the northern sky bloomed a purple-red lenticular cloud, and from that same direction we suddenly heard a raspy call. 'Kea! Kea! Kea!'

A big green mountain parrot came soaring down. The kea must have seen us from a distance. Its green wings were stretched out like a gymnast's arms and it landed with outstretched legs on a rock. Tilting its head from side to side, it studied us intently. It didn't appear to be afraid or anxious; I saw only curiosity and intelligence in its eyes.

'Hello,' said Peter, in a parrot-like voice.

The kea hopped closer with awkward little skips, then it sidled towards Peter's pack, which leaned against the rock. With its large bill, the bird pulled at a little cord. Then it looked at us again, and opened its beak. Its tongue moved swiftly, creating a peculiar chatter. We three sat there together for a while. It tried to eat the paper map that lay folded in the grass. Then, eventually, it flew away.

'Keas are extremely intelligent,' said Peter. 'There have been some studies done that showed they could even be as clever as chimpanzees. They were once common, but are endangered now and a protected species.'

In the still evening we could hear several kea calling to each other. The sound was so very beautiful and enchanting.

I felt a sense of relief when our trail reached Arthur's Pass and returned to the east side of the island, where it was drier. We traversed old forests and walked into barren, desert-like country. The landscape was round and curvy. It was not difficult to climb these mountains, but the distances were vast. From the high passes, we could see for many kilometres.

Some of the land we passed through had once been sheep stations, but was now part of the conservation estate. The forest in the valley floor had been burned a long time ago, but the native tussock grass now concealed any sign of the past. With the rocky outcrops and boulder-strewn streams and rivers, it was a very weather-beaten place.

Even though the Department of Conservation now took care of this land, the old musterers' huts were still there for the public to use. The four-by-four-metre huts were made out of stone or wood. They were very basic, but provided good shelter from rain or snow. There was always a table, on which we played chess, and an old cupboard with books, which we read with delight, and tin jars filled with musty tea leaves. The musterers' names were carved into the wood, reminding us of a time that was now a distant memory.

We were walking along the banks of a clear river one day when we heard a piercing cry: a falcon stood atop a tall pillar of rock, guarding its nest. We wanted to give it a wide berth, but we were caught between the rock face and the river. With our walking sticks crossed above our heads, Peter and I entered the falcon's territory. When we came closer to its stone tower, the bird screeched fiercely, then launched itself into the air and dived towards our heads. Luckily, our sticks were a sufficient defence. While the falcon made several attempts on us, Peter began telling a story about a friend who had once gone too close to a falcon's nest—he had been attacked and ended up with an ugly scar on his face. I was now very nervous and wondered whether a second falcon might soon appear.

It was obvious that the angry bird wouldn't hesitate to strike us if it had the chance, and we warily shuffled out of its territory. While Peter glanced ahead to look for an approaching female falcon, I walked backwards in case the male decided to attack us from behind. When the falcon rose again, I realised that it was not its strength or size that asserted its dominance; it was its fearlessness.

Our trail eventually left the DOC land and continued over a private farm track. Everything was neatly fenced off, but there were no sheep or cows, because there was no grass. Rabbits had eaten it all. As far as the eye could see, rabbit holes peppered the sandy soil and dozens of small rabbits ran about. I had heard stories of farmers who had been forced to walk away from their land because of the destruction wrought by rabbits, but now I saw for myself just what damage a plague of these seemingly harmless creatures could do.

We lost track of days and dates and walked endless kilometres through the mountains. Sometimes it took more than two weeks to come across a road, so we had to load our packs with food, making them heavy. The sections were longer than in the North Island, but over the months we slowly got stronger and stronger. Some days, we were extremely exhausted; some days, we felt energetic. When we were lucky enough to have wild meat, we soon felt our moods and energy levels rising.

I also knew the importance of rest: the body needs enough recovery time to repair muscle tissue and ligaments, and to prevent long-term damage. I carefully watched for any sign of fatigue or over-training in both Peter and myself, and we didn't suffer from any illness, chronic pain or injury. Nor did we ever hurt ourselves. Walking the entire trail in sandals helped me greatly, because it forced me to walk slowly and carefully.

The two big barriers we came across along the Te Araroa route were both huge rivers. When we reached the Rakaia, we looked at the braided river from a distance. Between the channels was sand and gravel, and sometimes grass and trees. The walk across would be about five kilometres, but some of the channels looked very deep and swift. So we hitchhiked more than 40 kilometres to a bridge, then back up the other side again to rejoin the Te Araroa trail. The country roads were so quiet that we had to walk most of the way. A week later, we did the same thing to get across the second river—the Rangitata.

One hot day, we left the forested valley behind and climbed up towards a pass over the Two Thumb Range. Around us, the landscape was golden brown with tussock, some bushes and an occasional rocky outcrop. The sun was so fierce that I walked in a hat and a light blouse to protect my skin against the strong light.

We thought we saw wild sheep on the tops, but when we came closer we discovered it was a big herd of wild tahr peacefully grazing the alpine vegetation. In their summer coats, these magnificent creatures were remarkably well camouflaged. Some were eating, while others were looking out. They seemed to cooperate without effort.

We walked over the pass and descended until we found a good place to camp. The evening was very still and beautiful. The air was slightly cool and the sky had a scarlet tint, which promised a good day tomorrow. Rosehips grew among the speargrass and tussock, and the beautiful perfume of the pink flowers was carried on the slight breeze up the valley. We built a stone circle and lit a fire with the roots of alpine shrubs. We cooked a small meal of rice and lentils. I was just cleaning the pot with sand in the riverbed when, out of the corner of my eye, I saw a rabbit hopping in the distance. The three previous evenings, I had been hunting without success. Now that a rabbit was right here, I anxiously searched for my gun.

I crept 30 metres through the tussock. Lacking enough cover to get any closer, I was forced to shoot from a long distance. The bullet hit the rabbit's leg, but didn't kill it.

'It's still alive!' shouted Peter after my first shot.

I tried to shoot again, but missed. The wounded rabbit started to crawl away. I stumbled to my feet and ran between big tussocks to the creek. In my hurry, I slipped off a rock and nearly fell in the water. Wildly panting, I made it across and sped as fast as I could to the rabbit. When I got closer I felt for my pocketknife, but it wasn't there—I had forgotten it. I had to take a close-up shot.

Pfeeeew.

The bullet went through the rabbit, hit a stone and ricocheted. It flew just past me.

I froze. I felt dazed, almost paralysed. I realised the bullet had very nearly hit me.

Peter stood motionless beside the fire. He was looking at me. It was as if the whole world stood still for a moment. The tussock had never been more tranquil underneath the calm evening sky. The silent rocky mountain had never been more serene. I could feel the pulse, the rhythm and the heartbeat of life itself. As I stood there, I was reminded of the fragility of life—my life.

I picked up the rabbit, and my feet slowly found their way down the steep rockslide.

When I reached the water, I scooped a handful out of the swift creek. It tasted sweet.

The sun sank silently behind the mountain, leaving a last red glow along the tops of the mountains.

Peter had his first encounter with civilisation in four months when we walked into the small, friendly town of Twizel.

'Wow, it's so different!' Peter was gazing around, as we entered a field edged with flower beds and benches. 'You know what's most amazing?' he asked. 'It's all made for humans. The road, footpath, shops, seats, food—even those flowers are planted for our enjoyment. Marvellous, isn't it?'

I smiled at him striding around with a spring in his step. I went to check my email, but Peter said he'd rather talk to people face-to-face.

'Good luck!' I ran to the computer. On my way, I caught sight of myself in a mirror. Two big green eyes glared at me, as if they didn't belong to me. My face was tanned and weather-beaten, with lines around my eyes from looking into the sun. My head looked a lot bigger than I remembered. I guess my body had become smaller. I had lost a lot of fat and my muscles were quite pronounced.

Around midsummer, when the days seemed endless and the nights were short, Peter suggested taking a detour away from Te Araroa into a forested valley. To reach this wild place, we had to climb over a rugged pass. It was an exhausting scramble in the heat. It took all morning to arrive at the top, but the view was breathtaking. The mountains around us were sharp, rocky peaks. The clear river far below ran through a pristine forest. This valley had no road or track. Looking at it from this great height, I could sense the pure wildness. The air was still and everything so silent that even an approaching bumblebee sounded loud.

On the way down the steep, rocky crags and shingle slides, we walked past big white Mount Cook lilies. They were lush compared to the other alpine flowers. Between the rocks and gravel, beds of sweet snowberries hid, and we ate them with relish. When we reached the river, we strolled through grassy clearings and old forest alive with birdsong. We followed small animal tracks along the water's edge, until the banks slowly rose into a steep gorge. In the deep pools we saw rainbow trout, but without a fly-fishing rod we could not catch them. As it lowered behind us, the sun cast deep shadows over the sparkling water. It was undoubtedly the most peaceful and pristine valley I had ever seen in New Zealand.

———

One night we found a soft campsite underneath some old trees. We lit a fire with the abundant driftwood to cook our hare stew. Since it was such a beautifully still evening, we went for a little walk after dinner. We ambled through high grass and yellow flowers, and sat down on a big outcrop. The air was a little hazy and heavy with the fullness of summer. The subtle perfume of wild flowers drifted upstream. In the warm evening sun, everything glowed golden.

'On days like today, when the world is extraordinarily beautiful, I think of death,' said Peter. 'Because I hope I'll die in a beautiful natural place like this.'

His words hung in the air between us.

'One day, my sweet Miriam, I'll die, and you will live,' he said tenderly. 'It's very sad and tragic in a way, but that's the price we pay for our life together.'

'Yes.' I put my elbow round his leg and my head on his knee.

'To love someone is to give the other space to put down roots, grow tall and to flower,' he said. 'A flower blossoms for maybe a week, maybe for a long summer, but eventually it will finish blooming. The colours will fade and the plant will wane.'

We fell silent and I watched the long grass move in the wind.

Peter turned to me. 'Don't look so sad. I'm not going yet. I still have a lot of energy left. I can do many things for many years. But one day I will have to rest, while you will go on. And one day, like the flowers, you will have to let me go when I die.'

I looked at the coarse grey rock underneath my feet. My throat hurt. Tears were welling up.

'Maybe, long before that time, you might want to go off on your own. I might have to let you go.' He gazed up at the mountaintops.

'I won't go away,' I said softly.

'You don't know that. You might. You're strong, and you've got a lot of energy. You can go anywhere in the world. You might want to travel on your own, or do things that I can't do. You are free to go any time, if you so wish. Of course you're free—you know that, don't you?'

I stroked his knee, and then I held it tightly against my chest.

'I just don't want to hold you back, you know,' he said quietly.

The river below me became blurry. Tears were in my eyes. I shook my head. 'You don't hold me back, sweetie.'

'I hope not.' He kissed my arm.

We looked in silence at the beauty around us.

'It occurred to me the other day,' he said at last, 'that, when I see the place where I'll die, I'd like to think that I'll recognise it. Then I'll know the time has come to stay in one place. Maybe it will be a quiet spot by a lake in the mountains, where I'll live out my life until I have to leave this earth. It might be just a foolish idea, but it would be nice.' His hand rested on my back.

'But not yet, eh?' I whispered.

'Not yet, no. Don't cry now,' he said when he saw my watery eyes.

I covered my face with my hand. A tear rolled through my fingers and fell on the rock.

'Look at that tree.' Peter pointed to a fallen beech below us. 'The tree dies and falls over, and makes light and space for the new seeds. In a way, life and death are one.'

We quietly enjoyed the beautiful evening, which suddenly had become very precious. Little insects flashed brightly in the lowering light. A wind-feather in the west lit up with the colours of the sunset. The clouds turned pink and purple, before the dusky sky slowly became grey.

We wandered down many unknown valleys. We explored hidden side creeks, lit fires to cook our wild meat, and camped under stands of trees that had probably never seen humans before. We were living the nomadic life we had dreamed of. It felt natural to walk onwards and be comfortable in any given place. The feeling of being on an ongoing journey was wonderful. It felt as if we were moving at the same pace as the animals, the growing plants, and the coming and going seasons.

We eventually arrived at Lake Hawea. Situated in Otago, the lake and its surroundings were barren and bone dry. We camped beneath some eucalyptus trees on the edge of the lake, and in the morning I woke up to the chorus of many birds. I drowsily gathered my clothes in the half dark and crawled out of my sleeping bag. I took my empty pack and walked along the dusty road towards the town for a resupply, hoping an early traveller might pick me up on the way. The whole world seemed at peace, slowly awakening to a brand-new day. The air was dry and fresh, and a soft breeze carried the scent of eucalyptus and pine.

I had slept well and I felt very refreshed. The flat road I was striding along was easy compared to the terrain we had just covered. My body felt as strong as that cheetah we had seen at Wellington Zoo. To be so fit, to have such boundless energy, to feel so comfortable in my body was an almost intoxicatingly joyful experience. I felt like I could jump up and reach the highest branches. I looked at my feet and hands, and for a short moment I was so surprised that I existed in a body; that I was able to experience the world in a physical sense.

The lake was azure blue—an extravagant colour, a pleasure for the eyes. All round the lake were steep mountains. The sunrise created a spectacular red glow on the rocky cliffs. But it wasn't just the view that made me feel like I was walking through heaven. The dry earth, with its brown grass and dusty air, reminded me of Africa. In this warm climate I could sit in the dry grass without getting dirty. If I washed my clothes they would dry in minutes, and if it rained I wouldn't freeze to death.

Scenery, I realised, was only a small part of enjoying a place. We had walked through so many different landscapes. All had their own plants, trees, flowers, animals and therefore beauty. A rabbit beneath a scented pine was as beautiful to me as seeing a kea in a high tree overlooking lush valleys and grand glaciers.

I walked more than 10 kilometres before the first car picked me up. On the way back to our campsite, I had to walk the same distance again. When I approached our camp, I noticed ominous hogsback clouds with sharp edges coming from the northwest: strong winds would soon be upon us. We went to bed and had hardly slept an hour when the storm arrived.

The area had been dry for a long time and the lake level was quite low, which exposed a lot of sand. The bright moonlight revealed eddies of dust spinning over the lake's edge. The surrounding trees protected us from the worst winds, but slowly everything became covered in a layer of dust. I could taste the sand in my mouth and throat; even the sleeping bags in the tent were coated. The wind worsened and the trees above us began to groan and squeak. We looked anxiously outside the tent.

'You see those branches above us?' said Peter. 'They used to call eucalyptus trees widow-makers. If these trees decide to drop a branch, it could kill us.'

I grew afraid when I heard gales galloping down the mountains and across the lake. When the gusts reached our tent, the poles bent in all directions and the fabric was flicked up with a whipping noise that sounded similar to gunshots. It was so deafening that I blocked my ears every time I heard a gust coming. I wondered how long the tent would stand these gales; it could rip apart at any time. Sometimes a small branch or leaf hit the tent and gave me a horrible fright.

'This is like Russian roulette!' I called over the noise of the groaning branches. I was quite terrified. As I lay there, I thought of all the other people in the world who were also lying awake in fear at that same moment—not out of fear of falling branches, though, but of falling bombs, bullets or missiles. 'Shall we pick up our sleeping bags and move away from the trees?'

'And sit in a sandstorm without a tent?' Peter said. 'I don't know what's worse.'

After a sleepless night and at the first sign of dawn, I crawled out of the tent. The wind had died down and everything was covered in a film of brown dust. I walked to the lake to wash all the sand off my body and hair. I looked up when the first sunlight hit the tops of the mountains. Another day had come: a day to be grateful for.

Our journey through the South Island was enormously diverse. Some days we hiked through wild and remote areas; other days we strolled through suburbs of expensive holiday homes. The town of Wanaka was a natural delight. It was midsummer, and round every corner we found wild apricot, plum and other fruit trees. At night we hid in the pine trees, and in the morning we followed an easy track round the lake, which we shared with cyclists and people with dogs.

We were just sitting in the shade of a big rock when we met, for the first time, two other Te Araroa walkers. We greeted them as though they were long-lost friends, and asked them all about their journey. They were walking the entire trail in one season. With their light packs, boots and gaiters, Nordic poles, water filter, GPS and other equipment on their chest, they looked very professional compared to us. Just when I was about to suggest we share a cup of tea, the young man said they had no time. 'We're already a day behind schedule, and we've only got another three weeks to complete our journey.'

'Three weeks?' I was astonished, as it seemed there was still an awful long way to Invercargill.

'Oh, I wish we could have more time, but we've got to get back to work.' He smiled. 'Back to the real world.'

'But this *is* the real world!' I laughed and pointed at the exquisite mountains.

When we had said goodbye, Peter and I continued our journey. The rocky hills and distant mountains beyond the tranquil lake formed a remarkable view. While gazing at the natural wonder, we spoke about the luxury of not having a schedule. We could take as long as we wanted. Even if we didn't reach Invercargill for three years, it wouldn't matter. This suddenly felt like such a luxury: having time.

We soon saw a young woman walking in our direction. She looked fresh and washed, and her face was still a little pale. She smelled of sunscreen and deodorant, and her clothes were not faded, stained or ripped. She looked like a serious hiker, but had obviously only just begun her journey.

'Are you a Nobo?' I asked with a friendly smile, as she was about to walk past.

'Nobo?' She took off her sunglasses and we met with two blue eyes.

'North-bound Te Araroa walker?' I clarified.

'Oh, yes.' She smiled broadly. 'I'm walking to Cape Reinga.'

'Are you not afraid to walk on your own?' I asked.

'Well, I only started in Queenstown, and so far I've stayed in huts and campgrounds on the way. Tonight will be my first night alone. It's a little scary.'

I nodded sympathetically. I had great respect for this young woman walking the trail alone. We exchanged some practical information, and she appeared very confident. I recognised in her the same enthusiastic courage and innocent optimism as I have.

The track to the high pass didn't follow the natural contour of the land with a comfortable gradient, but went up and down into every gully and stream. By the time we finally reached the first of three passes, we were exhausted. It began to rain. The track went steeply down a barren spur. The mud on the track caked my sandals, and several times I slipped, which made me cautious and wary. The combination of my waterlogged pack with the sleeting rain in my face made me very grumpy.

We descended several hundred metres, and when we reached a little creek Peter pointed to the trail. It went sharply up again. The whole face of the mountain was muddy and looked very uninviting. The stony creek that ran down the valley seemed much easier. When Peter suggested we should go off track and find our own way down, I readily agreed. The first 50 metres in the stream were indeed easy. The gravel was flat and the creek was gentle, and I washed the mud off my sandals.

Then the stream dropped swiftly between boulders so big that the water cascaded over them. We slid down the smooth rocks and soon were in a canyon. After climbing for some time, we suddenly found ourselves staring over a big waterfall. We had little choice but to climb out of the gorge and on to the side of the mountain.

On the left was a sheer cliff, interrupted by another vertical gorge. In between the ravines were huge spires of rock. This astonishing canyon was full of forbidding peaks and sharp pinnacles. Wisps of mist swirled between the chasms, like ghosts in castles. I felt we were in the remotest wilderness you could imagine.

On the right was another steep slope clad in bushes and shrubs.

I climbed on to a gravel wall and reached for a bush. As I pulled myself up, the pebbles started to crumble under my sandals. The shrub held my weight, but when I tried to rise my pack hit the bush above me. While perched with one foot in the wall, I had to remove my pack in order to climb on to the bank. Everything was gruellingly difficult.

The rain had eased when we sidled round the steep mountain, and that made hiking a little easier. But time and time again we came to narrow gullies that looked like dangerous crevasses. To stop myself from falling, I held on to the wet vegetation. Everything seemed enormous in this valley. Plants that I had seen growing modestly in other places seemed to appear here in monstrous proportions. The normally small hemlock was so big that it held my entire weight. Even the wet grass came up to my hips. The treacherous journey through the gorge demanded all my attention, all of my senses and abilities. It demanded responsibility. There was no space for sour moods or grumpiness; there was only space for awareness.

After many hours toiling we saw, to my relief, some forest in the distance. We would finally be able to stop, pitch the tent, light a fire and dry out. We descended back into the gorge and found a flat spot under the trees to camp. With grey rock faces all around us, it felt as if we were in a secret place. A merry little waterfall came down from the tops and, while the last soft light shone through the gorge, a small robin welcomed us loudly to its private empire.

Even though the forest was dripping, we found dry firewood by shaving woodchips from the bottom of a fallen log. With a few dry pieces and some resinous leaves, we were able to make a flame. We carefully fed tiny twigs into the fire. It took a long time, but eventually we had a fire big enough to dry everything out. Over the years we had mastered the art of lighting a fire. We always carried several match-boxes, a lighter and a candle. For emergencies, we carried waterproof matches and a flint. Even in the most precarious and wet situations we could light a fire. It was a skill we often had to rely on.

'There is a huge difference between following a track and finding our own way through the wilderness,' I said. 'I mean, it feels very different, don't you think?'

'Oh yes,' Peter said. 'I feel so much more alive when I'm off the beaten track.' His eyes shone brightly with the sense of adventure.

'Me too, but why should that be?'

'Maybe because if you follow a track you don't have to do anything any more—just blindly obey it.'

'Yes,' I said. 'Whereas in places like this we have to use all our senses to find our way.' I was holding my wet pack and shorts near the fire. Steam started to rise from them. After a while, I asked, 'What happens when you take yourself away from society and the established order and live in nature?'

Peter looked thoughtful. 'Well, what has happened to you?'

'My sight and smell have become better, and other intuitive senses I never knew existed have come back to life.' I thought for a moment. 'I also feel more open. If I look at the person I was, say, ten years ago, then I must say I feel more connected. Not only with nature, but also with other people.'

'It sounds like a contradiction,' said Peter. 'To live in the remote wilderness in order to be more connected—but, yes, it seems to be true.'

'What has happened to you in the last six years of living in nature?' I asked him.

'Compared to ten years ago, I'm physically a lot stronger. It's a great feeling to be fit and flexible enough to sleep on the ground and sit on rocks.' He reached for his wet shorts and held them near the warmth of the fire. 'In the world of academia, thought, concepts and ideas are quite overwhelming. It almost becomes more real than the natural world. But I don't think there is order to be found in an abstract world. Even though outwardly the wilderness looks chaotic, I think it is within the natural realm that we find true order.'

We came out of the gorge at the Arrow River, where we saw many people looking for gold. Some were busy with small pans; others had huge machinery to sift through tonnes of sand. On the riverbanks were old gold-miners' cottages from the nineteenth century, surrounded by gooseberries and raspberries that we could still enjoy more than a hundred years after they had first been planted.

Our Te Araroa trail went through Arrowtown and crossed a beautiful golf course with big trees and colourful flower beds. We were walking along a neat little path in between green hills when Peter was nearly hit by a golf ball—the white projectile missed his head by only 10 centimetres. We had no idea where it had come from, nor did we ever see anyone playing, but it could have been a nasty accident.

We followed the trail right past the brown sewage ponds outside Queenstown, then over big asphalt roads through ugly industrial areas and past rubbish recycling compounds with screeching seagulls. Eventually we found ourselves on the side of a highway, where men were working with noisy machinery to broaden the busy road. A few hours later, we came out in the centre of Queenstown, where hundreds of people were sunbathing on the edge of the pristine Lake Wakatipu. The place was humming with people from all over the world. We thought it was marvellous. We talked with many strangers, ate exotic street food and picked wild plums on the side of the footpath. With our polished walking sticks and packs adorned with enamel cups and pocketknives, we stood out so much that some tourists took pictures of us. We must have looked quite outlandish.

In the late afternoon we boarded a ferry across the deep blue lake, and admired the surrounding mountains. During the long ride I grew increasingly excited about the last part of our journey. The moment we reached land again, we felt the same silence that we had experienced two years previously. We were back in Southland. Instead of following the main trail, we went into a lesser-known, quieter valley. Grassy river flats yielded to patches of old forest. One day, when the sun was high in the sky, we rested near the river. We lit a small fire on the rocks and made tea and flatbread.

A kingfisher sat quietly in a nearby tree. Its turquoise back was one of the most beautiful colours I had ever seen. It was difficult to find anything ugly here, for everything in nature seemed a magnificent form of art. A dark cloud was slowly sailing in from the south. When it started to rain, we dragged our packs underneath a big tree to stay dry for a little longer.

'What do you think is the most important thing in life?' I asked Peter.

He grinned. 'I could answer a hundred things.'

'Well, give me one of those hundred.'

'Courage is important. Humankind evolved and survived through courage, not through fear. Imagine what it was like to hunt a huge mammoth during the Ice Age! You would need courage to overcome fear and step into the unknown.' He threw a little stone into the river. 'What do you think is most important?'

'Maybe clarity,' I said, after some time. 'You need a clear mind in order to see what is important. You need clarity to know what you're going to be courageous about, and you need clarity to question reality.'

We watched the big raindrops fall on the river's surface. Each drop created a little hollow on the water. When it began to rain more heavily, the surface looked like a thousand mirrors. Our little fire in the riverbed slowly weakened with every drop, until there was only smoke.

When the shower passed, we followed the river south. Sometimes we walked through desert-like mountains with broad tussock-covered valleys; at other times we moved through lush farmland with hundreds of wild paradise ducks. We walked for days through sheep stations so big that we never saw any sign of farmers.

We had good weather until the first of the autumn rains began. One morning, the whole sky grew dark and a little later we walked into a band of showers. As the hours passed, I felt my pack growing heavier and I wondered whether the sky would ever be clear again. We stopped under a stand of pine trees. We allowed ourselves only six crackers with peanut butter, because we were at the tail end of our rations; I would hitchhike the next day to town for our final food supply.

After our meagre lunch, I was still very hungry. When Peter walked into the trees to pee, I thought of other things to eat. I tried some dried onion, which tasted a bit like chips. I ate some dried seaweed and a handful of instant potato powder, which was also delicious. Just when I was about to throw another handful into my mouth, Peter returned and caught me.

'Are you eating dried-potato powder?' He rolled his eyes at my powdery face.

'Only a very little,' I lied.

'We might need that tonight.'

The bags inside our packs had got damp by this point too. I was feeling very cold and started to shiver. *How are we going to set up camp in this rain?* I felt this was the beginning of autumn in Southland, and nothing would dry out any more. We followed the trail out of the forest into farmland. Then we had to climb over a stile. This would have been easy in normal conditions, but the mere sight of the wooden steps over the fence made me sigh. The planks were wet and slippery, my pack heavy and it took an enormous amount of energy just to step on to the one-metre-high stile. I held on to the pole, but the farmer hadn't hammered it in properly. I swung from left to right, my pack pulling me off balance. I nearly touched the electric wire as I climbed over. *I'm so tired*, I thought.

'I'm so tired,' said Peter a second later. 'If we weren't just a hundred kilometres from the end, I would give up now. My body has had enough. I feel like I need several months' rest. Anywhere would be good, as long as I'm not walking.'

A few days later, we entered the last forest of our journey. The old trees had created their own reality and there was no sense of an outside world. We were walking between trees that carried so much moss that it looked like a stunted goblin forest. At night, we slept very well. It was like the trees absorbed all our thoughts. The forest felt protective, as if the trunks were the walls and the canopy the roof of a gentle house.

There was one more hut before the end of the trail. We had not used many public huts, but since it would be an opportunity to meet other Te Araroa walkers we aimed to spend the night there. It was an old, broken-down shelter, and I pitched the tent in a small clearing.

In the late afternoon, a handsome but shy young French man emerged from the forest. His skin was tanned, and he had elegant features and a calm vibe. He was a pleasure to look at. He told us his name was Emmanuel. Since he had little food and we had more than enough, Peter and I cooked enough dhal for three people. Just when we were about to eat, we heard a voice from the forest.

A tall, bearded young man with long, curly hair, a ripped shirt and muddy trousers turned up with a big smile. 'How are you doing?' he called from a distance. His name was Isaac and he was born in Israel. Compared to Emmanuel, he was a tornado. After he cheerfully shook our hands, he looked in the hut for anything edible left behind by others. He had nothing to eat, so I made extra flatbread and divided the dhal into four portions, which was still plenty for all of us.

'What would you have done if you hadn't found any food?' I asked.

'Oh, it wouldn't have mattered. Tomorrow night I'll be eating a good meal in the pub at Colac Bay.' He smiled. 'I hope they'll let me in.'

I glanced at the sole of his right shoe. It had completely come off.

'Why don't you wear shorts, so that you don't rip and dirty your trousers?' I pointed at the mud that came up to his thighs.

'Because I don't want to get my legs dirty!' he exclaimed.

I realised that he—unlike me—did not identify his clothes with himself. It was quite a different and liberating point of view. After a few minutes, I couldn't help liking this man who was the personification of the word 'boisterous'. Isaac had walked the entire trail with a mini guitar strapped to his pack. When he played and sang, the music sounded beautiful in the forest.

When it was nearly dark, a young French woman came down the path. 'Smelly Jesus!' she called when she saw Isaac sitting with us round the fire.

Isaac smiled. 'I didn't make that name up,' he explained, somewhat sheepishly. 'Another Te Araroa walker did.'

'Et bonjour, Emmanuel,' she greeted her countryman. They all knew each other, because they had stayed in the same mountain huts and campgrounds along the trail.

Laura had started out this morning where we had left three days ago. She was slim, energetic and astonishingly fit. I guessed the adrenaline had fired her up, because she was hardly able to put her pack down. After a few hours she boiled a cup of water on her gas cooker and mixed instant potatoes into her small cup. I asked whether she was hungry or tired. 'Not at all!' She laughed and seemed surprised at the question.

We had walked for so long, but this was the first time I was conscious of belonging to a sub-culture: long walkers. I liked it. Hiking for thousands of kilometres was such an exceptional undertaking that only other long walkers could really understand the extreme physical effort of toiling with a pack over mountains to witness the extraordinary beauty of the landscape, and the satisfaction of completing a trail.

The next morning Laura looked quite different from the night before. She said she felt she was living in the body of an old woman, and was looking forward to reaching the end of her journey. She, Isaac and Emmanuel all left while I was still busy lighting a fire to cook breakfast. The sun was high in the sky by the time Peter and I finally walked out of the forest and down the valley towards the sea.

A soft breeze came to meet us where we stood on top of the dune. We had seen the sea from the high mountains, but the space and magnificence still came as a surprise. It was astonishing to be in such an open place after the enclosing forest and narrow valleys. It felt as if we had arrived at the end of the world. I took a deep breath. 'The Southern Ocean—at last.'

Peter leaned on his two walking sticks. 'The mother of all rivers,' he said. 'She's holding the land in her ceaseless embrace.'

I looked at Peter and grinned.

We saw nobody when we walked over the cobbled beach towards our last spot for the night. Huge lone rocks shaped by the wind stood solemnly on the grassy hills overlooking the ocean. We found refuge from the wind behind one tall pillar. We lit a fire and ate our meal while looking out over the blue-green ocean. Small, shy waves were trying to crawl on to the land, and the gentle sea pulled them carefully back.

Stewart Island lay about 40 kilometres to the south, and looked very mysterious with its dark blue mountains. The salt and mist above the sea made the island look as though it was floating.

It was such a quiet, peaceful evening.

Then we were treated to a remarkable spectacle: thousands of black seabirds with sharp wings were moving in a figure-eight formation very close to the shore. Each one would dive down into the sea for fish then reappear a little further along. The birds moved as one unit. The pattern was ordered and graceful, and as smooth as a flowing river. We silently watched this wonder.

'If you go in that direction—' Peter pointed east— 'the only land you'll see is Tierra del Fuego. The first place after that is this very point where we are sitting right now.'

I suddenly felt like stepping into a boat and sailing this ocean. 'Do you think we might meet somebody with a boat tomorrow?'

'Maybe. We'll see.' Peter looked at me with a little smile on his face. 'Tomorrow is the first day of the next chapter in our lives.'

'What do you think will happen to us?' I remembered asking that same question on our first day in the wilderness more than six years before. Once again, it felt as if we had no future—just a big void ahead of us.

Peter laughed. 'I don't know, but something will happen.'

We sat in silence and watched the coming and going of the clouds.

'This is not an expedition after which we go home,' Peter said.

'No, we don't have a home.' I smiled. 'Our life will keep unfolding in front of our eyes.'

The next morning we planned to walk to the city of Invercargill to see whether we would decide to fly or sail away to another country. Eager to get on the move, I started to pack my sleeping bag.

'We're not going anywhere in the rain,' Peter stated.

I looked out of the tent. Huge dark clouds loomed over the land. Big drops were falling. The blue sky felt very far away. I lay down again and listened to the rain for a while. When Peter went back to sleep, I crawled out of the tent into the warm rain, and dressed in my top and shorts. The rock next to our tent had been carved by wind and water over millions of years. The four-metre-high stone gave me some protection from the rain, and I leaned against it to keep my back dry. The pillar seemed to have its own energy.

The waves had grown wild overnight. White foam flicked up into the air, and a wall of spray came with every wave. I listened to the rhythm of the rolling waves and reflected on the last six years in the wilderness.

I had learned to endure, like the rocks in a river. I had learned to be flexible, like willows in the wind. I had learned to walk, to live a nomadic life. As a hunter, I had become wild and fierce. I had hunted for food by understanding—almost becoming—the animal I wanted to find. I had made its skin my skin by sewing clothes and blankets. I had learned to collect herbs and grow food. All these skills felt like a wealth I would always carry with me.

I placed our pots, plates and cups underneath the rock to collect the water. The sound of the drops falling in my cup was very satisfying. Soon I would have enough water to make tea. I lit a fire against the walls of the rock. While the rain soaked my back, the fire dried me at the same time. The wood that was burning had been floating in the ocean for a long time, and only the hardest parts of the log had survived. The flames on the old wood were a deep orange. I looked into the heart of the fire, and I felt it was a mirror of my own body.

I had grown hard over the years, and I had grown soft too. A receptive heart had opened and bloomed. The woman in me had grown like a lily in the mountains. I had learned to love by giving space to a precious flower—space to grow, space to blossom and, one day, space to die.

Mist covered the mountains and the distant island had disappeared behind a dim curtain. I stood with my sandals in a pool of water and my back against the rock. I looked at the great bull kelp that whirled contentedly with the ocean's currents. Birds flew slowly above the surface of the water. Nothing seemed worried about the rain. Everything surrendered to whatever was coming. I had learned to look at fear and surrendered to my shadows on the wall. I wasn't afraid to look again, and again.

The rain slowly soaked through my clothes. *This is the earth, and this is the rain*, I thought. By accepting completely what was given, there was order and the world opened up to me. I felt vulnerable because I didn't know what the future would bring, but I also felt the strongest I had ever been because there was nothing I could lose.

Many years ago, I had felt that everything had a place except for me. Yet, as I stood here on the earth, I felt for the first time that my feet were connected to the ground. *I have a place: it's here. I feel long roots growing out of the backs of my heels. I am firmly secured to the earth I was born into.*

The wind strengthened and pushed me against the rock. I looked up at the misty mountains, the approaching clouds and moving waves. I felt the wilderness wasn't just touching my skin; it was passing through my whole body.

My heart is like a wide-open window through which everything can blow free.

—— EPILOGUE ——

'Peter, have a look at this!' I am sitting behind a computer at the Invercargill library. When he leans over my shoulder, I smell the wood smoke in his hair and clothing.

'I've got an email from a book publisher—Allen and Unwin. The lady asks if I'm interested in writing a book about our life in the wilderness!'

Peter moves closer to the screen to read the email.

'A whole book!' I look at him with wide eyes. 'I'm not a writer. English was my worst subject at school.' I instantly feel nervous.

Peter looks at me. 'Well, I guess if you can learn how to hunt with a bow and arrow, you can learn how to write a book.'

I laugh when I see his shining eyes.

'It's an open door!'

The next great adventure has just begun.

——— ACKNOWLEDGEMENTS ———

It was Scott Eastham who revealed to me the power of literacy.
His wife, Mary, gifted me the pen.
Then Jenny Hellen handed me the paper,
And so I was inspired to write a book.

When I began my abstract journey,
Pete Horsley handed me the right rhythm,
My father sent me the subtle fragrance,
My mother brought me a new melody,
And Sofie was there to show me a clear mirror.

And while I was writing, day and night,
Peter watched the trees lose their leaves in the autumn wind.
'Look out there, Miriam,' he'd say to me.
'The natural world is the one thing the mind didn't make.'

When I hitchhiked down the road one day, Kim Batchelor picked me up,
And kindly offered us the old cook's cottage on her sheep station for the
    winter months.
Wayne Jansen also deserves great thanks for his hut in the forest, which we
    stayed in while I completed the last chapters.
Thank you all for your help
And, most importantly,
Thank you for reading.

ABOUT THE AUTHOR

Miriam Lancewood was born in 1983 and grew up in a loving home in a small village in the Netherlands. Nature, theatre, art and music were the pillars of her childhood. At the age of thirteen, Miriam started pole-vaulting and, as a result of many hours spent training, she won a number of competitions. It was, therefore, an obvious choice for her to study Physical Education when she left high school. At 21, upon completing her Bachelor's degree, she set off for Zimbabwe to spend a year volunteering in a school. From Africa, she flew to India, where she met her partner and companion, Peter. Together they travelled for several years throughout Asia and Papua New Guinea, and eventually arrived in Aotearoa New Zealand, Peter's home country. Miriam and Peter then made the decision to live in the most primitive manner in the wilderness of the Southern Alps.